Contextualization and Syncretism
Navigating Cultural Currents

Editor:
Dr. Gailyn Van Rheenen

Evangelical
Missiological
Society
Series
Number 13

WILLIAM CAREY
LIBRARY

EMS Series No. 13

Cover & Text Design: Todd Thomas

Published by William Carey Library

1605 E. Elizabeth St.

Pasadena, California 91104

www.WCLBooks.com

William Carey Library is a Ministry of the
U.S. Center for World Mission, Pasadena, California.

ISBN 0-87808-387-1

Printed in the United States of America

Contents

Case Studies: Contextualization and Syncretism in Living Contexts

Foreword

For many years I have contended that the largest vacuum in Missiology is the study of *syncretism* and the interrelated perspectives toward *contextualization*. I am happy to edit a volume which addresses these issues.

The book is timely. We are seeing many changes—from print media to oral transmission, from ahistorical to tradition, from propositionalism to narrative, from rationalism to embodiment, from market to mission, from rallies to relationship (Webber 2002, 7-8). Change permeates the very air we breathe. A few years ago Walter Brueggemann described this developing transition as the creation of a "new interpretive situation" resulting from "a radical shift of categories of culture, for which interpreters of faith in the West have not been well prepared" (1993, 1). Thus, as we transition from a modern to a postmodern era, the issues of contextualization and syncretism are exceptionally significant. Christianity's typical response to times of cataclysmic change is to so accommodate to the culture that the Christian message loses its divine essence.

Such accommodation is not new. Modernity's enthroning humanity and demoting God led Christians to become practicing deists. Because they could not be perceived, studied, and analyzed by the five senses, Biblical teachings about angels, demons, and Satan were considered myths. Even God was relegated to the spiritual realm, where he was allowed little authority over the world he created. Only "natural" powers which can be empirically analyzed were thought to operate in the "natural" world. Paradoxically, people viewed themselves as self-sufficient, not in need of God in the world that he created. Their world was a "closed universe" because natural powers were thought to operate with no interference from the spiritual realm. Even the social sciences, as described by Paul Hiebert in chapter 2, are rooted in humanistic, modern assumptions that either compartmentalize the natural and the supernatural or negate the spiritual realm altogether.

Culture's influence upon Christianity is easier to discern in retrospect than in prospect. If history is our guide, one thing is sure: This age will be as syncretistic as any other. Ancient Israel frequently syncretized the worship of God with that of the gods. Modern, "enlightenment" philosophies focused on the human and disregarded the spiritual. How is the gospel being contextualized in the contemporary world? To what degree are these new contextualizations syncretistic? This book attempts to answer these questions by defining and analyzing contextualization and syncretism.

Read carefully Steve Strauss' seminal writings on the role of context in shaping theology and the need to engage in intercultural theologizing. Examine my definitions of contextualization and syncretism and recontextualizations of the contemporary church in

North America to reflect the mission and kingdom of God and overcome the syncretism of Modernity. Consider David Hesselgrave's belief that inducements to syncretism are built into certain missionary paradigms. Give attention as Scott Moreau addresses the syncretism implicit in certain perspectives and forms of spiritual warfare. Ponder Dudley Woodberry's important discussion of C-4 and C-5 evangelism among Muslims. Critique the syncretistic nature of suburban evangelical individualism in North America in Nelson Jennings' analysis of Harvey Conn's writings. Other articles describe the reason for the rise of paganism in North America (Cooper); syncretism in Manila (Strong and Strong); revelation in Chinese characters (How Chuang Chua); how contextualization becomes syncretism among some Messianic Jews (Posten); how legalism creates syncretism in Romanian churches (Barbosu); millenarianism as ethnic defense among the Bayano Kuna of Panama (Moeller); and building Bridges to Muslims (Cockerill).

This book would not have been completed without the help of Todd and Teresa Thomas. They faithfully worked with my wife Becky and me to edit the manuscript and prepare it for publication. We appreciate them for their dedication and focus. I also thank Scott Moreau and innumerable other leaders of the Evangelical Missiological Society for their frequent help and encouragement during a period that we began a new ministry and lost our son Jonathan, who died five days short of his 35th birthday and left behind two beautiful children Eli, age 20 months, and Eva, age 8 months. I thank Rick Kruse of William Carey Library for guiding this book through to publication. Above all, I am thankful to God who is faithful even in times of sorrow.

Dr. Gailyn Van Rheenen
Facilitator of Church Planting
Mission Alive www.missionalive.org

Works Cited

Brueggemann, Walter.   1993.   *Notes under Negotiation: The Bible and Postmodern Imagination*. Minneapolis: Fortress Press.

Webber, Robert E. 2002. *The Younger Evangelicals: Facing the   Challenges of the New World*. Grand Rapids: Baker.

warfare), and technology in missions (especially information technology and the use of the Internet).

Larry Poston is Chair of the Department of Religion and Professor of Religion at Nyack College in Nyack, New York. He and his wife Linda lived for several years in Saffle, Sweden, where Larry taught at Greater Europe Mission's Nordic Bible Institute. He holds a Ph.D. in the History of Religions from Northwestern University (Evanston, Illinois) and is the author of Islamic Da'wah in the West: Muslim Missionary Activity and the Dynamics of Conversion to Islam (Oxford University Press, 1992) and The Changing Face of Islam in America (Horizon Books, 2000), as well as numerous articles.

Ron Stansell is Professor of Religious Studies and Missions at George Fox University in Newberg, Oregon (21 years) and a former missionary with the evangelical Friends Church in Bolivia, South America (18 years). He holds a D.Miss from Trinity Evangelical Divinity School and an MDiv. from Western Evangelical Seminary. He is currently the Director of the South American Studies Program for George Fox University, located in Santa Cruz, Bolivia in conjunction with the Bolivian Evangelical University. He serves as Director of the Evangelical Friends International Council and in that capacity travels regularly to Asia, Europe, Latin America and Africa to encourage leaders and leadership training and where he has served as a visiting professor.

Steve Strauss served for almost twenty years as a missionary with SIM (Serving in Mission) in Nigeria and Ethiopia, where he helped begin the Evangelical Theological College of Addis Ababa (ETC) and the Ethiopian Graduate School of Theology (EGST). He served as the Principal of ETC, as instructor in contextual theology at both ETC and EGST, and on the pastoral staff of the International Evangelical Church of Addis Ababa. Steve holds the PhD in Intercultural Studies from Trinity International University and since 2001 has been the United States Director for SIM. He is married to Marcia; the Strausses have three adult children.

Cynthia A. Strong, Associate Professor of Missiology, and **David K. Strong**, Frances P. Owen Distinguished Professor of Missiology, have served at Simpson University in Redding, California for the past ten years. Cindi studied at the University of California, Santa Barbara (B.A.), and with Dudley Woodberry at Fuller Theological Seminary (M.A., Ph.D.), receiving the Arthur Glasser Award, the David Allan Hubbard Award, and the Islamic Studies Award. David studied at the University of California, Los Angeles (B.A), Dallas Theological Seminary (Th.M.), and with Paul Hiebert at Fuller Theological Seminary (M.A.,

Ph.D.), where he received the David Allan Hubbard Award. Before coming to Simpson the Strongs served four years with the Christian and Missionary Alliance in Korea and five years at the Alliance Biblical Seminary in Manila.

Gailyn Van Rheenen served as missionary to East Africa for 14 years, taught missions and evangelism at Abilene Christian University for 17 years, and is currently Director of *Mission Alive*, a ministry dedicated to training talented, motivated Christian leaders as evangelists and church planters in urban contexts (www.missionalive.org). His books *Missions: Biblical Foundations and Contemporary Perspectives* (Zondervan, 1996), *Communicating Christ in Animistic Contexts* (William Carey Library, 1991), *The Status of Missions: A Nationwide Survey of Churches of Christ* (ACU Press, 2002) are widely used by both students and practitioners of missions. His web site (www.missiology.org) provides "resources for missions education" for local church leaders, field missionaries, and teachers of missions.

J. Dudley Woodberry is Dean Emeritus and Professor of Islamic Studies at the School of Intercultural Studies, Fuller Theological Seminary. His major mission service was at the Christian Study Centre in Pakistan and pastoring churches in Kabul, Afghanistan, and Riyadh, Saudi Arabia. He has been an editor of Muslims and Christians on the Emmaus Road (MARC/World Vision, 1989), Missiological Education for the 21st Century (Orbis, 1996), Reaching the Resistant (William Carey, 1998), Muslim and Christian Reflections on Peace (University Press of America, 2005), and From the Straight Path to the Narrow Way (Authentic, 2006).

1

Syncretism and Contextualization:
The Church on a Journey Defining Itself

Gailyn Van Rheenen

I am continually awed by the creativity of humans to mix and match various religious beliefs and rituals to suit their changing worldview inclinations.

I sat in an African house, full of people worshipping God. The mud-walled, thatched-roof house measured fifteen paces from rounded wall to rounded wall. Some sat around the circumference in chairs, others on stools, many on mats on the floor. About half an hour into a time of praise, a gaunt, nervous woman named Takwanya entered the house. Spotting the empty chair beside me, she sat down and whispered in the local language, "I want to be baptized." I nodded politely. After a stirring evening of song, praise, and preaching, those who had not yet accepted the way of Jesus Christ were invited to do so. Takwanya announced, this time publicly, "I want to be baptized!" I was surprised when the elders stated that they would pray for the sister and guide her on the way of Jesus. Later I learned from both Takwanya and the church leaders that she had been sick for many months. She was desperate. Non-Christian relatives, noticing the transformation of new Christians, had told her that if she were baptized in the church, she would be healed. Takwanya, viewing baptism as a magical rite of healing rather than a participation in the death, burial, and resurrection of Jesus, decided to try the "Christian way."

Two years ago Jim planted an evangelical Bible church. The guiding question forming his strategy was "How can we meet the needs of the people of this community and make this church grow?" Jim developed a core team, launched with an attendance of 300 after six months of planning, and now has an average attendance of 900 people each Sunday. By all appearances he is very successful. However, Jim is inwardly perturbed. He acknowledges that his church attracts people because it caters to what people want. The church is more a vendor of goods and services than a community of the kingdom of God. Jim sees that those attending have mixed motives: Attending is their duty, a place to meet people of influence or where children receive moral instruction. Church attendance assuages guilt and declares to others (and to self) that "I am religious." A spiritual responsibility has been discharged. Therefore, all is well. Observing the worldliness of members leads him to privately ask, "What have I created?"

Julie lived with tension. She was fearful about the success of her children, the faithfulness of her husband, and her own vocational ability. She also felt guilt because of her neglect of spiritual things. Julie grew up in a Christian home but grew tired of what she considered "the emptiness" of Christianity. She did believe in God and loved to hear stories about Jesus, whom she considered the greatest man who ever lived. In the midst of a busy family and work life, paradoxically, she was very lonely. Eventually she joined a yoga meditation group and found peace by relaxing and accessing the god within her while imagining the Holy Spirit drawing her to oneness with Jesus.

These stories illustrate the many ways in which Christianity is mixed with folk religion, humanistic understandings, and Eastern conceptions. I have found that in the West Christian leaders readily see the syncretism of Takwanya and perhaps Julie but permit (and perhaps appreciate) the syncretism of Jim because his church is growing. Is it possible that such syncretism is also prevalent in the Western church, but we are simply too close to perceive its pervasiveness? The *Evangelical Movement,*

> **Syncretism is like "an odorless, tasteless gas, likened to carbon monoxide which is seeping into our atmosphere."**
>
> **(John Orme, 2004, 1)**

molded by modern rationalism and the desire for relevance, frequently truncates, abuses, and loses the essence of the gospel.

This chapter . . . .

> ➢ compares and contrasts varying meanings of *contextualization* and *syncretism.*
> ➢ traces the historical tendencies to syncretize the Judeo-Christian way with the gods of the nations and the customs of the nations.
> ➢ re-images the life of the church in a postmodern context.
> ➢ evaluates the role of the church as the matrix for worldview formation in order to overcome syncretism.

Defining Syncretism and Contextualization

Syncretism cannot be defined without an understanding of *contextualization* since the two processes are interrelated. The various chapters of this text illustrate that what is considered authentic contextualization by some may be interpreted as syncretism by others.

Contextualization

Definitions of contextualization differ depending on the emphasis placed upon *scripture* and *the cultural setting* (Moreau 2005, 335). Models emphasizing scripture usually define contextualization as the translation of biblical meanings into contemporary cultural contexts. Therefore, images, metaphors, rituals, and words that are current in the culture are used to make the message both understandable and impactful. This model "assigns control to Scripture but cherishes the 'contextualization' rubric because it reminds us that the Bible must be thought about, translated into and preached in categories relevant to the particular cultural context" (Carson 1987, 219-20).

When the cultural setting is prioritized, however, God's meaning is sought experientially within the culture using the Bible as a guide. This model more fully "assigns control to the context; the operative term is praxis, which serves as a controlling grid to determine the meaning of Scripture" (Carson 1987, 219-20). The goal is to find what God is already doing in the culture rather than to communicate God's eternal message within the cultural context. For example, Vincent Donovan in *Christianity Rediscovered* (2003) describes anthropological inquiry as a "treasure hunt that uses Scripture as a map or guide to discover the treasures to be found in the culture" (Moreau 2005, 336; cf. Bevans 1992, 49).

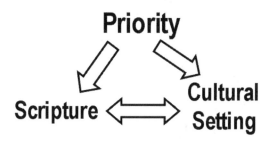

Figure 1: Varying Emphases in Contextualization Models

Evangelicals, who believe that God's revelation in Scripture is authoritative in life and ministry, view this second option as syncretistic. Scripture is marginalized in the contextualization process. According to Hesselgrave, "acceptable Contextualization is a direct result of ascertaining the meaning of the biblical text, consciously submitting to its authority, and applying or appropriating that meaning to a given situation. The results of this process may vary in form and intensity, but they will always remain within the scope of meaning prescribed by the biblical text" (1995). Tite Tiénou describes contextualization within the process of theology. He writes, "Contextualization is the inner dynamic of the theologizing process. It is not a matter of borrowing already existing forms or an established theology in order to fit them into various contexts. Rather contextualization is capturing the meaning of the gospel in such a way that a given society communicates with God. Therein theology is born." (1982, 51)

To Enoch Wan contextualization is derived from the dynamic relationship between gospel and culture, between "cultural relevancy" and "theological coherence." *Contextualization* is "the efforts of formulating, presenting and practicing the Christian faith in such a way that it is relevant to the cultural context of the target group in terms of conceptualization, expression and application; yet maintaining theological coherence, biblical integrity and theoretical consistency" (Wan 1999, 13). Wan then describes *Sino-theology* (ST), or a theology for China, as one such "contextual theology" and compares it to "Traditional Western Theology" (TWT). He says that Sino-Theology:

> is specifically designed for the Chinese people; not by transplanting Christianity in the "pot" of Western culture but by planting it in the Chinese cultural soil so it can take root, flourish and grow. ST should be done by using the Chinese cognitive pattern (e.g. shame culture vs. the guilt culture of TWT), Chinese cognitive process (e.g. synthetic vs. the dialectic of TWT), Chinese way of social interaction (e.g. relational/complementary vs. dichotomistic/ confrontational of TWT), Chinese vocabulary, topics, etc.
> (Wan 1999, 13)

Christianity, according to Enoch Wan, can be dressed in the garments of a shame culture, a synthetic cognitive process, Chinese ways of social interactions, communicated through the use of Chinese grammar, and expressed in terms of Chinese topics (Wan 1999, 13-16).

David Hesselgrave and Ed Rommen define *contextualization* as "the attempt to communicate the message of the person, works, Word, and will of God in a way that is faithful to God's revelation, especially as put forth in the teaching of Holy Scripture, and that is meaningful to respondents in their respective cultural and existential contexts" (1989, 200). The first part of this definition focuses on authentic understandings or faithfulness to scripture: "The adequacy of an attempted contextualization must be measured by the degree to which it faithfully reflects the meaning of the biblical text" (1989, 201). Contextualization thus involves conceptions of (1) *revelation* (God's communication of eternal truth in human linguistic and cultural categories); (2) *interpretation* ("the reader's or hearer's perception of the intended meaning"); and (3) *application* (including how "the interpreter formulates the logical implications of his understanding of the biblical text" and how he "decides to accept the validity of the text's implications" by totally accepting it, accepting some parts and rejecting others, or superimposing his own meanings upon the text (1989, 201-202).

> The New Testament has given us the pattern for cultural adaptation. The incarnation itself is a form of contextualization. The Son of God condescended to pitch his tent among us to make it possible for us to be redeemed (John 1:14).
>
> Byang Kato (1975, 1217)

The final phrase of the definition infers "effectiveness"--that communicating the gospel "grows out of an understanding of our respondents in their particular context and out of the active ministry of the Holy Spirit in us and in them" (1989, 199-200). Hesselgrave's seven-dimension grid (Worldview--ways of viewing the World; Cognitive processes--ways of thinking; Linguistic forms--ways of expressing ideas; Behavioral patterns-- ways of acting; Communication media--ways of channeling the message; Social structures--ways of interacting; Motivation sources--ways of deciding) provides tools for cultural analysis that equip the Christian missionary to effectively communicate the gospel (1989, 202-203). Hesselgrave and Rommen assert that *authentic contextualization* must be measured by its "faithfulness" to the meanings of the scripture and its "effectiveness" or "relevance" in communicating Christ within the recipient culture.

Charles Kraft defines contextualization in terms of the incarnation. He describes *contextualization* as "a process in which God is recognized as THE Contextualizer--who wants to be understood, and who reveals his purposes through both people and events. This process reaches its ultimate expression in Jesus Christ who uniquely communicates the Father's character and purpose--so that the Incarnation became the defining expression of all effective communication" (synthesis of ideas from Kraft 1989; cf. Taylor 2004). Kraft emphasizes "receptor-oriented" communication. God is relational. He takes the initiative to communicate with us and enters "the trappings of human contexts in order to reach those whose lives are lived within [the bounds of human] limitations" (Kraft 1989, 127). Each receptor is, therefore, "approached on his or her own terms" (Kraft 1989, 127). God works in and through human culture but seeks to meet felt needs "at a level deeper than culture." These needs include "forgiveness from sin, freedom from satanic oppression, and the security that can only come from a relationship with God" (Kraft 1989, 127). People are born "insecure, powerless, . . . at the mercy of suprahuman powers. A contextually oriented God chooses to address these subjects in terms intelligible at the deepest personal level" (Kraft 1989, 127).

I concur with Kraft that God is relational and self-revealing and that the greatest example of that contextualization is the incarnation of Christ. It is, however, inappropriate to describe God as operating in terms of human felt needs. Kraft's functional view of Anthropology eventually leads to syncretism because God is understood as working within a modern, humanistic paradigm. Frequently God's followers do not have their felt needs met. They experience with Paul "thorns in the flesh, instruments of Satan to hinder them." They suffer for their faith. They lament because God appears to be absent. Frequently atheological paradigms promote spurious syncretism instead of authentic contextualization.

These definitions establish the need for contextualization and illustrate that an over-emphasis upon the cultural context can lead to syncretism.

Syncretism

Syncretism occurs when Christian leaders accommodate, either consciously or unconsciously, the prevailing plausibility structures or worldviews of their culture. Syncretism, then, is *the conscious or unconscious reshaping of Christian plausibility structures, beliefs, and practices through cultural accommodation so that they reflect those of the dominant culture.* Or, stated in other terms, syncretism is the blending of

Christian beliefs and practices with those of the dominant culture so that Christianity loses it distinctiveness and speaks with a voice reflective of its culture (Van Rheenen 1997, 173).

Frequently syncretism is birthed out of a desire to make the gospel relevant. The Christian community attempts to make its message and life attractive and appealing to those outside the fellowship. Over the years these accommodations become routinized, integrated into the narrative of the Christian community and inseparable from its life. When major worldview changes occur within the culture, the church struggles to separate the eternals from the temporals. The church, swept along by the ebb and flow of cultural currents over a long period of time, loses her moorings. Thus syncretism occurs when Christianity opts into the major cultural assumptions of a society (Van Rheenen 1997, 173).

For example, my religious fellowship was born and grew to maturity during Modern times and reflects Enlightenment thinking. Salvation was understood as certain steps that individuals had to do to be saved; scripture was interpreted as a blue-print or a pattern to be logically followed; and the hermeneutic of "command, example, or necessary inference" formed our interpretive grid. Generally our movement followed the rationalism of Alexander Campbell rather than the revivalism of Barton W. Stone. Our emphasis was on *knowing about* God and Christianity rather than *relating to* Him personally as Father God. I acknowledge these syncretisms for a number of reasons. Biblically-based theology must form our identities and challenge our syncretisms. We must realize that we are always, to some degree, syncretistic, and acknowledge our syncretisms before God and fellow Christians.

Missiologists' writings tend to focus more on contextualization with only brief notations about syncretism. There are many reasons for this. Writing about contextualizing the message of the gospel in the life of the church is much more appealing than discussing excessive accommodation to the philosophies and practices of the dominant cultures. We also live in an age of tolerance. Few are willing to negatively critique the beliefs and practices of others. David Hesselgrave, however, does this frequently and with grace. For example, many of the authors of *Encountering New Religious Movements: A Holistic Evangelical Approach* encourage establishing *common ground* with participants of the new spiritualities. Satanists believe that people should not "follow the herd" as Christians do, but insatiably enjoy all of life. Within this context authentic Christians might be described as "Left-handed Christian philosophers," who think for themselves despite peer pressure. The message of the taro can be an archetype for sharing the gospel. The story line of the Bible can be communicated within the framework of the Wiccan Wheel of the Year myth. A theology of anointing forms the basis of creative outreach to aromatherapists. Hesselgrave, however, raises a significant caution flag.

> "Both philosophically and theologically, a communication approach that is over-dependent upon the discovery and utilization of similarities is open to question. *Dissimilarities* between beliefs and practices may, in fact, be more important and utilitarian in the long run . . . . If one's objective is to convert and disciple, both the number and importance of these differences will far outweigh the number and importance of supposed similarities."
>
> (Hesselgrave 2004, 147, 149)

Incorporating oils into Christian practice, for instance, does not necessarily Christianize an aromatherapist. Christian evangelists must, therefore, consider both points of contact and points of contrast. Although the authors of *Encountering New Religious Movements* rightly provide an incarnational model of engagement with occult practitioners, they must also ask, "When and how do we adopt the forms of New Religious Movements to both relate to the culture and communicate a distinctively Christian message?" Can the accommodations of today become the syncretisms of tomorrow?

The following case study illustrates the difficulty in distinguishing between authentic *contextualization* and *syncretism*. Why might one person's "contextualization" be considered "syncretism" by another? What are guiding principles to differentiate the two terms?

Translating God in Mongolia

In March 2003 a symposium of Christian leaders was held in Mongolia on the topic "Distinctively Christian . . . Distinctively Mongolian." This title was especially intriguing because it uniquely captured many of the issues concerning the tension between contextualization and syncretism.

During the seminar, all speakers were asked to lay the foundations of Christian formation without addressing the specific concern about the name for God. This issue had so polarized the Mongolian church that it would be impossible to have a symposium for the entire Evangelical community if this topic was on the agenda. When a presenter spoke about the various names for God employed in the Hebrew and Greek texts of the Bible, many Christians felt that they had been betrayed. A confrontation ensued, and the symposium was almost terminated. This situation demonstrates the volatility of emotions over the struggles relating to contextualization and syncretism.

One community of Christians in Mongolian use the generic term *Yertuntsiin Ezen* ("Lord of the Universe") when speaking of God. By using this term, "Christians are declaring that their God is unique and quite separate from any other god" (Voysey 2003, 2). They consider all specific Mongolian names for God, like *Burhan* or *Tenger*, to have pagan connotations and, therefore, are unable to capture the essence of the God of the Bible. They believe that the Bible is clear: "Do no invoke the names of other gods; do not let them be heard on our lips" (Ex. 23:13). Frequently, they quote non-Christian Mongolians who have been angered by the Christian use of *Burhan*. "The religion of the cross has been amalgamated with the Buddhist Religion," wrote A. Nerbish in the independent Mongolian newspaper *Il Tovchoo*. Byambajav, the Principal of the Lama Training College, said that when Christians use *Burhan* as the name for God, they are beginning a new religion, "a merging together of Christianity and *burhani shashin*." This group, therefore, advocates the use of a generic term since there is no term in the local language for creator God (Voysey 2003, 1-5).

Most Christians, however, use the term *Burhan* for God. They feel it wiser not to use a generic term but to use scripture to transform the meaning of a familiar indigenous term. According to P. Enkh-Amgalan, *burhan* was originally used by traditional Shamanistic Mongolians to mean deity. The word took on Buddhist meanings after the arrival of this religion about 1500 B.C. It came to mean "Buddha" (the enlightened one, idol, death, impersonal force). During the Communist decades the term maintained its Buddhist connotations but also was used to refer to deity in a general sense. The general use of *Burhan* as deity continues in "translations of western classics, contemporary dubbing of western films, and different deities of any religion" (Enkh-Amgalan, 3). This group would respond to the charge of syncretism by saying that it is abundantly clear from the context that *Burhan* as worshipped in Christian churches is distinct from Buddha or the idols that Buddhists worship. "There is clear evidence of true repentance and a new birth, a new heart and changed lives" (P. Enkh-Amgalan, 6).

What one group perceives to be syncretism is seen as authentic contextualization by other groups.

This case study evokes a number of significant questions regarding the relationship of contextualization and syncretism.

1. How do Christian communicators determine when it is best to use indigenous terms for God (or for other concepts like heaven, sin, Satan, and forgiveness), a generic phrase, or a term borrowed from another language or culture?
2. To what degree are meanings dynamic or static?
3. How do we interpret verses such as Exodus 23:13: "Do not invoke the names of other gods; do not let them be heard on your lips." Is this command focused on specific words or focused on allegiance within the hearts of people?
4. What role does human ego and identity play in the contextualization process?
5. What role do cross-cultural and multicultural relationships play in the process of communication? Do national leaders and missionaries minister as equals, mutually encouraging and helping each other?

Understanding Syncretism in Theological History

The theme of syncretism occurs so frequently in Scripture that it is like a thread interwoven through the fabric of scripture's kingdom narrative. In a very real sense, the Ten Commandments are injunctions against syncretism. The first three charge the Israelites to follow Yahweh exclusively--to distinctively stand before God without reliance on any other gods (Exod. 20:1-7). The oft-quoted and oft-memorized Shema likewise exhorts Israel to *hear* that Yahweh is one and to love Him with all her heart, soul, and strength (Deut. 6:4-5). The Israelites are exhorted not to listen to the animistic practitioners prevalent in the land of Canaan but to listen to "a prophet like Moses" (that is, Jesus), whom God would raise up (Deut. 18:9-15). In other words, Israel was to live distinctively, not fusing the way of God with the beliefs and customs of surrounding nations.

Israel, however, failed to heed the words of Yahweh. God's chosen people incessantly accommodated to the dominant cultures around her and blended their beliefs with hers. For example, Jereboam I, the first king of North Israel, built two golden calves because he feared that his followers might go to the Southern Kingdom and worship Yahweh in the temple.

Ahab and Jezebel introduced the Phoenician cult of Baalism into Israel. Manasseh of Judah rebuilt the high places that were torn down by his father Hezekiah, erected altars of Baal, practiced astrology, and burned his son as a sacrifice to Molech. Because of this idolatrous syncretism, God banished North Israel into Assyrian captivity (2 Kings 17:16-18) and exiled Judah in Babylon for 70 years (Jer. 11:9-13).

Various Old Testament scriptures describe the nature of syncretism. The Samaritans were a mixed-breed people who also blended their allegiance: "They worshiped the Lord, but they also served their own gods in accordance with the customs of the nations from which they had been brought" (2 Kings 17:33). The pre-exilic Jews followed Yahweh but also created for themselves idols out of wood and stone. God through Jeremiah said, "They have turned their backs to me but not their faces, yet when they are in trouble, they say, `Come and save us!'" (Jer. 2:27). Zephaniah described the dual allegiance of the people of Judah, who "bow down and swear by the Lord and who also swear by Molech" (Zeph. 1:5).

In his epistles to both the Ephesians and the Colossians Paul acknowledges and addresses the ease with which new Christians syncretize Christianity and traditional beliefs.

The Ephesians came to Christ in a culture that worshipped Artemis as a supreme deity of unsurpassed power-- a goddess who descended directly from heaven (Acts 19:35). People relied on the *Ephesia Grammata*, letters thought to be laden with magical power. Beliefs in magic and demons flourished (Arnold 1989, 15-16). Paul, therefore, encouraged Ephesian Christians to stay faithful to God by reminding them of their position in the heavenly realms. There they had received "every spiritual blessing in Christ" (1:3). Christ himself had been exalted and was seated at God's right hand in the heavenly realms, a place "far above" all principalities and powers (1:20-21). Christians, who once were dead in sin, were also now seated at Christ's right hand in the heavenly realms. This "change of place" occurred because they had been saved by grace through faith (2:1-8). The book concludes with a military metaphor depicting that Satan and his forces are at war with the church. The church, who dwells in "the heavenly realms," had allowed Satan to invade its realm because of sin and reversion. The church was instructed to "put on the full armor of God" to resist the principalities and powers (Eph. 6:10-18).

Syncretism is more overt in Paul's letter to the Colossians. Even after receiving Christ, Colossian Christians were tempted to follow the elementary principles of the powers, the *stoicheia* (2:8, 20; cf. Ga. 4:3). The *stoicheia* were the cultural building blocks of traditional society, the directives through which the powers had established legalistic control of society (2:8, 20; cf. Gal. 4:3). Within this context Paul called upon Christians to remember their conversion: "Just as you received Christ Jesus as Lord, continue to live in him, rooted and built up in him" (2:6). He then cautions them against returning to the old ways: "See to it that no one takes you captive through hollow and deceptive philosophy, which depends on human tradition and the basic principles ("*stoicheia*") of this world rather than on Christ" (2:8).

Paul knew that centering life on Christ provides a check on syncretism and facilitates authentic contextualization of the gospel. He reminded the Colossians of the fullness of Christ's sovereignty: "For in Christ all the fullness of the Deity lives in bodily form and you have been given fullness in Christ, who is the head over every power and authority" (2:9-10; cf. 1:19). The *stoicheia* of Paul's time were legalistic observances of the law, worship of angels, and returning to pre-Christian animistic practices (2:16-19). Paul asked, "If you have died with Christ to the elementary principles of the world, why do you submit to their decrees?" (2:20). Even after receiving Christ, Colossian Christians were still tempted to live in terms of their pre-Christian worldview.

> "It is odd (that's a polite word for hypocritical) that westerners who are so critical of people who practice alleged syncretism are themselves so syncretistic."
>
> **Russ Wood**

This short summary reveals one important theme: *The story line of the Bible illustrates that there is a tendency for people of God in all times and on all continents to blend their beliefs and practices with those of the dominant culture.* However, the nature of the syncretism varies depending on the dominant culture in which God's community finds itself.

Re-Imaging the Life of the Church in a Postmodern Context

Randy Harris, professor at Abilene Christian University, describes *imagination* as the spiritual gift whereby Christians reflect upon scripture and natural revelation within their life situations to envision what God wants. It is "seeing things as God sees them, catching a dream as big as God is" (Harris 2004). Using this gift, Christian leaders image alternative worlds. For example, Martin Luther King's "I Have a Dream" speech envisioned a world of equality, where black and white live in harmony, without discrimination.

The church has so greatly absorbed modern ideologies of self-reliance and rationalism that it has, in many ways, ceased to be the Church of Christ. Eddie Gibbs and Ryan Bolger comment, "The church is a modern institution in a postmodern world, a fact that is often widely overlooked. The church must embody the gospel with the culture of postmodernity for the Western church to survive the twenty-first century" (2005, 17). It is therefore time for us, with divine imagination, to deconstruct the syncretism of modernity and reconstruct a gospel identity for the postmodern era. I envision six fundamental transformations that the church must undergo in order to be faithful to God within increasingly post-modern, post-Christian, and post-denominational Western cultures. The transformations reflect the incipient syncretism of Christian forms and beliefs with Modernity and a fundamental response for authentic Christians living in Postmodernity.

Characteristics of Contemporary Western Cultures	
Post-modern	Christianity is typically perceived as a life to be lived rather than merely a system to be believed. People are skeptical of rational, segmented beliefs, which are disconnected from spiritual living.
Post-Christian	Rather than standing at the center of Western culture mediating ethical and moral values, Christianity has been de-centered to be one of many options within pluralistic urban cultures.
Post-denominational	Denominational boundaries, largely formed in the New World and then exported to the rest of the world, are crumbling. In a more tolerant postmodern context, where many world religions exist side-by-side, the commonalities of Christian beliefs and practices are more celebrated than their differences.

From a Cognitive Cathedral to a Holy People Walking with God

Churches developed during the Modern era generally exist to dispense information. Unbelievers become Christians by receiving new information and grow in Christ to become leaders through enhanced understandings. The role of the preaching minister or pastor is that of *teacher*, dispensing information to the flock. These churches are cognitive groups ascribing to a particular set of teachings and meeting for a few hours each week in a palace of bricks and mortar to receive additional teaching.

God, however, expects more. He desires that his people not only know *about* him but that they also walk personally *with* him.

Envision churches full of people whose lives exist in relationship with God, where members passionately, whole-heartedly pursue full devotion to Christ. As Christians look toward the glory of God, they are "being transformed into his likeness with ever increasing glory, which comes from the Lord" (2 Cor. 3:18). Like the early Christian church, they devote "themselves to the apostles' teaching and to fellowship, to the breaking of bread, and to prayer" (Acts 2:42).

From Attenders to Community

People "go to church" for many different reasons: Their parents expect it. At "church" they meet people of influence. It provides moral education for their children. Attending church assuages guilt and declares to self and others that they are religious. All is well because a responsibility has been discharged.

Turning to God, relating intimately with him in Christian

> We are living in the west among people who are increasingly becoming more post-modern, post-Christian and post-denominational, but our DNA heritage prepares us best to speak to people in a modern, Christian, denominationalized context. What do we do? Do we abandon our heritage and seek for something else? Or, do we continue on unchanged, demanding that those "out there" come into our world if they want to converse? I believe we are called . . . to return again and again to scripture with these new questions, these new orientations, and to seek God's will and God's way afresh. This seems to be the essence of restoration, not the outward restoring of physical practices, but the seeking of truth and understanding that connects our God of unchanging truth to a world that is continually changing, challenging and demanding relevance to the questions of life.
>
> Granberg 2006

15

community, discovering his will, and developing the discipline to implement a Christian lifestyle are frequently secondary motivations. Church is considered "a place" to go rather than a people of God in community.

Imagine churches where Christians are not merely spectators but live in community. Christians practice the "one-another" relationships descriptive of Christian fellowship in the Bible. They are God's holy people "clothed . . . with compassion, kindness, humility, gentleness, and patience." They "bear with each other and forgive whatever grievances [they] have against one another. [They] forgive as the Lord has forgiven [them]" (Col. 3:13). Love "binds them all together in perfect harmony" (Col. 3:14). The *church* is a community of God on a pilgrimage through life helping each other to continue as Christ's disciples and encouraging others to join them on the journey to reach heaven.

Consider, for example, Ted and Tammy, who are struggling with their marriage, their children, and relationships in the workplace. Ted is wrestling specifically with sins of pornography and pride and Tammy with depression and the fear of not being an adequate mother. Without the church their marriage will likely disintegrate. But as a one-another fellowship of the kingdom of God, the church enables them to overcome sins and provides direction in their relationships. Their fellowship, typically a small group in a larger congregation or a house church, gives them the spiritual direction to live as God's people.

From Members to Ministers

Frequently church is equated with a "place" to meet rather than a fellowship for equipping God's servants for works of service. Church strength is naively equated with church attendance. The result is that hundreds are mere spectators! Many "Christians" have merely "become members" by publicly declaring their affiliation or following a few easy steps to membership. These understandings of membership have little to do with genuine Christian discipleship.

The Kipsigis of Kenya have a proverb that says, "Magisiche logok si kebagach" ("We do not have children and then leave them."). Although obvious with biological children, the proverb is frequently applied to the spiritual formation of "baby Christians." In most churches, however, more attention is given to the "birth" than to the "rearing". In other words, the focus is on conversion or becoming members rather than on nurturing new Christians to walk with God and equipping them as participating ministers in the kingdom of God. The sad result the 15/85 pattern: 15 percent of the Christians in a typical church do 85 percent of its ministries.

Imagine churches where all members have a place of ministry within the body, where leaders focus on equipping God's people for works of ministry. In this process, according to Ephesians 4, Christ is the prime mover providing, by his grace and power, specific gifts to the body (4:7-9, 10). He gifted some to be apostles, others to be prophets, and still others to be evangelists, pastors, and teachers. These leaders function together "to prepare God's people for works of service, so that the body of Christ may be built up" (4:12). Note the progression in the text: The small initial body planted in a locality must be "built up" until it reaches "unity in the faith and in the knowledge of the Son of God" so that it becomes "mature, attaining to the whole measure of the fullness of Christ" (vs. 13). The church, then, is no longer composed of "infants, tossed back and forth by the waves and blown here and there by every wind of teaching and by the cunning and craftiness of men in their scheming" (vs. 14). "Instead, speaking the truth in love" enables the church to "grow up into him who is the Head, that is, Christ" (vs. 15). The result is a body *"joined and held together by every supporting ligament"* which *"grows and builds itself up in love, as each part does its work"* (vs. 16). Ephesians 4:16 thus describes a mature body, equipped by its leadership for ministry. Doug Murren reports that churches that grow 25% or more each year always have 60% of their attending adults serving in some form of ministry (Murren 2002).

Christians must be nurtured to become Christ-formed, Spirit-led participants in the kingdom of God.

From the Strong to the Weak

Because churches are voluntary associations of individuals, they aim to gain the loyalty of searchers and to maintain the loyalty of members. To accomplish these tasks, Evangelical churches typically opt into this market-driven culture by becoming "vendors of religious goods and services" (Guder 1998, 84). Generally, the focus is on the rich and powerful who have the ability to create and maintain expensive church structures and programs that draw people to "our church." The church, consequently, looks and sounds more like a business enterprise. Christian leaders begin to view themselves, despite disclaimers, as jars of gold, silver, or bronze.

Imagine churches whose theme is authenticity, where all confess their weaknesses and acknowledge God's sovereign leading. Envision churches reflecting God's nature by caring for the weak, i.e., the children and the poor, those with no means to survive on their own.

Imagine children of unbelievers feeling excitement about God and Jesus, an excitement that then ripples into the family and leads to the conversion of mother, father, and other relatives. Consequently, children's ministry serves as a catalyst for evangelism, an entry point into the church. Barna reports that 85 percent of those who come to Christ do so before the age of 15, and that human spiritual foundations are largely formed by age 9 (Barna 2003). Lisa Jones of Christ's Church of the Valley in Philadelphia says that parents have a natural inclination to be involved in their children's activities. These parents are invited to help with the children's ministry and willingly "do it for the kids." Searchers are then incorporated as helpers in the youth program because, "The best way to learn something is to teach it." An evangelistic children's ministry thus provides the relationships that serve to incorporate these searchers into small groups on their journey to know God (Jones 2004).

Envision churches with Jesus' compassion for the poor. At the inception of his ministry, Jesus quoted Isaiah, "The Spirit of the Lord is on me, because he has anointed me to preach good news to the poor. He has sent me to proclaim freedom for the prisoners and recovery of sight for the blind, and release the oppressed, to proclaim the year of the Lord's favor" (Luke 4:18-19). Acts of kindness toward the poor are in actuality done to Jesus because he lives among the poor (Matt. 25:31-46).

Paradoxically, much growth comes from the margins of society because of the church's concern for the weak.

In this ministry Christian leaders must posture themselves as fragile jars of clay (literally, clay lamps) through whom the light of the Gospel shines. Never should they portray themselves as prestigious powerhouses, jars of gold, silver, or bronze (2 Cor. 4:7).

From Cultural Accommodators to Kingdom Participants

Significant influence from enlightenment thinking has molded many churches to think in rational, propositional categories. In the process these churches failed to spiritually form followers of Christ to think of themselves as participants of God's mission and instruments of his kingdom. Christianity spoke with a voice reflective of its culture! The church began to lose it moorings and was swept here and there by the ebb and flow of cultural currents. This process continues today with devastating results.

Many Christians are practicing Deists. They diligently study the Bible without expecting God to act in the same way he did in Scripture. They pray for the sick, yet expect God to work only through doctors' hands. God—who created the world, selected Israel to become his chosen people, and gave resurrection power to his Son—is viewed as a clockmaker: "God wound up the clock of the world once and for all at the beginning, so that it now proceeds as world history without the need for his further involvement" (MacDonald 1984, 304-305). In these churches God's "truth is too distant, his grace is too ordinary, his judgment is too benign, his gospel is too easy, and his Christ is too common" (Wells 1994, 30). Thus, Christians who seek to be faithful to the God of the Bible must break from their Enlightenment heritage to believe that God is "majestic in holiness, awesome in glory, working wonders" (Ex. 15:11).

Church Growth practitioners also absorb this Modern stance. They focus on what humans do in missions and ministry (assuming that they can chart their way to success by their ingenuity and creativity) rather than on what God is doing. Although they advocate faithfulness to and guidance from God, decisions are based upon anthropological analysis and pragmatic strategies. Theological frameworks are not intentionally developed and are not formative to practical ministry. They assume the gospel rather than intentionally allowing the gospel to shape their identities and methodologies.

The church's propensity to accommodate the prevailing worldviews of popular culture requires that she consistently define herself in biblical terms. The church, although contextualized for the contemporary situation, must seek to restore God's intentions for the church in every era.

Imagine churches who perceive themselves to be part of the mission and kingdom of God. Church leaders base their identities upon scripture and then move from these theologies to practice. Their terminologies change. They do not "set the DNA" of churches, "build" the church, or "establish" the kingdom. Rather, they "enter into" the mission of God; they "serve" as participants in the kingdom of God (Guder 1998, 93-94).

Their understanding of the church also changes. The church is depicted in theological rather than human terms. The purpose of the church is to reflect the glory of God rather than to provide "religious goods and services." The church is understood to be "a unique community in the world created by God through the Spirit as both holy and human" (Love 2003) and as "a distinctive community formed by the calling and sending of God and reflecting the redemptive reign of God in Christ" (Guder 1998, 77-109). The church is composed of living stones built around the chief cornerstone to become "a spiritual house to be a holy priesthood, offering spiritual sacrifices acceptable to God through Jesus Christ." (1 Peter 2:4-5).

Paul uses multiple metaphors in Ephesians 2:19-22 to describe the nature of the church. The church is a *new nation*: Newly converted Christians are "no longer foreigners and aliens" but "fellow citizens" in a community of faith (2:19). The church is a *family*, or "God's household" (2:19). The church is a *holy temple*, well constructed with each part joined together and built around Jesus Christ, the chief cornerstone. This fellowship comes into existence through conversion: Those dead in sin (2:1-3) are made alive with Christ (2:4-7) by God's grace (2:8-10). Paul stacks metaphors one on another to illustrate a redeemed fellowship "brought together under . . . Christ" (1:3-11) and existing "for the praise of his glory" (1:12). These perspectives form an inspired picture of God's divine community.

From Monocultural to Multicultural

Despite the foundational Christian belief that "God does not show favoritism but accepts people from every nation who hear him and do what is right" (Acts 10:34-35), 11:00 a.m. on Sunday morning continues to be the most segregated hour of the week in North America. Social distance, alienation, and interracial suspicion in popular culture exist in the church. Christ, however, is "our peace" who brings together the nations, destroying the walls that divide them (Eph. 2:14).

Imagine fellowships where there is no "Jew or Gentile, bond or free." All are accepted in their rich cultural diversity within the church. Envision churches which borrow aspects from many cultures and incorporate them in unique ways. These churches draw from a collage of cultural metaphors, motifs, and parables from various world cultures to creatively depict a Christian worldview. The diversity of God's kingdom is also reflected in the multicultural nature of lay and full-time Christian leaders. George Yancey's *One Body, One Spirit: Principles of Successful Multiracial Churches* (2003) is a practical guide to help churches sensitively enter other cultures within a city and intentionally become God's community of nations in urban, multicultural contexts. To facilitate this transition, Christian leaders must view themselves as missionaries to the ethnicities and nations of our multicultural cities.

In summary, churches rooted in modernity will continue to stagnate and dwindle. Most are in the maintenance mode. They look inward, taking care of their own immediate needs. Seldom do they perceive themselves as God's people on the journey through life helping fellow travelers to be God's disciples and encouraging others to join them on this God-directed and Jesus-inspired journey.

God, however, is working through both church renewal and church planting. A recontextualization of the gospel is necessary to restore God's intention for his church. The church must focus on . . . .

- spiritual formation,
- community,
- equipping members for ministry,
- caring for the weak,

- a missional, kingdom identity,
- multicultural ministry

> ... *to restore God's intention for his church.*

The following cartoon appeared in the Easter Sunday edition of the Daily Nation, the major newspaper in Kenya, East Africa, soon after "The Passion of Christ" began showing in theatres (*Sunday Nation*, April 11).

The cartoonist's message was readily apparent: People are drawn to Christ but not the church. Only a few aged people attend; the young feel estranged.

The Role of the Church in Making Disciples

What then is the role of the church in overcoming syncretism and affirming a Christian worldview?

For those coming to Christ in non-Christian contexts, social forces, the languages people use and the social structure in which they function, work against the Christian view of reality. This is the meaning of *stoicheia* in Pauline writing. Satan and his powers had established control over the prevailing laws and social structures of culture. Christians were exhorted to resist these "elementary principles" and hold to Christ and Christ alone (Col. 2:8-10, 20-23). The church, teaching and modeling the "fullness of Christ" (Col. 1:19; 2:9-10), becomes the fundamental matrix of worldview change, the context in which new believers grow to become disciples of Christ. Berger and Luckmann write,

> It is only within the religious community, the *ecclesia*, that [one's] conversion can be effectively maintained as plausible. To have a conversion experience is nothing much. The real thing is to be able to keep on taking it seriously; to retain a sense of its plausibility. This is where the religious community comes in. It provides the plausibility structure for the new reality. In other words, Saul may have become Paul in the aloneness of religious ecstasy, but he could *remain* Paul only in the context of the Christian community that recognized him as such and confirmed the 'new being' in which he located this identity. . . . One cannot remain a Muslim outside the *'umma* of Islam, a Buddhist outside the *sangha*, and probably not a Hindu anywhere outside India. Religion requires a religious community, and to live in a religious world requires affiliation with that community.
> (Berger and Luckmann 1966, 145).

Competing worldviews grapple for allegiance both before and after people come to Christ. During these times, the Christian community affirms the Christian worldview and challenges competing worldviews through both story and ritual.

The Christian narrative is told and retold to reaffirm the Christian way of life. Lesslie Newbigin writes,

> Every person living in a 'modern' society is subject to an almost continuous bombardment of ideas, images, slogans, and stories which presuppose a plausibility structure radically different from that which is controlled by the Christian's understanding of human nature and destiny. The power of contemporary media to shape thought and imagination is very great. Even the most alert critical powers are easily overwhelmed. A Christian congregation is a community in which, through the constant remembering and rehearsing of the true story of human nature and destiny, an attitude of healthy skepticism can be sustained, a skepticism which enables one to take part in the life of society if the congregation is to function effectively as a community of truth, its manner of speaking the truth must not be aligned to the techniques of modern propaganda, but must have the modesty, the sobriety, and the realism which are proper to a disciple of Jesus. (1989)

Making disciples necessitates a change of story, a restorying of the historical narrative employed by the searcher to visualize the fabric of reality. The Christian says, "I once lived in darkness but now dwell in the light; once I was controlled by the sinful desires, controlled by Satan, but now I have come into the kingdom of God." Christians' personal stories begin to enfold and reflect the great story of God's kingdom work in history. Life is rescripted because it now reflects a new story—a story of God's in-breaking kingdom on earth progressing toward the ultimate consummation of his kingdom at the end of time. Our story begins to coincide with God's story.

Rituals, as well as stories, affirm the Christian way and help to overcome syncretism by affirming the core beliefs and values. Within the nurturing process these rituals (baptism, the Lord's Supper, blessing of children, repeated patterns of personal, family, and communal prayer and meditation, etc.) provide concrete, tangible expressions of the worldview. In fact, even when apart from Christian community the plausibility structure of the Christian way can be maintained by practicing some of these rituals of the community. Participation involves putting on new and different worldview glasses. Thus the making of rituals within Christian community is a fundamental missionary task.

During the Modern Era, these patterns of worldview affirmation were marginalized. The Christian way was explained rationally in topical, sequential categories. Protestantism rejected the visual symbols of Catholicism and focused almost exclusively on the rational study of the printed Word.

The church in this Post-Modern Era, however, must resurrect the ancient impulses for narrative and ritual. The church must affirm a Christian worldview by telling and retelling the story of God's work through his prophets and priests, his Son, and his Holy Spirit in human history. The church must employ rituals of remembrance and affirmation of God's work in our lives. Only then can the Modern church be retheologized (or "desecularized") to reflect God's presence among his created people.

Conclusion

My prayer is that this initial chapter in *Contextualization and Syncretism: Navigating Cultural Currents* provides beginning frameworks for understanding syncretism and better understandings of the nature of contextualization. I have attempted in this chapter to carefully compare and contrast meanings and understandings of both *contextualization* and *syncretism*. I have traced the historical tendencies to syncretize the Judeo-Christian way with the gods and customs of the dominant culture. I have tried to reconstruct the life of the church in a postmodern culture in a way that deconstructs the syncretisms of Modernity and reconstructs what I hope to be non-syncretistic practices for a Post-Modern Era. Finally, I have described the church as the matrix for worldview formation in order to overcome syncretism.

Sources Cited

Arnold, Clinton. 1989. *Ephesians: Power and Magic*. Grand Rapids: Baker.

Barna, George. 2003. "Research Shows that Spiritual Maturity Process Should Start at a Young Age," *Barna Update*, November 17.

_____. 2003. *Transforming Children into Spiritual Champions: Why Children Should be Your Church's #1 Priority*. Ventura, CA: Regal Books.

Berger, Peter L. and Thomas Luckmann. 1966. *The Social Construction of Reality: A Treatise in the Sociology of Knowledge*. New York: Anchor Books.

Bevans, Stephen B. 1992. *Models of Contextual Theology*. Maryknoll, NY: Orbis.

Carson, Don A. 1987. "Church and Mission: Reflections on Contextualization and the Third Horizon." In *The Church in the Bible and the World: An International Study*, ed. D. A. Carson, 213-257. Grand Rapids: Baker.

Donovan, Vincent J. 2003. *Christianity Rediscovered: 25th Anniversary Edition*. Maryknoll: Orbis Books.

Enkh-Amgalan, P. 2003. From a summary of an article sent by email by Markus Dubach, March 18.

Gibbs, Eddie and Ryan K. Bolger. 2005. *Emerging Churches: Creating Christian Community in Postmodern Cultures*. Grand Rapids: Baker Academic.

Gilliland, Dean S., ed. 1989. *The Word Among Us: Contextualizing Theology for Mission Today*. Dallas: Word Publishing.

Guder, Darrell L. Ed. 1998. *The Missional Church: A Vision for the Sending of the Church in North America*. Grand Rapids: Eerdmans.

Granberg, Stan. 2006. Northwest Church Planting Workshop. Email Communication. (Jan. 29).

Harris, Randy. 2004. Imagination. Speech at Mission Alive's Church Planters' Retreat, June 11, 2004.

Hesselgrave, David J. 1995. "Contextualization That Is Authentic and Relevant." *International Journal of Frontier Missions*. July, Volume 12:3, pp. 115-20. Accessed at: http://strategicnetwork.org/index.php?loc=kb&view=v&page=v&id=8530&mode=v&pagenum=1&lang=

_____. 2004. "Traditional Religion, New Religions, and the Communication of the Christian Faith." In *Encountering New Religious Movements: A Holistic Evangelical Approach*, eds. Hexham, Irving, Stephen Rost, and John W. Morehead II, 137-56. Grand Rapids: Kregel.

Hesselgrave, David J. and Edward Rommen. 1989. *Contextualization: Meanings, Methods, and Models*. Grand Rapids: Baker.

Hexham, Irving, Stephen Rost, and John W. Morehead II (eds). 2004. *Encountering New Religious Movements: A Holistic Evangelical Approach*. Grand Rapids: Kregel.

Jones, Lisa. 2004. Children's Ministry: The Best Thing You Can Do to Build a Healthy New Church. Stadia Workshop, April.

Kato, Byang H. 1975. "The Gospel, Cultural Context, and Religious Syncretism." In *Let the Earth Hear His Voice*, ed. J.D. Douglas, 1216-28. Minneapolis: World Wide Publications.

Kraft, Charles. 1989. "Contextualizing Communication." In *The Word Among Us: Contextualizing Theology for Mission Today*, ed. Dean S. Gilliland, 121-138. Dallas: Word Publishing.

Love, Mark. 2003. Lectures in BMIS 640 *The Church and Its Mission*. Spring.

MacDonald, Michael. 1984. "Deism." In *Evangelical Dictionary of Theology*, ed. Walter A Elwell. Grand Rapids, Baker.

Moreau, A. Scott. 2005. "Contextualization: From an Adapted Message to an Adapted Life." In *The Changing Face of World Missions*, by Michael Pocock, Gailyn Van Rheenen, and Douglas McConnell, 321-348. Grand Rapids: Baker Academic.

Murren, Doug. 2002. *Churches that Heal*. West Monroe, LA: Howard Publishing Co.

Newbigin, Lesslie. 1989. *The Gospel in a Pluralist Society*. Grand Rapids: Eerdmans.

Orme, John. 2004. IFMA News, Vol. 55, Summer 2004, No. 2.

Sunday Nation. 2004. Editorial Cartoon. April 11.

Taylor, William D. (Ed.). 2004. *Global Missiology for the 21st Century*. Grand Rapids: Baker Academic.

Tiénou, Tite. 1982. "Contextualization of Theology for Theological Education." *Evangelical Theological Education Today: 2 Agenda for Renewal*, ed. Paul Bowers, 42-52. Nairobi, Kenya: Evangel Publishing House.

Van Rheenen, Gailyn. 1997. "Modern and Postmodern Syncretism in Theology and Missions." In *The Holy Spirit and Mission Dynamics*, ed. C. Douglas McConnell, 164-207. Pasadena: Wm. Carey.

Voysey, Irene. 2003. Warning of a New Religion in Mongolia. Unpublished manuscript sent by author to Gailyn Van Rheenen. March 15.

Wan, Enoch. 1999. "Critiquing the Method of Traditional Western Theology and Calling for Sino-Theology." *Chinese Around the World*: 13-16. Accessed on-line on September 22, 2004, at http://www.missiology.org/missionchina/wan1-1.htm.

Wells, David. 1994. *God in the Wasteland: The Reality of Truth in a World of Fading Dreams*. Grand Rapids: Eerdmans.

Wood, Russ M. Contextualization: Where to from Here?

Yancey, George A. 2003. One Body, One Spirit: Principles of Successful Multiracial Churches. Downers Grove, IL: IVP.

2

Syncretism and Social Paradigms

Paul G. Hiebert

Our vision is to see the Kingdom of God come on earth as it is in heaven. Our mission is to manifest and make known the King and his kingdom to the world, particularly to those people who have not heard of it, and to invite them to become followers of Jesus Christ as their Lord. To carry out our mission we need to understand both the Kingdom of God and humans.

In the past we have focused our attention on the message, the Good News of the Gospel. This is essential, for without a message, we have no mission. We exegete the Bible carefully, and formulate our systematic and biblical theologies precisely. We preach sermons based on Scripture, and teach Christians to study the Bible.

The Mission has made us increasingly aware of the need to study humans as well. Too often we come with a good message, but little understanding of the people. Consequently, the Gospel, as we present it, makes little sense to the people, or they

> **Too often we come with a good message, but little understanding of the people.**

see it as foreign. Early missionaries realized they had to learn new languages and translate the Bible. Most assumed that people in different cultures live in the same world, but use different labels to speak of it. Consequently translations were literal. One simply found linguistic equivalents for the biblical words, adjusted the grammar, and the translations would be accurate. Similarly, worship forms, rituals such as baptism and the Lord's Supper, concepts of sin, and theology could be translated literally with little loss of meaning.

Over the years, as missionaries studied languages more deeply, they came to realize that people in different cultures do not live in the same world using different labels, they live in different worlds. Languages and cultures not only create different categories in ordering their worlds, they organize these at deeper levels in radically different ways. Putting the Gospel in human contexts does not only involve Bible translation that goes deeper than literal equivalence; it must involve conceptualizing rituals, ecclesiology, beliefs and even theology in terms of different categories, logics and worldviews. Moreover, if, as evangelicals, we believe that ordinary people should learn to read and study the Scripture for themselves, we must allow Christians in other cultures to take the lead in conceptualizing the Gospel in their settings. Donald Shultz writes, "The time is also past when Western theologians have all the 'definitive answers.' Asian theologians now bear the responsibility and willingly accept it. The latter have discovered that Western definitive answers do not automatically fit the Asian situation and often answer questions not asked in Asia." (1989, 23)

The study of humans raises difficult questions which we cannot avoid (Kirk and Vanhoozer 1999; Ramachandra 1999). How can we put the Gospel in human contexts and avoid cultural relativism? How can we work towards the unity of the Church when people and their societies are so different? How do we take into account the fact that not only are young Christians in sociocultural contexts, so, too, are we as missionaries and sending churches? Moreover, God's revelation to humans as recorded in Scripture was given in specific sociocultural and historical contexts. We must ask, therefore, to what extent our Christian ways and theologies are shaped by Scripture and to what extent by our cultures, and what are the social, economic, political and legal dimensions in our relationships with the people we serve. We must also ask what in Scripture is divine revelation, and what relates to the social and cultural context of its time.

The answer to these questions is not to only study Scripture and reject the study of humans for fear of losing the Gospel, nor is it to study humans and lose sight of the Gospel. It is to keep in mind that we have been entrusted with God's revelation, made known in human history and definitively manifested in Jesus Christ as recorded in the Bible. We understand the Gospel as humans in social, cultural, personal and historical contexts. Our understanding of revelation is always partial, and shaped by our contexts. Therefore we dare not equate our theologies fully with divine revelation. On the other hand, by careful study of Scripture and our human contexts we can understand the Gospel more fully. We may see through glasses darkly, but we can see enough to become followers of Jesus Christ as our Lord and King.

Studying Humans

To study humans we need theoretical frameworks. Just as systematic theologians draw on western philosophy, and biblical theologians draw on western history for the questions they ask, the data they examine and the methods they use, so missionaries often draw on western human sciences, notably chemistry and biology (for example in modern medicine, relief and development), psychology (in counseling), sociology (in social work), and anthropology (in Bible translation and contextualization). Christian missionaries need to be aware of the insights these various disciplines can offer. The study of anthropology is of critical importance because it deals with many of the same issues that missionaries do (Hiebert 1978). It takes a global perspective, not simply a western one. It studies and compares different social and cultural systems around the world, wrestles with the questions of fundamental human differences–of Others and Otherness, and seeks to understand what it means to be human.

Like academic studies, including biblical and systematic theologies, anthropology began as a western discipline (Barnard 2000). Over the past hundred years, anthropologists have developed different theories to understand humans, and, in varying degrees, missionaries have drawn on their insights to translate the Bible and to understand the people they serve. Like other western disciplines, these theories have cast light on the understanding of humans, but they are also culturally situated, and so have their limitations and biases.[1]

One of the first theories to emerge was biological and cultural evolution, a secular deviation from the Biblical story. It affirmed that meaning is found in a grand meta-narrative moving from simple beginnings to the complex present day human world and ending, hopefully, in an earthly utopia. It held that 'man' not God, is the measure of all things. In western missions, the influence of the theory of evolution was seen in beliefs in 'progress' and the church's responsibility to bring the Kingdom of God to earth – the kingdom defined in terms of human well being. But the great wars of the twentieth century, and the increase in injustice, oppression and evil undermined the vision of cultural evolution.

A second theory to emerge in anthropology was British Structural Functionalism which compared social systems around the world,[2] such as families, clans, tribes, and peasant societies. This helped us see that social systems are real and powerful–societies are not simply gatherings of individuals. It also showed us that humans organize their societies in very different ways, and gave us ways to compare social systems. These insights have important implications for missions. For example, polygamy in the west is seen as sin, but in other societies it is regarded as honorable, while anger, which is

---

[1] The same is true for Systematic and Biblical theologies. To say that the ones we use were developed in western sociocultural contexts is not to say that they are totally culturally shaped, wrong or relative. They do offer us deep and true insights into the deep structure and story of the Scriptures. However, their use of digital intrinsic categories, and abstract algorithmic logic has led them to divorce Truth from Beauty and Holiness (the cognitive from the affective and evaluative dimensions of culture), and to reduce worship and divine mysteries to philosophical categories and logic. Their perspective of outside observation rather than participants in the scene, often led theology to be the knowledge of truth, but not lives that lived out the Gospel.

[2] Many of the studies were done by British anthropologists in British colonies, often to help British administrators institute indirect rule through local governmental structures.

often tolerated in the west, is seen as a greater evil for it breaks the harmony of the community. In the west we expect individuals to make personal decisions to follow Christ, but in many parts of the world important decisions are made by the significant groups to which people belong–their families, or lineages. We translate the Bible, but we rarely think of conceptualizing ecclesiologies. Anglicans ordain bishops, Presbyterians appoint presbyteries and synods, and free churches hold elections, even if these forms of leadership cause confusion in societies where these are foreign.[3]

While social anthropology is important in the study of people, it has its limitations and distortions. It is often reductionist and linear in causality, explaining human realities basically in terms of social systems. For example, religions are seen as important to keep groups together, but not 'true' in any ontological sense. In its early stages it focused attention on small societies, and examined them as closed systems, largely unaffected by outside factors. Consequently, it had difficulties in understanding larger, complex societies, such as cities, and global systems. Social anthropology also saw societies as harmonious organic wholes, and change as bad. There was no place for oppression, injustice and human sinfulness. Consequently, missionaries were often castigated for changing cultures. Furthermore, in social anthropology there was no place for God and spiritual realities. Finally, early social anthropologists saw themselves as objective scientists analyzing humans using scientific categories, methods and logic. They were not in the scenes they described, nor did they see themselves as socially and culturally shaped. What the people thought, at first, was unimportant. What the scientist said was true. Shaped by the enlightenment, it placed humans at the center of reality

Over time, social anthropologists, such as Malinowski, realized the importance of understanding how the people

---

[3] For example, in rural South India, when elections were introduced in the churches, Christians learned that whoever had the most votes won, so candidates brought their relatives and friends, Christian and non-Christian, to church business meetings. Church politics became village politics. When told that only Christian members of the church could vote, they argued that they didn't want to drive non-Christians away by rejecting them.

they studied looked at the world (emic perspectives), and to differentiate between insider and outsider views of reality. This insight challenged the old belief that scientists are totally objective observers unaffected their own social and cultural contexts.

In North America, anthropologists often studied the Native Americans who had been overrun by white settlers and placed on reservations. They could not understand the Native Americans without taking history, outside forces and change into account. Moreover, while the social systems of the Native Americans had been radically altered, the Native Americans maintained a sense of cultural identity, even in the most difficult and oppressive situations.

Like other scientists of the time, American anthropologists came as outsiders, confident that their scientific categories and methods produced objective truth. They focused their attention on cultures as closed harmonious cognitive systems that explained and gave meaning to their lives, but did not see change as always evil. Consequently, anthropology was increasingly used in programs for advocating the rights of Native Americans, for human development, and in missions. Moreover, they became aware of the importance of seeing the world as the people did, and of their own cultural context and its shaping of their anthropological reflections.

Cultural anthropologists helped us in mission to understand the reality and power of cultural systems, including languages and other sign systems, patterns of behavior, rituals and myths, beliefs and worldviews. This has helped us move beyond literal Bible translations to dynamic equivalence translations sensitive to cultural differences. It has also made us aware of the need to contextualize worship services and rituals, and, more recently, local theologies, and to engage worldviews.

Cultural anthropology, too, had its distortions. It had a linear causality and reduced everything to cultural explanations. Moreover, those who used Saussurian semiotics saw cultures as essentially subjective–the arbitrary creations of human societies (Barnard 2000, 120-138). Consequently, all cultures are relative. None can stand in judgment of another. In this view there is no external objective Truth, and even if there is, it can only be known subjectively.[4] Secular cultural anthropology, moreover, had no place in its assumptions and categories for God or spiritual realities. Consequently, it did not take the ontological claims of religions seriously, and claimed a privileged stance, as a science, on the assessment of reality.

Marxist anthropology stressed the importance of a grand meta-narrative, the evils of oppression and exploitation in human social systems, and the need for transforming not only individuals but also whole social systems. Its solution was revolution, by violence if need be. But it could not guarantee that the new social order would be any less repressive than the old. It, too, had no place for God and spiritual realities, nor for personal and corporate redemption.

More recently, symbolic anthropology has made us aware of the power and importance of nondiscursive signs,[5] myths[6] and rituals in communicating deeper truths, feelings and judgments about reality as it is seen by the people involved (Turner 1969). These insights have great significance for missions, particularly as they seek to contextualize the Gospel in the worship and life of a community of believers, but we must go further and ask, "What is the Gospel that we are

---

[4]Ferdinand de Saussure argued that signs, such as words, do not point to external objective realities, but refer to subjective categories in people's minds. Consequently, in Bible translation, what is important is that 'meanings' are communicated in other cultures using dynamic equivalents. In contrast, Charles Peirce argued that signs are triadic. The word does refer to external objective realities and links these to images in the mind. Thus, the word "tree" refers to real trees and links these to images in the minds of the people. Therefore signs link objective realities to subjective perceptions. A Peircian approach to Bible translation would take both the subjective and the objective dimensions of signs, perceptions and meanings seriously. It would not totally reject the need for dynamic equivalence, but would limit this by keeping the objective nature of the message.

[5] Signs that point to realities which are beyond description using discursive signs such as words, that evoke the deepest feelings, and that embody the fundamental values–understandings of righteousness and sin, of a culture.

[6] Defined, not as fable, but in the technical sense as the meta-narrative believed to be true by which we understand the cosmic story of reality.

37

seeking to communicate and validate by these cultural means?"

In recent years some anthropologists such as Clifford Geertz (1988) argue that anthropology is the study of humans, and that humans cannot be reduced to purely objective scientific observation. Anthropology is more like the humanities in that it seeks to understand what is going on inside humans, and that involves the methods of hermeneutics. This is a move away from objective materialism to the "communication of lived-through experiences" (Harries-Jones 1985, 234). This helps us avoid reducing humans to purely objects and machines, and calls for us to enter into their lives and worlds, and then relate to them as humans to humans.

At the end of the twentieth century anthropologists, such as Peter Harries-Jones (1985, 224-248), challenged the very assumptions of the mid-twentieth-century approach to the study of humans, and provided a rationale and point to the direction which anthropology should take in the twenty-first century. Jacob Loewen writes,

> Harries-Jones observes that in the past anthropologists who enjoyed the hospitality of a people over a period of months or years usually wrote an ethnography as a return "gift." They wrote it, however, in the language and intellectual categories of the researcher's culture, not of the host culture. These researchers "piously" hoped for a "trickle-down" effect. That is, as more Westerners learned more about these exotic peoples, benefits from the academic industrialized world would trickle down to the former host society. This, says Harries-Jones, never happened! In fact, the anthropologists' work often exposed these societies to exploitation by the Western industrialized world. (1992, 42)

Harries-Jones notes that anthropological research is based on the assumption of an exchange of communication between human equals of two different cultures. In fact anthropologists saw the local people mainly as "informants," and "objects" to be studied, "as a mine whose product was extracted for export to the Western academic community (Harries-Jones 1985, 227; Loewen 1992, 47). Rarely is there a genuine two-way exchange of information and beliefs to discover reality. Moreover, ethnographic studies carry no commitment of responsibility on the part of the anthropologist.

Harries-Jones and others (Anderson 1985, 45-48; Maybury-Lewis 1985, 136-148) point out that the day of moral neutrality is over. Knowledge is used by the participants in the social, economic and political arenas of life. In the past, anthropologists have interpreted others from the point of view of western culture. Today they must also interpret the point of local peoples to those in power. Harries-Jones argues that anthropology can no longer be taught as an objective morally neutral description of culture. "[C]ultural knowledge carries with it responsibilities to facilitate mutually beneficial interaction between different social and racial groups" (Loewen 1992, 48). Consequently anthropologists must be advocates helping minority communities cope with the impact of majority cultures in a rapidly changing world (1985, 225).

Jacob Loewen notes (1992, 48) that on the whole missionaries have been less guilty than anthropologists of exploiting the societies they studied. They stayed, and sought to serve the people they learned to know. However, some missionaries collaborated with colonial governments–at least in the eyes of the local people, and even now many see ethnographic knowledge, not as a way of building deep mutual relationships, but as useful tools for carrying out their own agendas more efficiently. In missions we must now ask what do young churches have to teach sending churches, how can we, as missionaries, be advocates of our adopted churches to those in the West, and how can churches around the world join as fully equal partners in missions to a lost world (Loewen 1991, 49)?

There are many other anthropological, sociological, psychological, biological and historical theories that can help us understand different aspects of human beings. These which have been discussed are given only as illustrations of how human studies can help us understand our mission task better, and bear witness to the Gospel more effectively among peoples who have not heard it. Many of these theories can help us understand certain aspects of human life, but all of them need to be critiqued anthropologically. No one of these is fully adequate in helping us understand humans. Like in medicine, physics and other disciplines, further research may help us develop better models. But, as Christians we must also evaluate them from the perspective of a biblical worldview as best we understand it through a careful study of Scripture.[7]

Understanding the Gospel in Human Contexts

How can we understand the Gospel when we live in particular human contexts? We need to study Scripture to understand and bear witness to the Gospel, but studying Scripture alone does not help us see our sociocultural biases, and often leads to a failure in missions to communicate that Gospel so that the people understand and believe. We need to study humans to understand ourselves and others, and to communicate accurately, but studying humans alone leaves us with no Gospel to share. We need both–to study divine revelation and human contexts, and we need to communicate that revelation in ways that remain true to it, and are understood by people. Failure to do so leads to syncretism in which the truth of the Gospel is lost and the people go astray.

How can we communicate the Gospel in human contexts? First, it is important to note that our understandings of the Scriptures are limited by our humanness. We must not equate our theological reflections on revelation with a full and final understanding of revelation itself. Moreover, to understand complex realities we must use different theories or maps which complement one another on the essentials, but focus on different aspects of reality.[8] For example, to understand humans we can look at them as physical, biological, psychological, social, cultural and spiritual systems.

---

[7] The same is true in our use of philosophical and historical models and methods. Western systematic theology contributes much to our understanding of the structure of a biblical worldview, but also distorts the gospel in other ways. For example, in its search for objectivity, it has divorced cognition from affectivity and evaluation–truth from beauty and holiness. And its use of digital intrinsic categories has reduced salvation to a personal state, not a relationship, and divorced justification from sanctification.

[8] Complementarity is an essential part of a critical realist epistemology (Hiebert 1999). For a discussion of the theory of complementarity see D. M. MacKay, Complementarity in scientific and theological thinking. *Zygon* 9 (September 1974): 225-44.

While each of these adds insights to our understandings, none is the whole. On the other hand, taken together in a 'system of systems' view we begin to understand them more fully. This means that we need to work together as a hermeneutical community to gain a more comprehensive knowledge of the truth.

Second, we must keep in mind that our interpretations are shaped by our social, cultural, psychological and historical contexts. This is not to say that they are totally subjective or necessarily wrong. But, like glasses, they color how we see things. By studying these carefully, we can begin to see our particular perspectives, and grow in our knowledge of and obedience to the Gospel.

Third, God starts with us where we are, but our knowledge of him and the Gospel should keep growing. Conversion is to turn to follow Christ, but throughout life we must keep following more closely. We must not split justification from sanctification.

Fourth, it is important to remember that God revealed himself in Scripture in particular human contexts. That does not reduce the Gospel to particularities, or relativize it. Rather, we must seek to understand what God's revelation in those contexts has to say to us today in our contexts, and, indeed, for all humans everywhere and in all times.

Finally, we must seek the guidance of the Holy Spirit in our studies. Reason, in its many forms, is important, but it is the Holy Spirit that reveals to us through Scripture mysteries that transcend human knowledge.

In seeking to understand Scripture and to guard against the limitations and falsehoods of our cultures and societies, we need a meta-theology,[9] a transcultural framework that guides us in doing theology in different human contexts (Hiebert 1994). This has four steps. First, we need to study Scripture as the accurate, divinely inspired history of God's revelation to humans and let it shape our thinking (Pannenberg 1968; Morrison 2004). In doing so, we need to allow for different methods of analysis, in part because each

---

[9] The preface *meta* is used as Douglas Hofstadter uses it, as a position above two or more systems of the same level (*Godel, Escher, Bach: An Eternal Braid* [New York: Random House, 1980]. For further discussion see Hiebert 1994, 87).

throws light on certain aspects of Scripture but overlooks others, and in part because young churches around the world use their own philosophical methods in studying the Bible.[10] For example, modern Systematic Theology uses the western philosophical methods which use digital intrinsic categories, and abstract linear algorithmic logic to understand the underlying structure of Reality. Eastern Orthodox theologians use tropological reasoning and nondiscursive signs such as icons to speak about truths that cannot be reduced to words (Haleblian 2005). Indian theologians may use extrinsic, analogical categories and theologians in other cultures may use concrete functional logic (Luria 1976) in seeking to understand the Scriptures. Biblical theologians use the methods of history to understand the unfolding story of God's cosmic mission. Like different maps, these may be complementary if they are based on the texts, and do not contradict one another in fundamental ways.

It is important to use not only philosophical and historical methods in the study of scripture. To do so is to focus on truth (cognitive dimension of knowledge) and to divorce it from beauty (affective dimension) and holiness (evaluative dimension). We need truth, but unless it moves and transforms us, it remains lifeless. The Gospel must be understood as a whole, as truth, beauty, and holiness, and it must be lived out in daily life. We need also to do theological reflection liturgically–as leading to and as an essential part of our worship of God.

The second step is to study humans in their contexts. Local church leaders and missionaries lead the church in *uncritically* studying the local culture–gathering and analyzing the traditional beliefs and customs associated with the critical questions the church is facing using their local emic perspectives and worldview. If at this point, the missionaries show criticism of the customary beliefs and practices, the people will not talk to them freely for fear of being condemned, and we only drive the old ways underground.

In studying humans in their contexts, it is also important to study the context of the missionary or outsider participating

---

[10] For a discussion of categories and rational systems see Luria 1976, Wilson 1970, and Hiebert 1994.

in the study, seeking to understand their emic perspectives and worldviews to help separate the Gospel from their particular cultural viewpoints. This includes examining the worldviews behind modern theology and modern science.

Having studied both inside and outside views of the issues at hand, it is important to develop a metacultural framework to compare and evaluate these various perspectives. This framework is not itself a full culture, but a translating grid that enables participants in one culture to begin to understand other cultural perspectives. The formation of this framework is critical in building bridges of understanding, and all parties to the conversation must be heard. Each must agree that their views have been truly understood by outsiders as best as can be done in outside etic terms. It is here that anthropology can be of help, because it has sought to develop ways of translating and comparing social and cultural systems. Its frameworks are imperfect, and an ongoing dialogue between spokespersons for different cultures must continue in the construction of a metacultural framework.

The third step is for the people corporately to critically evaluate their own beliefs and practices in the light of their new biblical understandings, and to make decisions regarding their responses to their new-found truths. The gospel is not simply information to be communicated. It is a message to which the people must respond. Moreover, it is not enough that the leaders be convinced that changes are needed. They may share their convictions and point out the consequences of various decisions, but they and their people must together make and enforce decisions arrived at corporately. Only then will there be little likelihood of old beliefs and practices going underground and subverting the Gospel.

To involve people in evaluating their own culture in the light of new truth is to draw on their strength. They know their old culture better than does the missionary, and are in a better position to critique it and live transformed lives, once they have biblical instruction. Moreover, their involvement helps them to grow spiritually through learning discernment and applying scriptural teachings to their own lives. The priesthood of believers works in practice in a hermeneutical community.

Checks against Syncretism

What checks help us in this process of doing missional theology (Tiénou and Hiebert 2005) to guard against syncretism? It is important to remember that all our Christian understandings and life are in human contexts, and therefore partial. This does not mean they are necessarily wrong, but we need to be humble in our stance and to seek unity in the church "so that through the church the wisdom of God in its rich variety might be made known . . ." (Eph. 3:10, 4:1-3). But there is always the danger that when we put the Gospel in human contexts that the essence of the Gospel will be so distorted that it loses its message. God also starts with us where we are and reveals himself to us more fully as we grow in the knowledge of our Lord. In one sense syncretism is a message that has lost the heart of the Gospel. In another sense, it is moving in the wrong direction, away from a fuller knowledge of the Gospel.

The checks against both types of syncretisms lie in the metatheology we use in doing our theological reflections in life. We need to take the Bible seriously as the rule of faith and life. This may seem obvious, but we must constantly remind ourselves that biblical revelation is the standard against which our beliefs and practices must be measured. We need to recognize the work of the Holy Spirit in the lives of all believers open to God's leading. The church must act as a hermeneutical community seeking to understand God's word to it in its particular contexts. The priesthood of believers is not a license for theological "Lone-Rangerism." We need Christians from other cultures for they often see how our cultural biases have limited or distorted our interpretations of the Scriptures. This corporate nature of the church as a community of interpretation extends not only to the church in every culture, but also to the church in all ages. Through this community hermeneutic we seek a growing understanding, if not agreement, on key theological issues that can help us test our theologies and our practices. This will be an ongoing process in which the church constantly engages itself seeking to understand what the lordship of Christ and the Kingdom of God on earth are about.

Sources Cited

Anderson, David. 1985. "The Rubicon of Involvement–Social Work and Anthropology." In *Advocacy and Anthropology: First Encounter*, ed. Robert Paine, Pg. #s. St. Johns: Institute of Social and Economic Research.

Bernard, Alan. 2000. *History and Theory in Anthropology*. Cambridge: Cambridge University Press.

Geertz, Clifford. 1988. *Works and Lives: The Anthropologist as Author*. Stanford: Stanford University Press.

Haleblian, Krikor G. 2004. Art, theology and contextualization: the Armenian Orthodox experience. *Missiology: An International Review*. 3 (July):309-335.

Harries-Jones, Peter. 1985. From cultural translator to advocate: changing circles of interpretation. In *Advocacy and Anthropology: First Encounters*, ed. Robert Paine. St. Johns: Institute of Social and Economic Research.

Hiebert, Paul G. 1978. Missions and anthropology: a love/hate relationship. *Missiology*. 6 (April):165-189.

_____. 1994. *Anthropological Reflections on Missiological Issues*. Grand Rapids: Baker.

_____. 1999. *Missiological Implications of Epistemological Shifts: Affirming Truth in a Modern/ Postmodern World*. Harrisburg, PA: Trinity Press International.

Kirk, J.; Andrew and Kevin J. Vanhoozer, eds. 1999. *To Stake a Claim: Mission and the Western Crisis of Knowledge*. Maryknoll, NY: Orbis Books.

Laudin, Larry. 1996. *Beyond Positivism and Relativism: Theory, Method and Evidence*. Boulder, CO: Westview Press.

Loewen, Jacob. 1992. What is happening in anthropology? An example for missionaries and mission boards. *Mission Focus* 20:3:47 - 50.

Luria, Aleksandr R. 1976. *Cognitive Development: Its Cultural and Social Foundations*. Trans. M. Lopez-Moriallas and I. Solotaroff. Cambridge, MA.: Harvard University Press.

Mayberry-Lewis, David. 1985. Brazilian Indianist policy: some lessons from the Shavarite Project. In *Native Peoples and Economic Development: Six Case Studies from Latin America*, ed. Theodore Macdonald, Jr. Cambridge: Cultural Survival Occasional Paper No. 16.

Morrison, John. 2004. Barth, Barthians and Evangelicals: Reassessing the question of the relations of Holy Scripture and the Word of God. *Trinity Journal*. 25:187-213.

Pannenberg, Wolfhart, ed. 1968. *Revelation as History: A Proposal for a More Open Less Authoritarian View of an Important Theological Concept*. New York: Macmillan Company.

Ramachandra, Vinoth. 1999. *Faiths in Conflict? Christian Integrity in a Multicultural World*. Downers Grove, IL: InterVarsity Press.

Schultz, Donald L. 1989. *Developing an Asian Evangelical Theology*. Manila: Mandalyjyong

Turner, Harold. 1969. *The Ritual Process*. Harmondsworth: Penguin Books.

Wilson, Bryan R., ed. 1970. *Rationality*. New York: Harper Torchbooks.

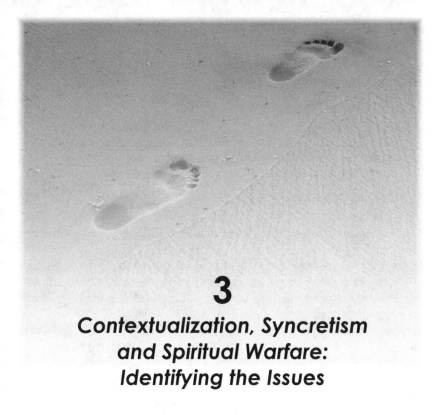

3
Contextualization, Syncretism and Spiritual Warfare: Identifying the Issues

Scott Moreau

In trying to trace the terrain of discussion on contextualization and syncretism in relation to spiritual warfare, we can start with opposing sets of questions that highlight the issues involved.

On one hand, we may ask the following: Is it syncretism when Christian missionaries march around a Hindu temple seven times and then declare God's victory? Is it syncretism when Christians gather at an ancient religious site to declare God's glory and break an ancient curse? Is it syncretism when Christians pray to bind Satan and all of his work? With equal validity, however, we may ask these questions: Is it syncretism when a Christian therapist treats disassociation with therapy and drugs without ever addressing demonic possibilities? Is it syncretism when seminaries prepare ministerial candidates with no training on spiritual warfare? Is it syncretism when Christians act as though there is no ongoing conflict between Satan and the body of Christ?

In setting the stage for the discussion to follow, we will do well to remember the oft-quoted statement from C. S. Lewis:

There are two equal and opposite errors about which our race can fall about the devils. One is to disbelieve in their existence. The other is to believe, and to feel an excessive and unhealthy interest in them. They themselves are equally pleased by both errors and hail a materialist or a magician with the same delight. (Lewis 1961, 9)

Today, though it is perhaps not as significantly on the forefront of discussion as in recent years, spiritual warfare is certainly still a subject that tends to divide more than to unify. In exploring the frame of syncretism in relation to spiritual warfare, our focus will be to explore the questions that need to be raised. Space to frame the answers would require a book-length treatment.

Syncretism Defined

Syncretism "has generally referred to the replacement or dilution of the essential truths of the Gospel through the incorporation of non-Christian elements" (Moreau, 2000). Key considerations include definitions of several terms. What is meant by "replacement" or the more pejorative "dilution"? When we talk about essential elements, what are those elements and who determines what they are? Recent theologians have noted that contextualization must include the whole of scripture, not just a "canon within the canon" of supracultural principles (see Carson 1983 and Conn 1988).

Unmasking Hidden Assumptions

If we are to make progress in resolving the thorny issues presented in this chapter, we must be willing to ask ourselves to what extent each of these "hidden assumptions" characterizes our approach to syncretism. As you read them, ask God to reveal to you ones that might be more true of you than he would like.

1. It is syncretism when *I* don't like what they are doing!
2. It is *my* job to determine what is syncretistic.
3. The biblical approach that *I* take is the correct one.
4. *It is possible* (and it is necessary) to eliminate all syncretism.
5. It is *always easy* to identify syncretism.

Selected Biblical Case Studies

In setting up the questions to follow, it will help to describe several case studies of spiritual warfare found in Scripture. Each offers insights into understanding syncretism and boundaries that are important to establish in spiritual warfare. Our point in citing them is not to try to develop complete explanations that either secularize or spiritualize what happens. Rather, it is to point out that in the Bible we do find examples of religious blending within apparent spiritual warfare contexts for which no overt condemnation is present.

Among the many examples from the Old Testament, we note three. First is God's command to Moses to make a bronze snake and place it high enough on a pole to be visible from a distance (Num. 21:4-9). Previously, God had sent venomous snakes in judgment for the grumbling of the Israelites in the wilderness. After the Israelites repented of their grumbling, God commanded Moses to make the snake so that those bitten could look at the bronze snake and be healed. This is certainly not a type of practice we would promote today—making an image of an unclean animal so that those who looked at it after being bitten would live! Indeed, eventually the bronze snake had to be destroyed because it became a source of idolatry (2 Kings 18:4).

The second example is one frequently cited as an illustration that the lines between syncretism and allowable worship are not as inflexible nor as clear as we would like. Namaan the Syrian was healed of leprosy. Before leaving to return to his home, he professed faith in God. However, he first made a request of Elisha:

> ". . . please let me, your servant, be given as much earth as a pair of mules can carry, for your servant will never again make burnt offerings and sacrifices to any other god but the Lord. But may the Lord forgive your servant for this one thing: When my master enters the temple of Rimmon to bow down and he is leaning on my arm and bow there also—when I bow down in the temple of Rimmon, may the Lord forgive your servant for this." (2 Kings 5:17-19)

We could expect anything but Elisha's response: "Go in peace" (v. 19).

The theological implications of this response are certainly debatable, but this also provides a case study to consider issues of significance in spiritual warfare.

A third example in the Old Testament is one that provides little context and no explanation. It is the divination cup possessed by Joseph and put into Benjamin's sack of grain so that Joseph had a pretense for arresting Benjamin and bringing him back to Egypt (Gen. 44:1-15). While we do not read of Joseph actually practicing divination, and certainly in other Old Testament texts that would not be allowed, Joseph uses the existence of the cup to remind his brothers (who do not yet know it is Joseph) that he can discover the fact of what he accused them of doing by divination (v. 15).

Several examples can also be found in the New Testament. Again, our intention is not to try to offer full explanations. Instead, we point to examples that bear further reflection as we wrestle with the issues being discussed in this paper.

First is Simon the sorcerer's offer to pay for spiritual power after seeing the gift of the Spirit bestowed through the ministry of Peter and John (Acts 8:9-24). Here the boundary is clear; paying for God's power demonstrates that Simon has no partnership in the Gospel. It is interesting that he frames his final request in terms of spiritual power, asking Peter to pray for him that none of the curses Peter announces would come to pass (v. 24).

A second example is the burning of the magical paraphernalia in Ephesus (Acts 19). This event takes place only *after* the botched exorcism of the sons of Sceva and the great fear that came on the church as a result. It certainly seems possible, especially

> **This seems to imply that new believers may be given some time for growth, though there will come a stage where a decision to truly break with magical ways must be made.**

given the magical reputation of Ephesus (Arnold 1992a), that the Christians there had those objects all along and only burned them when they saw that God was serious about dependence on Him alone. One may ask why Paul did not address this issue sooner. Perhaps he did not know that they kept their magical objects, or perhaps it was not a central issue of his concern in discipleship. It seems, however, that God brought them to a stage where they realized the destruction of the objects was crucial for their faith. This seems to imply that new believers may be given some time for growth, though there will come a stage where a decision to truly break with magical ways must be made.

A third example is Paul warning the Corinthians about eating meat that had been sacrificed to idols. On one hand, the mature believer should choose whether to eat such food on the basis of the conscience of those who see this as polluting or contaminating (1 Cor. 8: 1-13). On the other hand, Paul writes that we are not to be partakers of the Lord's table and the "table of demons" (1 Cor. 10:19-21). Once again we see clear evidence for boundaries, but that defining those carefully is not as easy as simply agreeing with the religious beliefs of believers who come from the background of idolatrous religious systems.

The fourth and final example is Paul's epistle dealing with the folk religious practices of the Colossians. Clinton Arnold aptly observes:

> Paul perceived a dangerous teaching was threatening the health and stability of the Colossian church. Although it is difficult to interpret the details of the aberration with certainty, it appears a group of people within the church were advocating that the rest of the church join them in a number of practices that were not a part of the Christian tradition or apostolic teaching. These practices seemed to be rooted in a syncretistic view of Christianity in which elements of mystery initiation, Jewish ritual observances and magical practices were combined with the gospel. In his letter Paul revealed the demonic nature of this false teaching and its accompanying practices. He called the church to a fresh commitment to the purity of the gospel. (Arnold 1992b, 139)

For each of the biblical examples, careful exegetical work needs to be done by the Christian community. It is quite clear that there are biblical boundaries on the extent of allowable religions intermingling—but that those boundaries are not always as easy to draw as we might think.

Dimensions of Religion, Contextualization, Syncretism and Spiritual Warfare

At this point we are ready to frame the types of questions we must ask to help provide clarity on syncretism and spiritual warfare. We will focus the rest of the chapter on these questions, placing them in the context of contextualization that helps us put perspective on each. To do that, we will utilize the outline for understanding contextualization that builds on the work of comparative religious scholar Ninian Smart (1996). Smart, after a lifetime of study, developed a set of dimensions of religion that can be used to unpack a religious tradition. These dimensions are all important for contextualization, which in evangelical circles has tended to focus almost exclusively on theology to the exclusion of other areas of Christian faith. We have provided an explanation of these dimensions in greater detail elsewhere (Moreau, 2005a and 2005b); here we will simply summarize each dimension and focus on questions raised in it.

The Doctrinal Dimension

The doctrinal dimension focuses on the way religions express what they consider to be the fundamental explanations about the world, the universe, and the relationship of people within the larger structures. The focus of the doctrinal dimension is "What is true?"

Multiple questions about theological teaching in spiritual warfare have been wrestled with recently. Particularly in terms of the two directions of syncretism we presented earlier (secularization and spiritism), we will note five such questions here. This does not exhaust the types of questions

> The focus of the doctrinal dimension is **"What is true?"**

that can be asked, but is offered as a starting point on areas that need further exploration.

First, are there territorial spirits? Following up on that, if such entities exist, what is meant by "territories"? Are there clear biblical guidelines in determining the answer to this question? If they do exist, we have a further question to ask, namely what is the Christian's responsibility towards such spirits (Arnold 1997; Moreau 2002; Page 1995; Reid 2002)?

A second question is whether modern psychotherapy can explain possession phenomena? Certainly for the Christian who believes that the Bible is the sole authority in all matters of faith and practice, it would be inappropriate to deny the reality of spirits' destructive work in the lives of people, but many from secular environments are more comfortable with explanations that conveniently explain demonic-appearing phenomena in terms of personal life history, genetic dispositions, and the choices that people make (Augsburger 1986; Bufford 1988).

A third question that looks at the same issue from the other side is this: To what extent can spiritual problems be reduced to spiritual warfare? For many, finding out that a demon (or many demons) is the source of their sin provides a sense of relief. The relief can be so great that there is a temptation to ascribe all of their sins and shortcomings to demonic influence. This type of reductionism is just as bad as that which completely excludes the demonic (Moreau 1995; see also Mungadze 2002)

The fourth question goes beyond the personal: To what extent may spiritual warfare be considered an explanation for what Westerners consider to be "natural" phenomena such as disease and disasters? If we live in a world infected with the demonic, and if demons possess powers parallel to the powers seen in angels in the book of Revelation, can a demonic explanation offer help in understanding what Westerners like to call "natural" disasters (see, for example, Winter 1998a and 1998b and Kraft 1989)?

Fifth, and finally, many have asserted on the basis of "sins passing on to the third and fourth generations" and findings that come from interrogation of demons that demons can "legally" pass from one generation to the next within families (Dickason 1987, 221). Is this an accurate biblical teaching?

The Ritual Dimension

Rituals are regularized ceremonies of life that provide places of security and identity. They are "cultural libraries" that act out, establish and preserve in symbolic form important religious truths. Unfortunately, Evangelicalism as a whole has tended to deny the power of ritual in religious life. Correctly noting that dead ritual leads to dead churches and traditions, we have tended to intellectually throw out all ritual. At the same time however, Evangelicals are big on quiet times, Sunday church attendance, baptisms, the Lord's supper, weekly discipleship meetings or Bible studies, prayer meetings, and so on. Every one of these (not to mention short-term missions trips!) is a ritual, and Evangelicals would greatly benefit from naming them as such and trying to understand more of the power they have in our lives. The picture given in Revelation clearly shows that heaven will include ritual (e.g., Rev. 4:8-11; 5:6-14), so obviously to pretend it is not important in our lives is to deny reality. With that in mind, what are some questions we can ask that will help us understand syncretism in spiritual warfare in ritual contexts? Here we identify four questions.

> **Every one of these is a ritual, and Evangelicals would greatly benefit from naming them as such and trying to understand more of the power they have in our lives.**

First, for those working in non-Christian contexts, can local rituals be "redeemed" for spiritual warfare purposes (Zahniser 1997)? While on the surface it seems an immediate "no" is required, we need to consider this question not just on the surface. In many cultures traditional transition rituals can be used to announce to the spirits that those who follow Christ no longer will look to the spirits for protection or guidance (e.g., Hiebert and Hiebert1987, 158-60). These would typically be one-time events in which a "good-bye" to the traditions is given.

Second, and following up on the first question, what roles might ritual play in helping people connect to spiritual warfare truths? Certainly Neil Anderson's "Steps to Freedom in Christ" (1993) involves a ritual, but typically such language is not used to describe the event. From the early church through the 18th century baptism typically included a renunciation of the devil and all of his works (e.g., Skarsaune and Engelsviken 2002, 78) so the power of such ritual was clearly recognized through much of the history of the church. What positive orientations towards ritual do we need to recover today, especially when we work in cultures that still affirm and understand the importance of ritual?

In addition to these questions, we may note several case studies of specific rituals. For example, Neil Anderson frames spiritual warfare in terms of "truth" encounters that focus exclusively on cognitive categories. The person seeking deliverance is walked through a thorough moral inventory in which he or she is asked to identify and confess sin, declare statements of faith, take stances against Satan and his schemes and so on. During the course of the inventory there may or may not be an emotional connection. In my work with Anderson's inventory, I have found that the less significant the emotional connection, the less significant the encounter. World view—in this case the emphasis of cognition over emotion—shapes the ritual.

Other case studies include the more recent phenomena of prayer vigils, walks, or journeys. In these a person or group of people enter into a season of prayer as led by God. This may include walking around a location (e.g., a temple or church) in which prayers are offered to God either for protection (church) or against Satan's work in holding people in bondage (temples, mosques).

Another type of case study in ritual is the reliance—or the avoidance—of patterned prayers. Such prayers have been part of the history of the church since the earliest days (the Lord's Prayer). Some feel uncomfortable with patterned prayers simply because of an implicit aversion to formal ritual. Others want to use pattern prayers because they have assurance that the words they are using are the correct ones. Each attitude is a movement towards syncretism that should be examined.

The Ethical Dimension

This is the application of religious values focusing on *how people are to behave*. It is closely related to the doctrinal dimension, which posits *why* people should behave in a particular way. In this sense, ethics are the application of truths expressed in doctrine. For example, one doctrine is that God exists and created humankind. An ethical implication is that we are to love God with all of our hearts, souls, minds, and strength.

Ethical systems are seen on the personal, group, and societal (systemic) levels. Evangelicals have generally been very consistent on calling people to personal righteousness, and for churches to live righteously in communities. However, we have not done as well in wrestling with systemic ethical systems, except perhaps when they frame personal moral issues (e.g., abortion).

We can identify several ethical issues in syncretism and spiritual warfare that bear further investigation. On the personal level, what are the ethics involved when people want to shed personal responsibility for sin or shameful acts and, in effect, say "The Devil made me do it"? This spiritistic approach opens the door to reductionistic excuses that enable perpetrators to get away with anything they do and never have to face personal responsibility. This is not to say that demonic control is not possible. Rather, it is to say that even when demonic control is evident, we still bear responsibilities for the sins we commit. The good news, of course, is that the price has already been paid.

A second question focuses on the oft-stated claim that there are demons tasked to personal immorality (alcohol, pornography, theft, and so on). Clearly we see instances in Scripture in which unnamed demons afflict people with specific disorders (the 'deaf and mute' spirit; Mark 9:25). However, we do not see clear examples of demons perpetrating specific vices among their victims (Powlison 1995, 66-69). However, does that necessarily mean that people who talk about "demon of alcohol' are necessarily incorrect? This certainly bears further discussion.

We may also ask questions on the systemic side. First, to what extent is it possible for a person or group to repent on behalf of a larger group? There have been examples of Japanese church leaders repenting before Korean church leaders, but to what extent does the Japanese church represent all of Japanese culture? It seems that to repent on behalf of someone effectively, the person repenting must truly represent the group. Certainly this bears further exploration, as identificational repentance is a method regularly used in some spiritual warfare circles (see Jørgensen 2002).

Second, is it possible to identify and come against systemic strongholds that are demonic in origin and maintenance? To what extent was there satanic influence in slave trade, the abortion industry, the Crusades, and even such things as the colonial enterprise? It is comfortable to challenge the first three areas for many evangelicals, while the fourth area would not be seen to fit as well. Were these nothing more than human destructiveness, or were there genuine demonic and satanic influences (and figures) that goaded their development, supported their entrenchment, and fought against change?

The Experiential Dimension

By the experiential dimension, we mean our encounters with the transcendent—including demonic and godly—and the mental maps we use to interpret those encounters. Contextualizing in this area feels uncomfortable to many, mainly because these experiences are not amenable to human control. At the same time, many cultures of the world recognize the interplay of what is seen with what is unseen, and if we ignore this dimension we ignore a potentially powerful tool for understanding syncretism in contextualization (Hiebert 1982).

> **How are we to evaluate phenomena such as words of wisdom, dreams, visions, revelations and so on?**

One significant question in the experiential dimension is this: How are we to evaluate phenomena such as words of wisdom, dreams, visions, revelations and so on? For many who grew up in more "secularized" cultures, such phenomena are more likely to be attributed to psychological or physiological health. We say, "I dreamed _____ because of the argument I had with my boss yesterday" or "I should not have eaten that much pizza; I had really weird dreams last night!" For people in the majority of world cultures, however, attributing dreams to purely secular sources is to miss their point entirely. For them it is during dream-time that the wall between the visible and the invisible is penetrable (see Kelsey 1978), and we should find the right interpretation of dream-phenomena when they occur.

Should we seek such experiences? One side attributes too much to dreams; the other too little. Both are reading the dream from their cultural perspective. In that sense both may be syncretistic.

In terms of syncretism and spiritual warfare, an important question is this: What is the real power of blessings and curses (Burnett 2000; Kraft 1989; Van Rheenen 1991)? Syncretism on the secular side attributes only psychosomatic power to such; syncretism on the spiritistic side attributes genuine power to the words—and the words must be exact to be powerful. Psychologists have recognized the power of words—but their orientation is that the power is psycho-social rather than spirit driven. This tends to be the world view of many Western Christians. In parallel with this question and with similar implications, we may ask whether prayers of power, especially prayers of binding and loosing so common in spiritual warfare, should be encouraged or discouraged (compare Wagner, 1986 with Wright, 1990, 185, 195; MacArthur, 1992, 146-7 and Moreau 1997)?

The Mythic Dimension

The mythic dimension refers to the corpus of narratives found in a society that reflect that society's thinking about the world, itself, its laws and values. This corpus is comprised of stories, proverbs, poems, songs and so on. The value of such stories is in the way they embody values that the society deems important. From a sociological perspective, the veracity of the stories is not as significant an issue as their influence. In that sense what is important is that the corpus of myth of a society concretizes important

> **The value of [myths] is in the way they embody values that the society deems important.**

cultural values and enables those values to be passed from generation to generation.

For this dimension, rather than asking the same questions we will briefly explore case studies of how North American myth can be found in spiritual warfare (see also Moreau 1995). The extent to which the mythic values and images drive spiritual warfare in our culture demonstrates the extent to which we have syncretized our cultural values into the practice of our faith.

First, part of the myth for many North American Christians is that the fun is in the fight (Hiebert 1992). The hero and the villain never learn—they are doomed to fight the same fights over and over throughout eternity (Wink, 1992, 18). For example, pay attention at the end of the next sports season. Typically one of the questions interviewers ask of the winning coach at the end of the season is "What about next year?" All too often, without missing a beat, the coach will say that he or she wants to enjoy this for a few weeks before worrying about next season. The implicit meaning is that "happily ever after" only lasts a short while, and then the real fun of planning for the next campaign begins. Often spiritual warfare practitioners focus their writing and speaking on engaging in the battle. Readers in North America expect this, and would not be as interested in the books or speakers if there were no battle accounts. Thankfully, spiritual warfare will one day cease to be, showing that the North American myth of the fun being in the fight is not a myth built on biblical values.

Embedded with the myth of the fun being in the fight is the mythic ideal that warfare is like a chess game (Hiebert, 1992), with the best strategist winning. Certainly we see that Satan has wiles and strategies and that we must combat them (2 Cor. 2:11). However, we also know that Christ's victory has already been won and in that sense Satan's current strategies are of little importance in the long run.

Closely related is our mythic understanding of the hero (see Wink 1992, 18-20). Though tempted, by the end of the story (s)he *always* makes the right choice. Heroes in North American mainstream society are not allowed final failure. Even death may only be temporary. Superman was killed in November of 1992 by DC Comics. However, he was resurrected not too long after. In the North American myth, the hero cannot truly die just as (s)he cannot truly lose the battle (see also Lawrence and Jewett 2002). This myth plagues spiritual warfare literature, seen especially in that the authors, as heroes, are not allowed to lose any battles. The sad truth is that not everyone is freed from demons, and not every story turns out well. The problem is that this reality is not often portrayed accurately. Further, our mythic heroes are often loners motivated by individual commitment to ideals (Superman, Lone Ranger) or revenge (Spiderman and Batman). They rarely question their own motivation; they always know that [they] are doing right. The means by which they overcome the enemies are violent ones—they never seek to redeem the enemy, only to destroy him . . . (Moreau 1995, 170).

The violence of the hero, however, is intrinsically "good," (after all, it is the hero's violence) while that of the villain is intrinsically "bad." Good violence may be used to overcome evil violence, especially if the enemy has drawn first blood (e.g., Rambo). Perhaps this is the most dangerous myth: good violence may be used to overcome evil violence. No one more clearly wrestles with the implications for this in spiritual warfare than Walter Wink (1992).

The Social Dimension

The social dimension of religions refers to the *religious* frame of social organization as seen through institutions and leadership in a society. It includes the social institutions found in every society: associations and kinship, education, economics, and law (or legal/political) (Hiebert and Meneses 1996; see also Harris and Moran 1982).

Association and Kinship

The associational system of a community refers to the multitude of ways people choose to group together. It includes people coming together to form such bodies as unions, clubs, societies, cooperatives, parties, and so on. These are often seen within the other types of social institutions (e.g., alumni associations, political parties, and economic cooperatives). Kinship is a subset of the associational system in which the relationship is less voluntary (for example, marriage may be voluntary, but descent lines are not). Every society must provide for the biological reproduction of new members and see that they are nourished and cared for during infancy and childhood. Nearly everywhere it is the family, whether nuclear or extended, that provides the basic context for the performance of these activities. Most of the early training and socialization of children also takes place within the family.

Questions related to syncretism and spiritual warfare seek to define the relationship between ethnocentrism and the demonic. To what extent does Satanic influence inform our perception of the significance of so-called racial divisions? To what extent can the exclusive homogeneity of many of our churches be considered syncretistic (taking an ungodly association pattern from our culture and incarnating it in our worship)? To what extent might this reality be caused by and amenable to spiritual warfare issues?

A related question is the extent to which demons might be "attached" to groups or institutions. For example, those in the Evangelical Missiological Society are all attached in some form to a mission agency, a mission-minded church, or a school where missions is taught. It should be a given that Satan would be interested in thwarting the efforts of such institutions, and would want to find "contextualized" ways to hinder, thwart and otherwise harass them. May we see some of the social tensions our institutions experience—and especially the destructive patterns we sometimes follow—as examples of Satanic influence? Might they be combated with spiritual warfare? It seems that Paul's many requests for prayer recognize this element (e.g., Eph. 6:19; Col. 3:3-4; 2 Thess. 3:2). Is it primarily the secularized syncretistic thinking found in so many Western Christian institutions that hinders us from seeing this more clearly?

Education

All types of educational processes—formal, non-formal, and informal—are institutionalized cultural elements necessary to every society. As an institutional term, education refers to all those activities which, in any way, directly or indirectly, contribute to providing new members, either by birth or immigration, with the knowledge, values and skills of the society. These are transmitted to members in order to prepare them to live and function within the society in a socially acceptable manner with some degree of independence. For Christians, this includes all elements of spiritual formation found within the church (e.g., discipleship programs, Sunday school, small group Bible studies, formal training colleges, and so on).

Within the educational context, we must ask to what extend cultural values and ideals frame our orientation towards the appropriateness (or inappropriateness) of spiritual warfare in the normal discipleship process. Why was this, at least until the 1980s, so typically ignored in Western seminaries and Bible colleges? Is this an example of syncretism in a secularized direction?

A related question is the analysis of current spiritual warfare methodologies. It is not surprising, for example, that Neil Anderson's cognitive therapy approach found in *Steps to Freedom* is so popular in the North American evangelical ethos. To what extent do cultural values and expectations so frame our approaches to spiritual warfare that they may be labeled as syncretistic—whether in secularized/rational or in spiritistic directions?

Economics

Every culture must have some way of producing and distributing the goods and services which sustain the lives of its members. The set of institutions and roles which are organized around the performance of these activities constitutes the economic system of the culture. Often there is an idealized portrait of what that system is which may not correspond to the actual events of life for the average person.

Given this as a description of the institution of economics, what is the level of satanic involvement in the economic materialism of the North American church? To put it more bluntly, is there a demon of money, and have we completely overlooked the demonic influence of materialism within our churches because of our more secularized outlook on economics?

Law and Politics

All communities or cultures must have some means of maintaining internal order and, at the same time, regulating their relations with other communities or cultures. Internal threats to a culture's—or religion's—existence come from the competition for power, here defined as the control over human, human-made, and natural resources. Since the availability of such resources has ultimate limits in any religious community, conflict over the use of those resources is inevitable. The political system in relation to religious systems, therefore, is the network of institutions and social roles within the religion which exist to control the competition for power. In Christian contexts, this institution entails such pragmatic issues as church polity, the selection of leadership, enforcement of church rules and regulations, and dealing with disputes over any of these.

One challenge being raised in certain portions of spiritual warfare literature is the allegation that there are satanic leaders who infiltrate Christian leadership circles. If this is true, what should Christians do to prevent this infiltration? Certainly some of the allegations are framed in conspiracy thinking, and should be treated as such. At the same time, a more "secularistic" orientation simply dismisses such allegations as paranoid. Would Paul have taken that stance?

Perhaps of more practical relevance is the issue of the appropriate means of oversight regarding deliverance ministry. In Roman Catholic circles, there is a well-developed set of rules and regulations, including people in official positions to perform the ministry of demonic deliverance. In Protestant circles such official recognition is almost completely absent. While para-church ministries of deliverance do exist, they are detached from denominational oversight and are often self-regulated. Even people within a church who minister in this way are not always accountable in formal ways to the church governing structure. Again, if syncretism is seen as the addition of non-Christian elements to the Christian faith, to what extent might this lack of oversight—and the potential dangers it exposes people to—be considered syncretistic?

The Material Dimension

The last dimension of religion discussed by Smart was the material or artistic. Following an orientation towards technology as any extension of humanity (see, for example, Postman 1993), this dimension has as its focus the multitude of ways we express religious themes, values, feelings, thoughts, and ideas through the "extensions" we develop. These include, but are not limited to, architecture, art of all types, literature, fashion, ritual paraphernalia, and so on.

One pervasive belief that is found in spiritual warfare literature and in many parts of the world is that objects have spiritual power or are infested with demons. To what extent might this be syncretistic and to what extent might it be biblical? We certainly see the early church burning objects of power (Acts 19:19). At the same time, as noted earlier, Paul tells the Corinthians "We know that an idol is nothing at all in the world and that there is no God but one." (1 Cor. 8:4). Later in the same epistle he states: "Do I mean then that a sacrifice offered to an idol is anything, or that an idol is anything? No, but the sacrifices of pagans are offered to demons, not to God, and I do not want you to be participants with demons" (1 Cor. 10:19-20). In each local setting wrestling with the implications of these and other passages that shed light on this question will be an important element of contextualizing the material dimension of spiritual warfare.

A second question in this area concerns artistic expressions. What role may artistic depictions of spiritual warfare—including such things as paintings, sculpture, architecture—play in the Church? To what extent are these even legitimate for the Christian (e.g., see J. I. Packer's 1973 critique of paintings and statues of Jesus)? Similar issues apply to spiritual warfare novels (e.g., Peretti 1986, 1989) and testimonies in book form (Onyango 1979).

Conclusion: A General Orientation

Syncretism is a broad word. In addition to contextualization, related terms include such ideas as borrowing, co-opting, adapting, blending, dilution, and interpenetration. It seems clear from some of the scriptural examples that God does allow—or at least tolerate—some forms of "borrowing" of ideas from other religions (2 Kings 5:17-19). However, it is also clear that there *are* boundaries on what is allowed (Exod. 23:23-33; Deut. 18:10-14). In fact, the sad statement found in 2 Kings 17:41: "Even while these people were worshiping the LORD, they were serving their idols" is a concise summary if Israel's participation in syncretism (Moreau 2001b).

Identifying and deciding how to draw these boundaries is not always as clear-cut as we might like. Part of the problem is that of objectivity. People from third world contexts, for example, note the syncretism they see in the Western church. "They ask who the judge is, and whether objectivity is possible. None of us think of ourselves as syncretistic—it is always the 'other' who's thinking incorporates inappropriate religious elements in the Gospel!" (Moreau 2001b).

Ultimately, however, we suggest that we focus our attention on the glory of God and growth in Christ-likeness of God's people as God's goal for all Christians. We are pilgrims on a path, not finished products. Indigenous-initiated and led movement away from syncretism—whether away from animism or away from secularism—is to be valued, encouraged and nurtured. How, then, do we grow in this direction? Four steps may be identified.

First...

be clear on identifying the ultimate goal of our faith...

Second...

as a community, identify and commit to biblically-framed non-negotiables.

Third...

develop the ability to really listen...

Fourth...

we should focus on empowering local decision-making...

First, be clear on identifying the ultimate goal of our faith, which is the growth of the local body of believers in Christ so as to glorify God.

Second, as a community, identify and commit to biblically-framed non-negotiables. For example, one of these must certainly be that the Bible is our normative standard for all issues of faith and practice.

Third—and this step is especially important for missionaries—develop the ability to *really* listen (a phenomenological approach). Too often our decisions have been made before we even know the problem. A phenomenological approach requires us to temporarily suspend truth issues until we know what we are actually facing (see Moreau 2001a).

Fourth, we should focus on empowering *local* decision-making to avoid the development of dependence. This should include the development of biblically-rooted *local* criteria for testing for syncretism. This may very well mean that people make decisions that make us uncomfortable. However, as long as they have the self-correcting frame of the Scriptures, opportunity for self-correction exists.

Sources Cited

Anderson, Neil. 1993. *Steps to Freedom in Christ*. La Habra, California: Freedom in Christ Ministries.

Arnold, Clinton. 1992a. *Ephesians: Power and Magic: The Concept of Power in Ephesians in Light of Its Historical Setting*. Grand Rapids: Baker.

_____1992b. *Powers of Darkness: Principalities and Powers in Paul's Letters*. Downers Grove: InterVarsity Press.

_____. 1997. *Three Crucial Questions about Spiritual Warfare*. Grand Rapids: Baker Books.

Augsburger, David W. 1986. *Pastoral Counseling across Cultures*. Philadelphia: Westminster Press.

Bufford, Rodger K. 1988. *Counseling and the Demonic*. Dallas, Texas: Word.

Burnett, David. 2000. *World of the Spirits*. London: Monarch Press.

Carson, Donald A. 1983. "Reflections on Contextualization: A Critical Appraisal of Daniel Von Allman's Birth of Theology." *East African Journal of Evangelical Theology* 3(1):16-59.

Conn, Harvie. 1988. "Normativity, Relevance, and Relativism." In *Inerrancy and Hermeneutic: A Tradition, a Challenge, a Debate*. Edited by Harvie M. Conn, 185-209. Grand Rapids: Baker.

Dickason, C. Fred. 1987. *Demon Possession & the Christian*. Chicago: Moody Press.

Harris, Philip R. and Moran, Robert T. 1982. "Understanding Cultural Differences." *In Intercultural Communication: A Reader*, 3rd ed. Edited by Richard E. Porter and Larry A. Samovar, 62-72. Belmont, California: Wadsworth.

Hiebert, Paul. 1992. "Spiritual Warfare: Biblical Perspectives." *Mission Focus* 20:3 (September): 41-46.

Hiebert, Paul and Eloise Hiebert Meneses. 1996. *Incarnational Mission: Planting Churches in Band, Tribal, Peasant, and Urban Societies*. Grand Rapids: Baker.

Hiebert, Paul and Frances Hiebert. 1987. *Case Studies in Missions.* Grand Rapids: Baker.

Jørgensen, Knud. "Spiritual Conflict in Socio-political Context." In *Deliver Us From Evil: An Uneasy Frontier in Christian Mission,* ed. by A. Scott Moreau, Tokunboh Adeyemo, David Burnett, Bryant Myers and Hwa Yung. 213-30. Monrovia, California: MARC.

Kelsey, Morton. 1978. *Dreams: A Way to Listen to God.* New York: Paulist Press.

Kraft, Charles. 1989. *Christianity with Power.* Ann Arbor, Michigan: Vine Books.

Lawrence, John Shelton and Robert Jewett. 2002. *The Myth of the American Superhero.* Grand Rapids: Eerdmans.

Lewis, Clive S. 1961. *The Screwtape Letters.* New York: MacMillan.

MacArthur, John. 1992. *How to Meet the Enemy: Arming Yourself for Spiritual Warfare.* Wheaton, Illinois: Victor Books, 1992.

Moreau, A. Scott. 1991. *The World of the Spirits.* Nairobi, Kenya: Evangel Publishing House.

_____. 1995. "Religious Borrowing as a Two-Way Street: An Introduction to Animistic Tendencies in the Euro-North American Context." In *Christianity and the Religions: A Biblical Theology of World Religions,* ed. Edward Rommen and Harold Netland, 166-82.

_____. 1997. *Essentials of Spiritual Warfare: Equipped to Win the Battle.* Wheaton: Harold Shaw Publishers.

_____. 2000. Evangelical Dictionary of World Mission, gen. ed. A. Scott Moreau, s.v. "Syncretism." Grand Rapids: Baker.

_____. 2001a. Evangelical Dictionary of Theology, rev. ed. Ed. Walter A. Elwell, s.v. "Phenomenology of Religion." Grand Rapids: Baker.

_____. 2001b. Evangelical Dictionary of Theology, rev. ed. Ed. Walter A. Elwell, s.v. "Syncretism." Grand Rapids: Baker.

_____. 2002. "Gaining Perspective on Territorial Spirits." In *Deliver Us From Evil: An Uneasy Frontier in Christian Mission*, ed. by A. Scott Moreau, Tokunboh Adeyemo, David Burnett, Bryant Myers and Hwa Yung. 263-78. Monrovia, California: MARC.

_____. 2005a. Contextualization: From an Adapted Message to an Adapted Life." In Engaging the Trends in the New Millennium, by Michael Pocock et al. Grand Rapids: Baker Books, forthcoming.

_____. 2005b. "Contextualization that Is Comprehensive." *Missiology: An International Review*, forthcoming.

Mungadze, Jerry. "Spiritual Conflict in Light of Psychology and Medicine." In *Deliver Us From Evil: An Uneasy Frontier in Christian Mission*, ed. by A. Scott Moreau, Tokunboh Adeyemo, David Burnett, Bryant Myers and Hwa Yung. 2203-12. Monrovia, California: MARC.

Onyango, Symons. 1979. *Set Free—from Demons*. Nairobi, Kenya: Evangel Publishing House.

Packer, James I. 1973. *Knowing God*. Downers Grove, IL: InterVarsity Press.

Page, Sydney. 1995. *Powers of Evil: A Biblical Study of Satan & Demons*. Grand Rapids: Baker.

Peretti, Frank. 1986 *This Present Darkness*. Westchester: Crossway Books.

_____. 1989. *Piercing the Darkness*. Westchester: Crossway Books.

Postman, Neil. 1993. *Technopoly: The Surrender of Culture to Technology*. New York: Vintage Books.

Powlison, David. 1995. *Power Encounters: Reclaiming Spiritual Warfare*. Grand Rapids: Baker Books.

Reid, Michael S. B. 2002. *Strategic Level Spiritual Warfare: A Modern Mythology?* Fairfax, Virginia: Xulon Press.

Skarsaune, Oskar and Engelsviken, Tormod. 2002. "Possession and Exorcism in the History of the Church." In *Deliver Us From Evil: An Uneasy Frontier in Christian Mission*, ed. by A. Scott

Moreau, Tokunboh Adeyemo, David Burnett, Bryant Myers and Hwa Yung. 65-87. Monrovia, California: MARC.

Smart, Ninian. 1996. *Dimensions of the Sacred: An Anatomy of the World's Beliefs*. Berkeley, CA: University of California Press.

Van Rheenen, Gailyn. 1991. *Communicating Christ in Animistic Contexts*. Grand Rapids: Baker.

Wagner, C. Peter, ed. 1986. "The Key to Victory is Binding the 'Strong Man'." *Ministries Today*. November-December, 1986, p. 84.

Wink, Walter. 1992. *Engaging the Powers: Discernment and Resistance in a World of Domination*. Philadelphia: Fortress Press.

Winter, Ralph. 1998a. "Editorial Comment: The Relationship between God, Satan and Evil, and How it Relates to Mission" *Mission Frontiers* (January/February):xx-xx.

_____. 1998b. "Editorial Comment: If Missionaries Do Not Preach about a God Who Is Interested in All Suffering, We Misrepresent the Full Scope of His Love and Concern." *Mission Frontiers* (June/July):xx-xx.

Wright, Nigel. 1990. *The Satan Syndrome: Putting the Power of Darkness in Its Place*. Grand Rapids: Zondervan.

Zahniser, A. H. Mathias. 1997. *Symbol and Ceremony: Making Disciples across Cultures*. Monrovia, California: MARC.

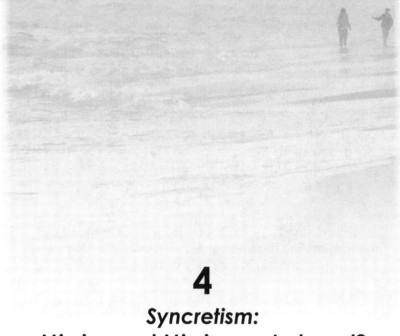

4

Syncretism: Mission and Missionary Induced?

David J. Hesselgrave

The topic of this essay is posed as a question. The question is not, *What is syncretism?* Neither is the question *How does syncretism occur?* Nor is it, *What is the result of syncretism?* Concerning such questions the authors of a recent book that focuses on missions in the context of folk religionists (though of much wider significance) say,

> The danger in responding to folk religions is not so much heresy as it is syncretism--combining elements of Christianity with folk beliefs and practices in such a way that the gospel loses its integrity and message. The problem here is not with old religious beliefs, but with the underlying assumptions on which they are built. The gospel must not only change beliefs, but also transform worldviews, otherwise the new beliefs will be reinterpreted in terms of the old worldviews. The result is Christopaganism.
>
> (Hiebert, Shaw and Tienou 1999, 378)

Most of my readers will agree with this definition of syncretism and will also be aware of the danger that syncretism poses. That frees us to concentrate on the main questions to be addressed here: namely, *Do those of us who are most involved in missions bear at least some responsibility for a pervasive syncretism; and, If so, what can we do to help remedy the situation?* In addressing these questions we will proceed by stating five propositions and, in connection with each proposition, introduce some preliminary considerations, elaborate some related contributors to syncretism, and propose some possible correctives.

Proposition #1: Syncretism is sometimes induced by underestimating the uniqueness of the Christian faith while overestimating the validity of competing faiths.

Some Preliminary Considerations

By "Christian faith" here I do not refer to personal faith but to the sum total of God's revelation in Christ and the Scripture—to what Jude spoke of as "the faith once for all delivered to the saints" (Jude 4). By "competing faiths" I refer to all other religions and faith systems.

Among varied comparisons between Christian and non-Christian faiths, Christian scholars have proposed two extremely different approaches. At one end of the spectrum are the proposals of people such as William Ernest Hocking, Paul Knitter and John Hick who minimize religious differences and depict the various religions as complementary ways of thinking about a final truth to which all religions aspire. For example, John Hick writes as follows:

> These resources [i.e., the various religions, ed.] have at their heart, I want to suggest, an awareness that the great purpose of religion is salvation, or liberation, as an actual transformation of human existence; and a recognition that this is taking place (though in conjunction with quite different systems of belief) Within other 'houses of faith' as well as one's own. (Hick 1985, 5)

At the opposite end of the spectrum is a perspective shared by the likes of Karl Barth, Hendrik Kraemer and Edmund

Perry. Perry expresses this basic viewpoint unequivocally in the following words:

> Religion is . . . first of all, the *generic* term comprehending the universal phenomenon of men individually and collectively being led away from God in manifold ways by divers claims and systems. Religion in this generic sense exists of course only in the *specific* religions, each of which is a concrete manifestation or actualization of a particular people being led away from God in a particular way by a particular schema, but as a descriptive term 'religion' expresses the unity of human life being oriented and organized away from the God of Gospel faith through the diversity of creeds, codes, myths, cults and ways of worship. [author's emphasis]
>
> (Perry 1956, 88)

Some Potential Contributors to Syncretism

Obviously, if the Christian faith and other faiths are *complementary*, some form of syncretism is to be welcomed as Hick implies. If they are *conflicting*, at least to the degree maintained by Barth, Kraemer and Perry, all forms of syncretism are to be deplored as Perry makes clear. Evangelicals would unhesitatingly distance themselves from the former approach but, at the same

> **"As a descriptive term 'religion' expresses the unity of human life being oriented and organized away from the God of Gospel faith."**
> **—Edmund Perry**

time, may have some misgivings with the latter. In so doing they may at least seem to be backing away from absolute uniqueness thereby risking some measure of syncretism.

Examples are easy to come by. Carl F. H. Henry argues for a "Christian rational presuppositionalism" according to which adherents of any or no religious faith can be convinced of a "creature-and-Creator" view of reality on rational as well as revelational bases. The laws of valid inference are elements of the *imago Dei* and therefore universal (Henry 1990, 108-14).

Christopher Little acknowledges that only special revelation is "redemptive." However, in agreement with Millard Erickson and others, he assigns special significance to general revelation grounded in the goodness of God. And he assigns perhaps even greater significance to "modalities of special revelation" such as divinely ordained dreams, visions, theophanies, and events outside of, though never in conflict with, God's special revelation in Christ and Scripture (Little 2000, 47-89).

Harold Netland disagrees with Hick's view that the various "houses of faith" are working at one and the same liberation task. Nevertheless he concurs with Hick's argument that, if a Christian is justified in believing that Christianity is *uniquely true*, then it follows that most of the religious beliefs of adherents of other religions are in fact false. Netland proceeds to deflect this odious inference by constructing an argument for some truth in other religions on the basis of what he (following Ninian Smart) calls a "soft natural theology" (Netland 2004, 16-39).

Mediating positions such as these certainly seem plausible. At the same time it seems to me that they do present evangelicals with a dilemma. We hold, on the one hand, that God's revelation in Christ and the Scriptures is truly *sui generis* and uniquely true. Adherents of other faiths must be converted to Christ and to Christ alone, to the Christian faith and to the Christian faith alone. On the other hand, we are inclined to admit that at least some ideas held by adherents of non-Christian faiths are true and some of their practices are good. But if that is correct, then it would seem to follow that those true beliefs and good practices should be welcomed as acceptable elements of a convert's new-found "Christian faith." To admit to that, however, is to either allow for syncretism or, at least, to run the risk of it.

Some Possible Correctives

Hendrik Kraemer avoids the foregoing "black and black" dilemma by noting (in line with Hiebert, Shaw and Tienou at this point) that particular ideas and practices of any religion grow out of its basic belief system (ideology, worldview) and, in intent or content or both, take their meanings from it. That being true, they cannot be extrapolated and evaluated or even understood in isolation. They are part and parcel of their "faith system" and along with the rest of that system are to be repented of, forsaken, and replaced by the faith of Christian revelation (Kraemer 1963, 134-36). It follows that even seemingly "good" and "noble" elements of non-Christian religions (perhaps good and noble elements *especially*!) must be reinterpreted and transformed if syncretism is to be avoided.

By way of examples, though Buddhist notions and practices connected with mercy, worship, prayer and meditation might seem to be intrinsically good and transferable, both the Christian missionary and the Buddhist convert should examine them carefully. Mercy, worship, prayer and meditation in Buddhism are not only very different from biblical mercy, worship, prayer and meditation, they are part and parcel of the larger Buddhist deception. To understand and practice them "as a Christian" is much different than to understand and practice them "as a Buddhist." Unless that is made plain, the result will be syncretism.

At least two problems accrue to this corrective. The first has to do with mediate proposals such as those of Henry, Little and Netland that may be in line with exclusivism but seem to run counter to absolute uniqueness. One solution to the kind of syncretism risked by these mediate proposals may well be found in the obvious distinction between a religious *system* and a religious *adherent*. What is true of the former is not necessarily true of the latter and vice versa. Rationalism as an element of the *imago Dei*, some kind of general revelation, and varied modalities of special revelation--insofar as these can be substantiated and validated by Scripture--can be true with regard to persons without being true of religious systems as such.

> **"Christianity ... is what it is and was what it was long before I was born and whether I like it or not."**
>
> — C. S. Lewis

As for the second problem, namely the insistence that Christianity is absolutely and uniquely true and therefore the beliefs of adherents of other religions are false: insofar as that is the case it is not so because we say it but because Christ and Scripture everywhere insist upon it. C. S. Lewis had it right when he said: ". . . I was not writing to expound something I could call 'my religion,' but to expound 'mere' Christianity, which is what it is and was what it was long before I was born and whether I like it or not" (Lewis 1960, viii).

Proposition #2: Syncretism often results from devoting too much attention to the outer layers of culture and not enough attention to its inner core or worldview.

Some Preliminary Considerations

Worldview has been variously defined but in this context the definition of Michael Kearney will serve us well: "The worldview of a people is their way of looking at reality. It consists of basic assumptions and images that provide a more or less coherent, though not necessarily accurate, way of thinking about the world" (Kearney 1984, 4).

Worldview, then, must be distinguished from culture. It is but part of culture albeit the most important part because it has to do with the cosmology, ideology and basic belief system that form the culture core. Of course, culture also includes the values and subsidiary beliefs, the institutions and institutional accoutrements, and the material goods and behavioral patterns that overlay the worldview core. But to get at the inner worldview core one must first peel away these surrounding layers much as one might peel away the layers of an onion in order to get to its "heart." The outer layers are more visible and available, but the inner core is more important and determinative.

Some potential contributors to syncretism.

Notice that the authors of the quotation with which we began this essay say,

> The problem here is not with old religious beliefs, but with the underlying assumptions on which they are built. The gospel must not only change beliefs, but also transform worldviews, otherwise the new beliefs will be reinterpreted in terms of the old worldviews. (Hiebert et. al. 1999, 378)

The almost universal tendency of missionaries is to deal first with respondent behaviors, institutions, beliefs and values that are most apparent and immediate. In the view of the missionary, those behaviors, institutions, beliefs and values connected with the old religion and most at odds with the Christian faith need to be abandoned. Those behaviors and beliefs that give evidence of an inner change—especially those connected with conversion such as "praying the sinner's prayer," Bible study, prayer, church attendance and so on—need to be adopted and demonstrated. But while all this is going on the old worldview that influences all else in ways not readily observable is allowed to remain more or less intact. The upshot is that missionaries need to be reminded repeatedly that "outer layer change" unaccompanied by a corresponding worldview transformation inevitably leads to syncretism.

A case from my early missionary experience may be helpful here. Long after my departure from Japan and appointment to Trinity I had occasion to revisit the home of a prominent and prosperous Japanese electronic engineer, Dr. K, who had hosted one of my Bible studies long years before. To my surprise and sorrow, Dr. K had passed away several weeks before my arrival. His widow apologized profusely for not being able to reach me during my travels. Then she ushered me to a large and exquisitely appointed *tatami* room. Centered on one wall was an elaborate lacquerware ancestral shelf with a large portrait of my late friend. Along with the usual Buddhist paraphernalia and immediately to one side of his portrait was the very New Testament he had used in those studies some twenty years before. It was cradled on a special stand and opened to the Gospel of John.

Anticipating my surprise and hesitating but a moment, Mrs. K turned to me and said,

> *Sensei*, my husband often said that out of all the religious books in the world, he trusted only one—the Bible. So I thought that I should certainly include it along with everything else. Please try to understand. After all, we are Japanese you know.

As I took leave of Mrs. K that day, I did so with the belated understanding that in the innocence of those early years I had not been wise in choosing the Gospel of John for an initial Bible study. What Dr. K had hoped for in requesting the weekly study was that many of the electronic engineers in his personal employ would be inculcated with the kind of moral values and work ethic he associated with Christianity. But what both he and they most needed was emancipation from the syncretistic admixture of Western secularism, Shinto nationalism, religious Buddhism and just plain ignorance and pride that blinded all of them to a biblical worldview and the gospel of Christ. Starting with the Gospel of John had occasioned far too many questions and problems that only a very basic knowledge of the Old Testament could resolve. Now Dr. K had died of a sudden heart attack and, if that ancestral shelf was indicative, he had died without really knowing Christ.

Some Possible Correctives

Missionaries everywhere need to learn what I had come to understand during the years that intervened between my first and final visit to Dr. K's home. Worldviews are based on big stories and little stories within a big story. At rock bottom, the Christian mission aims at an exchange of the worldview of Christian revelation for the worldview of this or that "other faith" whatever it might be. We missionaries encourage syncretism when we concentrate only or primarily on the ancillary values, beliefs and behaviors that constitute the externals and outer layers of culture. Our respondents embrace syncretism when they either fail to understand worldview differences or hesitate to choose between the Christian worldview and the worldview of their traditional religion(s).

If there was any justification for unawareness of the importance of all of this back in the 1950s, no such justification can be found today. We have, in the first place, new and renewed emphases on the importance of biblical theology, narrative theology, Bible survey and chronological Bible study in Christian education and missionizing. In the second place, there is a corresponding and corroborative body of materials on the place of history, myths and stories in the formation of worldviews.[1] And in the third place, we have numerous reports of the place that chronological Bible study and "cross-cultural storying of the gospel" has resulted in the conversion of the

---

[1] Cf. Tom A. Steffen, *Reconnecting God's Story to Ministry: Crosscultural Storytelling at Home and Abroad* (LaHabra, CA.: Center for Organizational & Ministry Development, 1996) and Everett Stowe, *Communicating Reality Through Symbols* (Philadelphia: Westminster, 1946, esp. 138-41).

various tribal groups such as the Mouk [2] and the Yali.[3] Also in the "re-conversion" of Luwuk-Banggai believers who had "become Christians in order to remain pagans" (cf. Weber 1957) and floundering Palawano Christians who had never really understood what it really meant to be Christian in the first place. (cf. McIlwain 1987) All of this and much more now undergirds and reinforces the notion that "the gospel must not only change beliefs, but also transform worldviews." An unwelcome alternative is some form of Christopaganism whether unsophisticated or sophisticated, unrecognized or recognized. For all their obvious cultural and educational differences, Dr. K and his research engineers needed precisely what Trevor McIlwain discovered tribalist Palawanos needed—the "big story" of Genesis, Exodus and the rest of the Old Testament apart from which John's Gospel is virtually impossible to fully understand.

Proposition #3: Both the under-contextualization and the over-contextualization of the Christian faith constitute open invitations to syncretism.

Some preliminary considerations.

Contextualization presents us with some "sticky wickets" when it comes to syncretism. The word "contextualization" is susceptible to differing definitions, procedures and objectives. And these differences relate as much to the background, expertise and interests of contextualizers as to anything else. Systematic theologians, cultural anthropologists and communication specialists, for example, tend to have their own particular biases and ways of looking at the subject.

Many years ago I attempted to show that, ultimately, revelational epistemology is largely determinative of one's approach to contextualization. I still believe that to be true. The contextualizer's understanding of the relative importance accorded to biblical revelation as over against cultural considerations filters through his or her basic theological orientation whether that be orthodox, neo-orthodox, neo-liberal or liberal. The end result of this process is a

---

[2] Cf. *Ee-Taow* video, New Tribes Mission.

[3] Cf. *The Yali Story* video, Gateway Films.

contextualization that is either more or less biblical, more or less justifiable. At the one end of the "contextualization continuum" a high view of Scripture lends itself to theological orthodoxy and a didactic contextualization that *eschews* syncretism. At the other end of the continuum an overly high view of culture lends itself to theological liberalism and a dialogical contextualization that *embraces* syncretism. (cf. Hesselgrave 1979, 8-26; Hesselgrave and Rommen 1989, 157)

Some Potential Contributors to Syncretism

Much of the more complete discussion referred to above must lie beyond our present purview but part of it is most germane. The problems to be pursued here have to do with contributors to syncretism emanating from the more evangelical and orthodox side of the contextualization continuum, especially from Western evangelical missions and missionaries. The authors of the quotation with which we began this essay touch on an aspect of this when they say, "They [Western missionaries, ed.] are in danger of reinterpreting the gospel in terms of their own cultural categories—of equating it with Western civilization, material prosperity, individualism, human rights and freedom." (Hiebert, et. al. 1999, 378-79) Norman Allison enlarges upon the same problem in a brief essay that introduces *Occasional Bulletin* readership to the Triennial of the IFMA, EFMA and EMS held in St. Louis in September, 2004. Referencing and quoting an article by Charles Kraft, he writes:

> 'The greatest risk of syncretism today, as in Jesus' day, comes not from those who are attempting to discover ways of expressing Christianity in non-western cultures (though there is great risk there). It comes, rather, from those who try, like the Pharisees and Judaizers, to preserve the foreign expressions of God's message. The risk of syncretism is, however, always present. This fact should not be ignored or taken lightly.' Charles Kraft wrote these words in an article for the *Evangelical Missions Quarterly* in 1978; however, they are no less true today than they were then.
>
> (Allison 2004, 3)

If I understand Kraft correctly, he is saying three things. First, those who attempt to express the Christian faith to people of non-Western cultures run the risk of syncretism by relying too much on foreign (Western) expressions of faith. Second, those who attempt to discover other and newer ways of expressing the Christian faith to those of other cultures also run the risk of syncretism. Third, the first group (let's call them "preservers" as contrasted with the second group or "innovators") run the greater risk of syncretism.

Now it is relatively easy to see how "preservers" can under-contextualize the gospel and thereby run the risk of syncretism. My experience with one Dr. K is a case in point so, if readers will permit just one additional illustration from my early experience in Japan, it may prove helpful here.

My family and I were sent to post-War Japan to help evangelize Japan and establish the Japan Evangelical Free Church. After a year of language study in the University of Minnesota and with little to inform our mission strategy other than pastoral experience in the U.S., we were catapulted into a land where the dominant religion had been discredited by failure in war and the dominant Protestant denomination deserved to be discredited by syncretism.[4]

After three months to get settled in, and in that completely new and challenging cultural context, we set out to preach the gospel, plant some churches, and begin an entirely new fellowship of churches. Even a very limited understanding of post-War Japan, the Evangelical Free Church of America and the International Federation of Free Churches will enable readers to understand something of what was involved in that task. There we were, neophyte missionary monoculturalists attempting to preach and teach the gospel in ways our culturally-distant respondents could understand; introducing and enjoining a statement of faith not yet translated into the Japanese language, and establishing fledgling independent/interdependent congregations that knew nothing of either Robert's Rules of Order or borrowings from New England town meeting procedures that had come to attend the workings of Free Church polity in the U.S.! To say the very least *over*-contextualization was hardly an option!

---

[4]By way of illustration, organizers had reported its formation to Amaterasu Omikami the Sun Goddess at the national shrine in Ise and asked for her blessing. During the war, church members often faced the Imperial Palace in an attitude of worship and sang from hymnbooks from which references to the Second Coming of Christ had been excised.

Some might say that ours was a mistaken mission from the first. But those who know something of the history of the Japan Evangelical Free Church will be hesitant to come to that conclusion. By virtue of the grace of God and the commitment of national leaders, the JEFC not only survived those shaky beginnings but has grown and matured to become the kind of salt and light to both Japan and some overseas mission fields that it is today.

This bit if my personal history is not entirely typical, of course, but it does illustrate an all-too-typical problem. It goes without saying that evangelical missionary-evangelists are ever and always products of their own culture; are necessarily beholden to supporting churches and missions; and, in ways of which they themselves may or may not be fully aware, are responsible for preserving biblical faith as well as disseminating it. Some of them may indeed be compared to those first-century Pharisees and Judaizers. But, I am persuaded, most of them are more like Peter and his monocultural colleagues who were burdened by cultural overhang but nevertheless commissioned to preach the gospel and build the church of Christ in cultures other than their own. That, like those early apostles, contemporary missionaries risk syncretism as a byproduct of *under*-contextualizing the faith is not at all surprising. That the early apostles should have been more culture-sensitive in their day and contemporary missionaries should be more culture-sensitive in our day goes without saying.

Nevertheless, "preserver" missionaries are not alone in running the risk of contributing to syncretism. "Innovator" missionaries and missiologists who are prone to *over*-contextualizing the gospel run the same risk. In fact, in advocating the "transculturation" approach put forward in his *magnum opus, Christianity and Culture* (1979), Kraft himself runs that risk. In that work Kraft makes the ingenious but quite startling proposal that gospel contextualization should be designed so as to reproduce in the hearers/readers of today's cultures the kind of *impact* experienced by the hearers/readers of the first century in response to the original communication. For example, Paul's statements to the effect

> **Both "preservers" and "innovators" run the risk of contributing to syncretism.**

that a church elder should be the husband of one wife and able to manage his household well (1 Tim. 3:2, 4) are said to have mirrored first century Greco-Roman values and therefore gained respect for the church. To earn that kind of respect in current American culture the requirements might be better stated as "faithful to one spouse," and "manage one's household well" might well be put lower on a scale of relative importance. In the Higi culture of northeastern Nigeria the requirements might be contextualized as "manage a (polygamous) household well" because the Higi people do not think that it requires much leadership ability for a man to manage a household that has only one wife! Kraft recognizes that contextualization is an ongoing process and that over time "tranculturations" such as these may need still further revision (Kraft 1979, 322-27).[5]

Taking leave of Kraft's quarter-century old contextualization proposal, turn with me to a very recent elucidation of, and apologetic for, the so-called C5 Messianic Muslim movement as offered by Joshua Massey (Massey 2004, 296-304). In doing so, it is important to note that the C5-Spectrum theology of mission (John Travis) does not lay claim to being an evangelistic strategy as such. Rather, it has to do with recognizing the "love-relationship with Jesus" enjoyed by certain Muslims who do not want to become "proselytes" by turning their back on their culture and nation but who, nevertheless, want to "follow Jesus as Muslims."

Various arguments are offered by Massey in an effort to get conservative evangelicals to suspend judgment and recognize the validity of the C5 approach. His concern grows out of the twin facts that C-5 advocates in general are very suspicious of the ability of Westerners to understand Muslim cultures, and especially because the "true nature" of orthodox confessions of faith largely owe their development to the Western church. They say that Greco-Roman categories used as tests of orthodoxy required several centuries to develop and possess but limited validity when used as tests of the authenticity of Messianic Muslim and similar movements today.

---

[5] I would suggest that a contemporary case in point might have to do with the re-definition of marriage in North American culture. "Faithful to spouse" accommodates divorce and female leadership but offers no corrective in the current debate on gay marriage, so Kraft's reservation was well taken!

Rather, Messianic Muslims should be given time (even considerable time) to develop their own "orthodoxy" and in categories provided by the Qur'an and Islamic culture. Accordingly, C-5 advocates believe that they are right in being more concerned about encouraging Christ-centered "insider" movements than about developing churches as such. They believe they are right in being more concerned about "planting the leaven of Jesus' rule and reign within Islam" than in what they refer to as "contextualizing *Western* Christianity." They also believe that a rethinking and redefining of Islam is already taking place within the Messianic Muslim movement and that this offers hope that, over time and in a manner reminiscent of developments in the Western churches of the early centuries, Messianic Muslims will develop their own "language of orthodoxy."

Some Possible Correctives

What needs to be said regarding the foregoing? First, without recrimination and with Christian humility, let all of us admit that both "preservers" and "innovators" run the very real risk of fostering syncretism. The risk of syncretism may be greater among missionaries who are not familiar with cultural constructs and therefore remain dependent upon understandings and approaches emanating from their own culture. But the risk of syncretism is also great among missionaries who are culturally astute and may be overly confident of their ability to contextualize the gospel in accord with the characteristics and workings of respondent cultures. In fact, over-dependence on the materials of a receptor culture can be just as dangerous as over-dependence upon the materials of a source culture.

Second, both practitioners and theorists do well to remember that there was, and is, such a thing as "all that Jesus commanded" (Matt. 28:18-20), "apostolic doctrine" (Acts 2:42) and the "faith once for all delivered to the saints" (Jude 3). The various creeds, confessions and statements of faith of the last twenty centuries are valid only insofar as they are true to this deposit of biblical faith and understandable only when interpreted in the light of the historic conditions that gave rise to them. Whether these confessions emanate from the West or from the East, they are significant and useful only to the degree that the Christian churches and communities that employ them have subjected their articles to the test of Scripture, reflected on them in the light of historic confessions, and agree to them as bases of their own discipline, fellowship and witness.

Third, it is not incumbent upon Christian contextualizers to innovate in such a way as to make the communication of the gospel "*impactful*" as Kraft might define impact. Neither is it incumbent upon them to endorse the efforts of indigenes to make the claims of Christ less costly and more "*sufferable*" (my word) as Massey seems to be saying. Inherent in the task of gospel contextualization is rather the goal of making the gospel "*meaningful*"—the responsibility of going to the Scripture text; doing our best to determine the intended meaning of its authors; and communicating that meaning as clearly as possible in the language and thought-forms of receptor culture peoples. We can appreciate the sensitivity with which missionaries to Africa must deal with polygamy and various other such aspects of African societies and cultures. We can appreciate the life and death consequences that often attend Christian conversion and witness in Islamic cultures and nations. We can appreciate what Massey is saying when he writes, "Advocates of C5 insider movements are equally concerned about the dangers of syncretism and lazy intolerance..." (Massey 2004, 300). At the same time, here also we could wish for a different choice of words, words that encourage dialogue rather than squelching it. All intolerance is not lazy. Some intolerance is laudable. A contextualization that takes too high a view of culture and is overly dependent on predilections and conditions presented by receptor cultures and their peoples can be as dangerous as no contextualization at all. As a matter of fact, Islamic messianism not only runs the risk of syncretism, it may *be* syncretism already!

Perhaps it is significant that Caner and Pruitt's *The Costly Call* comes to the kingdom for such a time as this (cf. Caner and Pruitt 2005). In this book former Muslims who now follow Christ bear witness, not to a foreign-imposed faith, but to Spirit-imparted faith that is remarkably like the faith of true Christians of all times and places. Reading both "Misunderstanding C5" and *The Costly Call* will raise questions that cannot be probed here. All we can do here is encourage continuing and cautionary dialogue. We missionaries are *disseminators* by definition. But we are also *preservers* and *innovators*, if not by definition then by job description. We do best in our role as disseminators when we listen to, and learn from, each other in our endeavors as preservers and innovators.

Proposition #4: Syncretism is sometimes occasioned by an over-emphasis on power encounter and a corresponding under-emphasis on truth encounter.

Some Preliminary Considerations

Gary McGee draws attention to a *tete-a-tete* that occurred long ago between a Southern Baptist missionary to North Africa, E. F. Baldwin, and Fanny E. Guinness, an editor working with the Regions Beyond Missionary Union. Baldwin believed that in Matthew 10 Jesus established an enduring missionary pattern for all missionaries: namely, that the preaching of the gospel is to be accompanied by supernatural signs. Guinness responded quite tersely to the effect that, for the heathen "miracles cannot enlighten their dark minds, or soften their hard hearts . . . . Our aim is to enlighten, not to astonish" (McGee 1997, 79).

That particular exchange took place in 1889! The debate had a taken on a different cast, but it had not abated but only intensified by the time McGee reported it over a century later in 1997. By that time a renewed interest in power encounter thinking had not only exploded on the missiological scene, its meaning and scope had dramatically expanded. Traditionally power encounter primarily had to do with open demonstrations of divine power as when Elijah challenged the prophets of Baal on Mount Carmel. It was largely confined to missionary situations as when Boniface defied the Thundergod by chopping down the Sacred Oak at Geismar. As presently conceived, however, power encounter often includes a wide variety of practices having to do with engaging in "spiritual warfare," exercising "spiritual gifts" and living a "victorious Christian life." It includes the employment of "signs and wonders," speaking in tongues, the interpretation of tongues, healing the sick, and neutralizing poisonous bites. It extends to extraordinary ministries related to spiritual mapping, prayer

86

walks, exorcising territorial spirits, raising the dead, and still more.

Some Potential Contributors to Syncretism

Like the demonstrations of divine power, the communication of revealed truth has been part and parcel of the practice of Christian mission from the very beginning. However, the term "truth encounter" does not enjoy the recognition and popularity that "power encounter" does. In fact, though the *Evangelical Dictionary of World Missions* includes an article on "truth" that speaks of "truth and missions," the author does not mention "truth encounter" per se (Scott 2000, 972-73) and the *Dictionary* does not include an entry under that designation. Nevertheless, it is certainly legitimate to subsume Bible translation and proclamation, teaching and preaching, debate and dialogue, storying the gospel, chronological Bible study and so on under the category "truth encounter." Especially in a missiological context where we do not hesitate to speak of allegiance, empirical love and prayer encounters as well as power encounters. In fact, I am inclined to believe that some significant measure of syncretism on the mission field results from our failure to deal adequately with the relationship between power encounter and truth encounter at both theological and practical levels.

Items:

1) Consider Boniface's determination to cut down the Sacred Oak of Thor way back in the Dark Ages. Was the Oak "sacred" to Boniface or just to his "pagan" respondents? The way in which we answer this question is largely determinative of the kind of "power encounter" involved, and also of the potential for syncretism had Boniface *not* cut it down or had he incorrectly explained his action when he *did* cut it down!

2) Now ponder the problem of a contemporary Honduran peasant farmer who wants to know whether or not the missionary's God can grow corn. At first blush, that question is a no-brainer for the missionary, but it is a matter of life and death from the worldview perspective of the pagan

peasant. The "natural" answer "Of course he can" accompanied by an absence of special prayer that God "give a good crop this year" would be an open invitation to some sort of syncretism. Why?

3) What about the kind of syncretism evidenced when in the light of day a Christian Congolese mother goes to her pastor with an urgent request for prayer for her sick baby only to resort to a local witchdoctor's "cure" under the cover of darkness. This kind of syncretism is all too frequent, not only in Africa but throughout the world of folk religion. Why? What is to be done about it?

4) In the very different context of a church in Taipei, consider the deafening silence that attends the fact that a number of church members have secreted away their family godshelf with its ancestral tablets, talismans and incense burners "just in case." Should this be a matter of concern?

5) Finally, what about the ambivalence of a Christian couple in Sapporo, Japan. Their family doctor wants to refer their troubled daughter to a prominent (unbelieving) psychiatrist of that city. But the author of a Christian book on "deliverance" they have been reading ascribes her symptoms to demon possession. How does the missionary or pastor involved respond to their plight in order to minimize the risk of syncretism?

If cases such as the foregoing admitted of easy answers syncretism would not be the problem that it is and these paragraphs would not be as necessary as they are! It seems to me that there are certain keys essential to responding to these questions in ways that encourage understanding and discourage syncretism.

Some Possible Correctives

Gailyn Van Rheenen is entirely correct when he writes, "When Christianity is reduced to power, the Christian message is always significantly distorted. God's power must always be seen in a broader theological framework" (1997, 198). The natural inability of men and women to explain God's decision to act or not to act; the readiness of unbelievers to attribute divine power to another source; the inability of many witnesses to view the works of God in the context of larger history; the failure of some of God's servants to give proper glory to God—

all of this and more make it essential that power encounter be attended by truth encounter.

Take another look at the record of the early church and mission in this regard. Note the following:

1) The response of unbelievers to the exercise of the gift of tongues on Pentecost was both amazement and puzzlement. They said, "What does this mean?" Only after hearing Peter's sermon based on the prophecy of Joel were they convicted and led to inquire, "Brethren, what shall we do?" (Acts 2:1-41).

2) The healing of the lame beggar at the gate of the temple called Beautiful so astonished the people that a large crowd gathered. Once again Peter addressed the crowd, this time tracing revelation from Abraham to the "Author of life," Jesus Christ whom God had raised from the dead. The very Christ that crowd had denied and delivered to death was the Christ who had given the lame man "perfect health" (Acts 3:1-26).

3) Both the preaching of the gospel and the healing of the lame man infuriated priests, Sadducees, scribes and elders. So within a couple of days the apostles were interrogated. The primary question was, "By what power or by what name did you do this?" In their blindness the accusers had asked just the right question! And the apostles were prepared with just the right answer! "There is salvation in no one else, for there is no other name under heaven given among men by which we must be saved." The accusers were astonished, not just by the apostles' miracles but also by the apostles' wisdom because the apostles were perceived as "uneducated and common men" (Acts 4:1-22).

4) Finally, note that the last section of Acts chapter four is indeed remarkable in the way it relates both power and truth to the corporate witness and life of the early believers. Luke notes that believers were convinced that all that had just happened was in accordance with the objectively communicated plan of God; that because of this believers were encouraged "to continue to speak the word with boldness"; and that only then were believers

> **Truth and power.**
> **Power and truth.**
> **Always married.**
> **Never divorced.**

confirmed in their faith and commitment by two signs—an earthquake and the filling of the Holy Spirit (Acts 4:23-31).

Truth and power. Power and truth. Always married. Never divorced. That seems to be the pattern from the beginning. It is as though Peter's words on Pentecost constituted something of a "formula:" This is that which was spoken by the prophet! Review the record. The judgment of Ananias and Sapphira; deliverances from the Jewish authorities; the vision of Stephen; the revival in Samaria; the conversion of Simon the Magician—all such demonstrations of divine power were either preceded or succeeded by revealed truth that explained their true Source and meaning lest they be misunderstood, misinterpreted and misapplied!

Divine demonstrations call for Divine explications. But the truth is that the 1889 debate between Baldwin and Guinness is still with us. All Christian missionaries believe that the name of Jesus is above all names and that all authority in heaven and earth has been given to him. All believe it when they pray "Thine is the kingdom, and the power and the glory forever and ever." Nevertheless, Pentecostal and charismatic missionaries are likely to believe that extraordinary demonstrations of supernatural power are essential to mission while cessationist missionaries are constrained to believe otherwise. Some missionaries believe that God can and will intervene supernaturally but only when it suits his divine will and purpose. Others believe that it is always his will to do so if his people will only believe and pray. Some missionaries seek power encounters. Others seek to avoid them. Let each be persuaded in his or her own mind and proceed accordingly. But let all know that the only trustworthy answers to the syncretism that accrues to either the presence or absence (!) of Spirit-empowered interventions are to be found in Spirit-inspired revelation. In the final analysis every power encounter turns out to be a truth encounter as well and it is the truth that sets men and women free and delivers them from skepticism, secularism, syncretism and just plain sin!

Proposition #5: Syncretism sometimes results from a failure to come to grips with the true nature of Christian conversion and the spiritual decision-making process.

Some Preliminary Considerations

Faced with the "three P's" options in missionary evangelism, most conservative evangelicals have few questions. They do not believe that it is enough just to "be present" as Christians on the mission field though they do believe that a missionary *presence* is important if not essential. They accept the idea that the gospel must be proclaimed though they likely will not agree that missionary responsibility stops with *proclamation*. Most will insist that, in one way or another, presence and proclamation should culminate in *persuasion*. With the apostle Paul, they believe that missionaries should attempt to persuade people to be reconciled to God (1 Cor. 5:20-21).

Here again we say "So far so good." But at that point, Western Christians in general, and Western evangelists and missionaries in particular, encounter real problems—sometimes without recognizing them and often without facing up to them. The passion and pressure to secure "commitments to Christ," (whether for the satisfaction of the Christian persuader or the salvation of the non-Christian persuadee) is so great as to eclipse other considerations. The results are patently predictable and everywhere present. One of them is syncretism.

Some Potential Contributors to Syncretism

Sometimes missionaries and evangelists fault converts for their syncretistic inclinations. In actuality, the evangelist or missionary may be more culpable. Why? For many reasons, most of which readily fall into one or the other of two categories: theological and methodological.

Theologically, missionary-evangelists often find it expedient to give short shrift to repentance and the "turning from" aspect of Christian conversion. Jesus spoke to a Jewish audience and said (twice), "Unless you repent you will all likewise perish" (Luke 13:3, 5). Paul spoke to an audience of pagan Gentiles and said that God "commands all people everywhere to repent" (Acts 17:30). Nevertheless, many contemporary pastors, evangelists and missionaries "preach the gospel" with barely a mention of the necessity for repentance—of the need for recognizing the old ways of believing and behaving as sinful, of seeking forgiveness for them, and of forsaking them in order to follow Christ! The closest they come to preaching repentance is a general reference to the fact that all are sinners and in need of forgiveness and salvation. But that is not enough. As a matter of fact, failure to deal with the old way of life and thinking, the old gods or no-gods, and the old beliefs and practices is tantamount to inviting at least some of them into a life that, according to Scripture, should be totally "new."

"Turning from" is, of course, to be accompanied by a "turning to." This presents its own challenges. Christ and Bible authors use a variety of words and phrases to describe it: "turning to God," "turning to the light," "receiving Christ," "believing in Christ," "believing the gospel," "obeying the gospel," "taking up one's cross and following Jesus," "confessing with the mouth and believing in the heart that Jesus Christ is Lord," and so on. At first we might wonder why the Spirit employed such an array of words and phrases. Why not just one or two simple formulae? Why if not because what is actually involved is so basic and so profound that, even when selected and employed by the Holy Spirit himself, no one prescription could do justice to the transaction involved?

If that be true of the Holy Spirit's choice of words, we can be sure that the same is true in the case of the missionary-evangelist. The invitation to "accept Christ" (our favored phraseology) must at least be accompanied by the sort of explanation that prepares the convert for other biblical ways of thinking about and expressing what is actually involved in becoming a true Christian. For example, it must be clear that "only trust him" also means, "trust him only." Both express deep theological truths, but though the distinction may seem to be "simply semantic," it is much more than semantic. Biblically, conversion leads *away from* syncretism as it leads *to* salvation.

To take another example, we might make reference to the so-called "lordship controversy." It seems to me that the idea of even temporarily divorcing the acceptance of Christ as Savior from the acknowledgement of Christ as Lord is theologically suspect. Be that as it may, the divorce has obvious implications as far as syncretism is concerned. The religious world is full of saviors so it is not enough to accept Christ as *a* Savior as though he were one among many. But to persuade people to believe that he is the *only* Savior is no easier—or, indeed, not much different than—persuading them that he is also Lord!

Now to some methodological issues. No generation of missionaries/missiologists has had ready access to more information on the decision-making process than this one. Innovation and change, and motivation and decision-making, have been carefully analyzed from a variety of perspectives— anthropological, psychological, rhetorical, political, managerial, marketing and so on. Methodologically, missionaries have found it helpful to understand conversion in terms of process as well as point, group decision as well as individual decision, worldview change as well as behavioral change, etc. Illustrations abound: group (or multi-individual) decision in Donald McGavran's church growth theory, James Engel's so-called "Engel Scale" built on a marketing model, the Maslowan "Motivational Pyramid," Homer Barnett's innovation approach to cultural change, Leon Festinger's dissonance theory, and George Homan's gain-loss economic model. Most of these and more have at one time or another become rather common coin in missiological discussions.

There is, as indicated above, a very positive side to this linkage with the sciences such as has occurred since the World War II. But there is a negative side as well. New ideas from the social sciences have sometimes been accepted uncritically with the result that our theories and practices themselves have become syncretistic. For instance, missionary appeals become something less than worthy when people are appealed to on the bases of yes-yes sales techniques, self-fulfillment motivations, or prosperity aspirations. At the same time and on the other hand, in some cases we have been first attracted, then beholden, and ultimately forgetful of some worthy lessons from the sciences with the result that we revert to asking for premature decisions, or bypass the real decision-makers, or disregard the dissonance that almost invariably follows a decision point. Any or all of this tends to undercut the true significance of Christian conversion and promotes, as one consequence, syncretism.

Some Possible Correctives

In my own missiological pilgrimage, Alan Tippett did as much as anyone to enlarge my understanding of conversion and the decision-making process. He himself acknowledged a debt to Homer Barnett and his studies of innovation as the basis of culture change. In fact, Tippett once wrote that "Anthropology has helped me more in this [understanding of conversion, ed.] than anything I had in seminary" (Tippett 1987, 7). Nevertheless, Tippett was a first class theologian and approached the subject of conversion from a theological as well as an anthropological perspective. He thought of conversion as both an act of God (the work of the Spirit) and an act of mankind (decision-making). His mission theory entailed what he termed "verdict theology" and he spoke and wrote pointedly and clearly on the subject (Tippett 1987, 74-75).[6]

I am indebted to Tippett for some of the ideas expressed above and believe all of them to be important. In fact, as I have indicated, important correctives to syncretism are to be found in rethinking and redoing conversion appeals in ways that are both biblical and "scientific." However, rather than pausing to rehearse and recast the above ideas in a positive and remedial mode, I prefer to close this part of our discussion with a simple but profound analysis of the spiritual decision-making process that first came to my attention in one of Tippett's lectures. Tippett elaborated four logical possibilities open to gospel hearers as follows:

Conversion: rejecting the old and accepting the new.
Rejection: retaining the old and rejecting the new.
Secularism: rejecting the old and rejecting the new.
Syncretism: retaining the old and accepting the new.

It was Tippett's contention that what is taken by missionaries to be either conversion or rejection very often is neither of them but actually amounts to either secularism or syncretism. As a result of hearing the gospel some hearers lose confidence in their traditional gods and beliefs and therefore turn from the "old ways" but without accepting Christ and the "new way." They become secularists. In other cases, hearers are attracted to Christ and the Christian way and "accept" it, but for whatever reason are not willing to break with their old

---

[6] See also Alan R. Tippett, *Verdict Theology in Missionary Theory*, 2nd ed., (Pasadena: William Carey, 1973).

beliefs and practices. They do not become real Christians. They become syncretists. Tippett was of the opinion that the Christian missionary movement has often been a significant force for both secularism and syncretism.

It may be, and usually is, assumed that conversion is the one aspect of evangelism and mission that is best understood by all Christians, especially Christian "professionals." Missionary experience indicates otherwise. It is hyperbole, of course, but I am sometimes led to say that, if all Japanese who were reported as having "received Christ" in post-War Japan had actually become Christians, most of the Japanese population would have been converted at least once and some of them twice! In actuality, however, the percentage of Japanese who profess to be Christians today is still considerably less than one per cent—not many more than was the case before the War! Only the Lord himself knows the number of Japanese who have settled for some form of "Christian syncretism" in a society that is religiously syncretistic to the core.

To avoid, or at least minimize, the inroads of syncretism it would be well to re-examine the biblical theology of conversion and devote more attention to numerous and helpful studies of Christian conversion and the conversion process such as those of Tippett (1974), Kasdorf (1980) and Johnson and Malony (1981).

Conclusion

We began this essay with a question, but an open-ended one. It is appropriate that we end it with an answer, but a partial one. Our approach has not been one of recrimination but one of reconsideration. Are we as missionaries and mission leaders at least partly responsible for an always present and sometimes rampant syncretism? The answer must be, *"Yes, we are."* What should we do about it? The answer should be, *"We will take syncretism seriously, study the record carefully, and respond to divine guidance obediently."* Syncretism is always present to some degree, but Hiebert, Shaw and Tienou are correct. There is a point at which syncretism becomes Christopaganism.

Sources Cited

Allison, Norman. 2004. "Contextualization or Syncretism?" *EMS Occasional Bulletin* 7 (Fall): 3.

Caner, Emir Fethi, and H. Edward Pruitt. 2005. *The Costly Call.* Grand Rapids: Kregel.

Henry, Carl F. H. 1990. *Toward a Recovery of Christian Belief: The Rutherford Lectures.* Wheaton: Crossways.

Hesselgrave, David J. 1979. "The Contextualization Continuum." *Gospel in Context* 2 (July): 8-26.

Hesselgrave, David J. and Edward Rommen. 1989. *Contextualization: Meaning, Methods and Models.* Grand Rapids: Baker.

Hick, John. 1985. "Religious Diversity as Challenge and Promise." In *The Experience of Religious Diversity*, eds. John Hick and Hasan Askari, 3-24. Brookfield, Vt.: Gower.

Hiebert, Paul G., Daniel R. Shaw and Tite Tienou. 1999. *Understanding Folk Religion: A Christian Response to Popular Beliefs and Practices.* Grand Rapids: Baker.

Johnson, Cedric B. and H. Newton Malony. 1981. *Christian Conversion: Biblical and Psychological Perspectives.* Grand Rapids: Baker.

Kasdorf, Hans. 1980. *Christian Conversion in Context.* Scottsdale, Pa.: Harold.

Kearney, Michael. 1984. *World View.* Novato, Calif.: Chandler and Sharpe.

Kraemer, Hendrik. 1963. *The Christian Message in a Non-Christian World.* Grand Rapids: Kregel.

Kraft, Charles H. 1979. *Christianity in Culture: A Study in Dynamic Biblical Theologizing in Cross-Cultural Perspective.* Maryknoll, N.Y.: Orbis.

Lewis, C. S. 1960. *Mere Christianity.* New York: Macmillan.

Little, Christopher R. 2000. *The Revelation of God Among the Unevangelized: An Evangelical Appraisal and Missiological Contribution.* Pasadena: William Carey.

Massey, Joshua. 2004. "Misunderstanding C5: His Ways Are Not Our Orthodoxy." *Evangelical Missions Quarterly* 40 (July): 296-304.

McGee, Gary B. 1997. "The Radical Strategy in Modern Mission: The Linkage of Paranormal Phenomena with Evangelism." In *The Holy Spirit and Mission Dynamics,* ed. C. Douglas McConnell, 69-95. Pasadena: William Carey.

McIlwain, Trevor. 1986. *Building on Firm Foundations,* Vol. 1. *Guidelines for Evangelism and Teaching Believers.* Sanford, Fl.: New Tribes.

Netland, Harold A. 2004. "Religious Pluralism and the Question of Truth." In *Biblical Faith and Other Religions: An Evangelical Assessment,* ed. David W. Baker, 16-39 (?). Grand Rapids: Kregel.

Perry, Edmund. 1958. *The Gospel in Dispute: The Relation of Christian Faith to Other Missionary Religions.* Garden City, N.Y.: Doubleday.

Scott, J. Julius, Jr. 2000. *Evangelical Dictionary of World Missions,* gen. ed. A. Scott Moreau, s.v. "Truth." Grand Rapids: Baker.

Steffen, Tom A. 1996. *Reconnecting God's Story to Ministry: Crosscultural Storytelling at Home and Abroad.* La Habra, Calif.: Center for Organizational & Ministry Development.

Stowe, Everett. 1946. *Communicating Reality Through Symbols*. Philadelphia: Westminster.

Tippett, Alan R. 1973. *Verdict Theology in Missionary Theory*, 2nd ed. Pasadena: William Carey.

Tippett, Alan R. 1987. *Introduction to Missiology*. Pasadena: William Carey.

Van Rheenen, Gailyn. 1997. "Modern and Postmodern Syncretism in Theology and Missions." In *The Holy Spirit and Mission Dynamics*, ed. C. Douglas McConnell, 164-201. Pasadena: William Carey.

Weber, Hans-Ruedi. 1957. *The Communication of the Gospel to Illiterates: Based on a Missionary Experience in Indonesia*. London: SCM.

5

The Role of Context in Shaping Theology

Steve Strauss

The idea of *contextual*[1] theology provokes uncertainty among many evangelical theologians. On the one hand, evangelicals know that theology should be based primarily on the Bible, which is absolute, perfectly truthful, and sufficient to shape the lives and thinking of believers of every culture and every historical era (2 Peter 1:3).[2] Since their theology is based on an

> **...evangelicals recognize that no individual's theology is absolute. Only the Bible itself is absolute.**

---

[1] "Context" in this sentence and throughout most of the article refers to the context of modern theologians and not the context of the text with which they are working. This context is everything that has shaped theologians and the way they think: their culture, the historical era in which they live, their theological background, personal circumstances, even the language they speak.

[2] See, for example, Millard Erickson, *Christian Theology* (1985, Grand Rapids: Baker), 21, who says theology should be "based primarily on the Scriptures" and Wayne Grudem, *Systematic Theology: An Introduction to*

absolutely truthful and fully sufficient Bible, and since they employ a hermeneutic that assumes God's Word can be understood and applied in every culture, it seems natural to assume that theology itself is equally truthful and equally sufficient for all people in every place and every time. To suggest that theology varies according to cultural and historical contexts seems to introduce a dangerous element of relativism that contradicts the certainties and absoluteness of Scripture.

On the other hand, evangelicals recognize that no individual's theology is absolute. Only the Bible itself is absolute. They recognize that theology is certainly not *equal* to God's revelation, but is the reflection on God by the Christian community *through* his self-revelation, primarily in the Scriptures. And even if they have had little exposure to other cultures, most evangelicals recognize that reflection on God takes place in the light of the ever-changing human context.[3] In some way culture, history, and personal circumstances affect the development of theology. But to talk of theology itself as being *contextual* seems to throw the theological process into a swamp of relativity. Some of the most prominent contextual theologians seem to base their theologies more in culture or political ideologies than on the Bible. The theologies they develop seem to contradict theologies historically accepted as orthodox, further confirming suspicion that the whole idea of contextual theology is suspect.[4] For many

---

Biblical Doctrine (1994, Grand Rapids: Zondervan), 73-138, who identifies the four characteristics of Scripture as authoritative, inerrant, clear, and sufficient.

[3] Erickson is a good example, defining theology as "that discipline which strives to give a coherent statement of the doctrines of the Christian faith, based primarily on the Scriptures, placed in the context of culture in general, worded in a contemporary idiom, and related to issues of life" (1985, 21). Grant Osborne agrees, defining systematic theology as "a contextualization of biblical theology, filtered through the history of dogma but recontextualized for the contemporary situation and both organized and expressed in current thought patterns" (*The Hermeneutical Spiral: A Comprehensive Introduction to Biblical Interpretation* [1991, Downers Grove, IL: InterVarsity]), 309.

[4] See, for example, Virginia Fabella, "Contextualization," 58-59, Samuel Ryan, "Decolonizing Theology," 66, and Nestor Oscar Miquez, "Hermeneutical Circle," 97, in Virginia Fabella and R. S. Sugirtharajah,

evangelicals, it seems safer to say, as one missionary told his students in Ethiopia, "Culture is relative. Theology is absolute."

What should be the role of context in the process of theologizing? Erickson divides contextual theologians into *transformers* and *translators* (Erickson 1985, 112-120). Transformers generally reject the idea that the Bible is God's revelation that is normative for all time and which must be, therefore, the primary source of theology. Though many transformers use the Bible in their theologizing, they use it primarily as an example of how God revealed himself in the past. When God speaks today, they believe, he speaks primarily through the encounters of his people with culture, political circumstances, or personal experience.[5] Translators, on the other hand, believe that the Bible is God's revelatory message for all people in all times, but that God's people in every generation and every culture must understand and express that message in ways that clearly and accurately speak to them. This article will develop a translation model for contextual theology. All theologies can and should be rooted in the absolute truthfulness and full sufficiency of the Bible. At the same time, all theologies are in some sense contextual in that they are shaped by context.

Scripture as the Basis for Contextual Theology

To say that theology is contextual is not necessarily to reject the Bible as the authoritative source for theologizing. Instead, a responsible translation model of the role of context in shaping theology begins with the very assumptions that the Bible makes about itself: that it is God's message for people of all contexts. In spite of a plethora of contextual preunderstandings that readers bring to the text, people from

---

eds., *Dictionary of Third World Theologies* (2000, Maryknoll, NY: Orbis Books), and J. Scott Horrell's review in *Bibliotheca Sacra*, 633 (January-March 2000): 117-118.

[5] Gordon Kaufman identifies himself as a transformer in his proposals for doing theology. For Kaufman, theologies have been "essentially works of the human imagination, bringing into being new meaning as they continually transformed what had been inherited from the past." The Bible is just one of these many traditions which have been inherited from the past. As a result, Kaufman admits, theology has no claim to be uniquely authorized by divine revelation" (1991, 413-14).

every culture and era can understand its essential message. Theology built on the message of Scripture will be both authoritative and relevant.[6]

The Bible Was Written as God's Message to People of All Contexts

The Bible claims to be a unique revelation from God which was given in a particular historical setting, but which continues to speak to people in every time and culture. Not only do the writers of Scripture claim to speak a revelatory message from God to their own generation;[7] biblical authors also treat Scripture written to contexts different from their own as both understandable and relevant. Isaiah understood that his audience could understand and should have responded to the declarations that God made to previous generations (Isaiah 48:1-11, especially verses 3, 6, 8). Ezra and the postexilic Levites treated the Law, written hundreds of years earlier, as both understandable and relevant to their own generation (Nehemiah 8:7-8). The Apostle Paul affirmed that *all* Scripture— even that originally written at a different time and to a different audience—could be understood by Timothy. It was relevant for his context, (2 Timothy 3:14-17) and consequently should be taught to the people to whom he ministered (1 Timothy 4:13; 2 Timothy 4:2). Paul specifically applied a New Testament text written to a different person and a different context to Timothy and his congregation (1 Timothy 5:17-18). Peter said that the "certain" word of Old Testament prophecy retained relevance for his New Testament readers, and they should, consequently, pay careful attention to it (2 Peter 1:19). The writer to the Hebrews told his readers that the exhortation to enter into God's rest—given to the Hebrews in the

---

[6] It is beyond the scope of this article to survey and compare the sources of theology or outline the entire process of theologizing, which would require a full-scale text on hermeneutics and prolegomena. See Osborne, 286-317 for an introductory discussion of the preparatory role of gathering of relevant texts, exegesis, and biblical theology.

[7] Wayne Gruden, "Scripture's Self-Attestation and the Problem of Formulating a Doctrine of Scripture," in *Scripture and Truth*, eds. D. A. Carson and John D. Woodbridge (1983, Grand Rapids: Zondervan), 19-59, presents a thorough overview of the Bible's claim to be a revelatory word from God.

wilderness—applied not only to a later generation of Israelites; it also applied to them in their contemporary context hundreds of years later (Hebrews 3:7-4:3). The frequent quotations of the Old Testament throughout the New Testament are ample evidence that New Testament writers understood that the Old Testament message remained understandable and relevant, even though their culture, historical circumstances, and covenantal status before God was different (e.g., Romans 3:10-18; 4:6-8; 8:36). It is clear that biblical writers themselves embraced Scripture as God's message to be read, understood and obeyed by God's people throughout history and in a variety of cultures.

As God's revelation for all people of all times, the Scriptures are more than a model of ongoing revelation or a model of "successful local theologies" that "have stood the test of time" (Bevans 1985, 197). Many contextual theologies go wrong at this point. They regard the cultural, historical, or political milieu as the primary source of theology. They may use Scripture as a methodological model, but not as revelation with "supernatural authority." Instead of being God's primary way of speaking to them in their context, the Bible is reduced to a "casebook" of God's encounters with his people and of their subsequent theologizing.[8]

> **It is clear that biblical writers themselves embraced Scripture as God's message to be read, understood and obeyed by God's people throughout history and in a variety of cultures.**

But how can people from different cultures and eras understand and build relevant theology from a scriptural message given in an entirely different culture and period of history? Theologians are affected by the preunderstandings they bring to the text. Won't their theologies be merely reflections of these presuppositions and cultural biases? These questions can be answered both hermeneutically and anthropologically.

---

[8] Though there is much to be learned from Charles Kraft's proposals for contextualization, his emphasis on the Bible as primarily "God's inspired casebook" leads him to underemphasize the nature of Scripture as permanently revelatory for all cultures and times, whether it has been heard and responded to or not (Kraft 1979, 194-215).

Hermeneutically: A Model for Adequate Shared Understanding

God has communicated the truth of his word in such a way that interpreters in every culture can have an "adequate, though nonabsolute, understanding of supracultural truth" (Kraft 1979, 129).[9] Their "apprehension or expression of absolute truth is of course incomplete and partial, but that does not make such apprehension or expression relative" (Larkin 1988, 241). Interpreters will understand in slightly different ways because of their unique contexts and preunderstandings, but, through a careful reading of the *whole* of a biblical passage and a *wide* reading of the Bible in general, interpreters and theologians from any time and culture can adequately understand the essential message of any text.

E. D. Hirsch presents a model of understanding that can be adapted to show how interpreters can understand texts differently but not disparately. Hirsch describes the meaning of a message as a "willed type" (Hirsch 1967, 49). Different interpreters may each notice or emphasize different "traits" (i.e., implications) of that type while all still correctly discern the "intrinsic genre" or meaning of the whole type (Hirsch 1967, 86). "The peculiarity of a whole meaning is that it retains its integrity and completeness even if all its implications have not been articulated" (Hirsch 1967, 64). In fact, no two interpreters or theologians will ever identify all of the same traits of a type, but that does not prevent them from sharing the same essential understanding of a text. "Their mutual compatibility is not based on their incompleteness or partiality, but quite the contrary on the identity of the whole meaning to which they refer" (Hirsch 1967, 132). Applied to biblical hermeneutics and contextual theologizing, Hirsch's model shows how interpreters from different cultures may each observe different traits of a passage of Scripture, but as long as they share the same

---

[9] Kraft's concept of "supracultural truth" is potentially confusing, because human beings can never truly understand any truth outside of culture. The truth God expresses in Scripture, though communicated through one cultural context, finds its source in a God who is supracultural and can, thus, be expressed in any cultural context. However, no human being will ever grasp that truth "supraculturally."

intrinsic genre of that passage, each has adequately understood its essential meaning.[10]

Hirsch's model may be further developed by identifying certain traits of a type as "defining traits"[11] or "defining implications" (Johnson 1990, 138). These are the traits of a text which must be held in common for a listener or reader to understand the same essential message as that intended by a speaker or the author. They are also the traits that must be held in common by two readers of a text (possibly from two different cultures) for them to share a common understanding of that text. The defining traits of any type will vary with the context of the message.[12] But so long as those defining traits are shared, people can communicate.

For example, a North American working in a rural part of the third world might be talking with a local friend about "freeways" in his home country. If the person to whom he was talking had seen a paved road, but had never seen a divided, high-speed, limited-access highway, he would not understand

---

[10] Anthropologist Clifford Geertz demonstrates how, even though it is impossible for a person from one culture to climb inside the mind of a person from another culture, by analyzing what the symbolic forms of a culture actually mean to the people themselves, it is possible "to produce an interpretation of the way a people lives which is neither imprisoned within their mental horizons . . . nor systematically deaf to the distinctive tonalities of their existence" (1983, 57). Geertz's analysis of culture is astonishingly parallel to Hirsch's discussion of hermeneutics. In the same way that individuals can adequately understand other cultures by carefully observing their symbolic "art texts" and then relating those symbols to what they know in general about the culture, so theologians can come to understand the essential message of a passage of Scripture by carefully observing the details of a text and fitting those into the broader context.

[11] Hirsch briefly refers to the concept of traits "by which a type is defined" and which must be shared for meaning to be shared, but he does not extensively develop the model.
[12] Johnson (1990) describes "defining implications" as those which are "necessarily related to the use of the construction in its base sense" and "diagnostic implications" as "component meanings...necessary to comprehend the sense of the construction as used in the text." However, because in actual speech or written communication words are always used in a context, it seems best to conclude that, in actual communication, the necessary or "defining implications" will always be diagnostic and will always vary according to the context.

all the "traits" of the "type" (i.e., "freeway") in the mind of the speaker. However, depending on the American speaker's whole message (e.g., the possibility of rapid travel between great distances), he could describe enough of the traits of the type ("freeway") to convey his essential message. As long as his listener shared those "defining" traits, the listener could adequately (though not completely) understand his American friend's essential message.

How does this hermeneutical model relate to contextual theology? The assumption of the biblical writers is that God's Word is revelatory communication for all people, in all cultures, throughout history. Though written in one context, their message can be understood and acted on by people in another context. This characteristic strongly implies that God wrote Scripture in such a way that people from all contexts can share the defining traits—and so understand the essential message—that God communicates through his Word.

Anthropologically: The Essential Commonality of All People

Though the study of anthropology highlights cultural and sociological differences between people, it also confirms their essential commonality and the possibility of communication in spite of vast cultural differences. An intrinsic genre may be shared by people across culture and history because of the essential commonality of all human beings. People of all times and places are alike biologically, psychologically, spiritually and, to a large degree, socio-culturally.[13] Though human languages vary widely and are integrally linked to culture, all cultures and languages seem to share a universal frame of conceptual reference. This frame of reference includes semantic relationships such as comparison, contrast, synonymy and exemplification. Because these semantic relationships are shared, all people of different times and cultures can communicate with one another (Hesselgrave and Rommen 1989, 161-65; Thiselton, 1977, 87). Human beings from one culture also share common life experiences—jokes, pain, remorse, sincerity, lying, reflecting on the past—with people from every other culture (Thiselton 1992, 249, 541-43).

---

[13] See Kraft, 84-88 for a full discussion of the nature of these similarities. Cf. also Larkin, *Culture*, 198-200.

The work of anthropologists demonstrates both a basic unity among human beings and that people of different cultures can understand one another (Geertz 1973, 14, 35-36; Geertz 1983, 41-48, 56-57.)

It is these basic human commonalities that enable all people to understand the essential message of Scripture and for Scripture to be the abiding authoritative source of theology for people from every culture and every era. Some cultures will understand certain traits; other cultures will understand other traits. Only God, the Author of Scripture, will fathom every trait of each "willed type," or message in Scripture. But because of the commonalities of humankind around the world, all can understand the essential message of Scripture.

The Problem of Preunderstanding: Horizons of Understanding Can and Must Be Extended

In spite of the commonalities that unite all people and the assumption of the writers of Scripture that their message could be understood and acted upon by people in other contexts, some contextual theologians have followed the thinking of philosophers such as Gadamer, Wittgenstein, and Heidegger and speculated that interpreters will never adequately be able to understand the message of the text itself.

> **Readers of Scripture are not doomed simply to confirm what they already know and believe, but can have their preunderstanding reshaped by the message of the text.**

They assume that the cultural, historical, and theological preunderstanding of Bible readers so shapes their minds that they will necessarily read into the text the meaning that they themselves bring to it. Consequently, these contextual theologians reject the idea that the Bible can be an authoritative and relevant source of theology for all contexts.

J. Severino Croatto exemplifies such theologians who are captivated by the power of the new hermeneutic, claiming that "exegesis is eisegesis, and anybody who claims to be doing only the former is, wittingly or unwittingly, engaged in subterfuge" (Croatto 1981, 2). Croatto believes that all theologians are so strongly influenced by their own context that it is impossible for modern readers to understand the essential message of any text of Scripture. Consequently, it is foolish to attempt to make Scripture the starting point for theology. As a result, instead of being a reflection of God's authoritative, revelatory message for today, theology is, as Kaufman summarizes, "essentially a creative activity of the human imagination, seeking to provide more adequate orientation for human life in face of the new problems confronting each new generation" (Kaufman 1991, 410). Hermeneutical theory such as that proposed by Croatto and Kaufman has led to radical contextual theologies that make no effort to read the text the way it was meant to be read, because they assume such a reading is impossible. It is this very approach to contextual theology that has led many evangelicals to become suspicious of the entire process of contextual theologizing.

Anthony Thiselton has responded to the philosophy of doubt in the new hermeneutic by pointing out that it is possible for interpreters and theologians to extend the horizons of their own context and unite them with the horizon of the text. Readers of Scripture are not doomed simply to confirm what they already know and believe, but can have their preunderstanding reshaped by the message of the text.

> We approach questions of knowledge, or we seek to understand, from within horizons already bounded by our finite situatedness within the flow of history. But it is possible for these finite and historically conditioned horizons to be enlarged, and to expand. In actualizations of understanding or encounter between readers and texts, the boundaries of horizons may be extended and moved, and thus come to constitute new horizons . . . . Is this not . . . one of the most fundamental functions which biblical texts can perform?
>
> (Thiselton 1992, 6)

Thiselton demonstrates in a number of ways that interpreters can adequately read scriptural texts the way they were meant to be read: (1) Students of secular history and past literature assume that the past can be understood even though the present is different than the past (Thiselton 1980, 80, 314). (2) People routinely learn new things from conversations and texts that are very different from their own context. "In Gadamer's own words, in conversation a content 'arises' or 'emerges', which was not in our minds or assumptions beforehand; . . . we 'see each other's point'," and so learn about the unique point of view and inner emotions of others (Thiselton 1992, 396, 398). (3) People change their minds based on the reading of texts. Sometimes people change their minds to radically different ideas, in spite of rigid opposition, and in the face of tremendous emotional turmoil. Texts can "surprise, contradict, or even reverse" the horizons of expectation that readers bring to them (Thiselton 1992, 34; see also 589). Though no one can ever claim to understand a text exhaustively, history, literature, the nature of learning, and changed minds are all proof that interpreters are not bound simply to read back into scriptural texts their contextual preunderstandings. It is possible to adequately read them the way they were intended to be read.[14]

For theologians such as Croatto and Kaufman, theology is successful if it is relevant, even though it has lost all claim of being authoritative. Having surrendered to the presuppositions of the new hermeneutic, they feel free to dismiss much of the thinking of the biblical writers as merely the "cultural scaffolding" of their thoughts. They then pick and choose between biblical ideas, ignoring the larger message being communicated in a biblical text in order to reshape it for relevance to their own reading community.

But these theologians have ignored the Bible's own assumption (summarized above) that it can be understood and should be applied by people of varying times and cultures. Not only is it *possible* for theologians first to understand the essential message of the text; these presuppositions of Scripture *demand* that they seek to understand the text. Biblical texts claim to be interpersonal communication— revelation from God to human beings—offering "*external norms of judgement over against their readers*," (Thiselton 1992,

---

[14] Other evangelical interpreters who skillfully respond to the "new hermeneutic" in the context of contextual theology are Osborne (1991, 366-415) and Larkin (1988, 300-312. To extend one's horizons in the direction of the text, Thiselton warns against "a premature fusion of horizons which fails to preserve any tension between the past and the present" (1980, 319). To read the text the way it was meant to be read, theologians and interpreters must first "distance" themselves from the horizon of the text (Thiselton 1980, 326; Thiselton 1992, 8) by identifying their own pre-understandings, particularly the "tensions" between their horizons and those of the text (Thiselton 1977, 317).

473; italics original) and subsequent writers continued to understand them as such. Interpreters and theologians must not be content with theology that is merely relevant; following the pattern of the Bible itself, they can theologize based on a revelatory message from God that continues to speak with his authority. Therefore, regardless of the theologian's culture or historical context, theologizing must begin by seeking the meaning of the text. The interpreters' initial "task is to let the text speak, whether they agree with it or not, and this demands that they understand what the text meant in its original situation . . . . No interpreters, regardless of their culture, are free to make the text say whatever they want it to say" (Padilla 1980, 71).

Context Affects Awareness of Aspects of the Text

Even though interpreters and theologians from different times and places can discern the same essential message of Scripture, their particular cultural, historical, and personal contexts will affect their awareness of aspects of the text. Positively, their context will sensitize them to details that readers from another context might ignore. Negatively, their context will limit their awareness of details of the text that theologians from other contexts will see. Their context will always shape the questions that they bring to a text from Scripture.

Every Context Will Increase Awareness of Aspects of the Text

"Every culture possesses positive elements, favorable to the understanding of the Gospel" (Padilla 1980, 65). The worldview, values, and images of each culture will help its readers see things in Scripture that readers from other cultures may miss. Applying this principle to the African situation, Sundkler says, "In the theological encounter in Africa there are certain aspects of the Biblical message which tend to carry a particular emphasis, and which take on overtones that are partially lacking in other Churches" (1978, 494). Every context shapes the interpreter to see traits of biblical texts that interpreters in other contexts may not adequately emphasize or may overlook altogether.

Robertson McQuilken provides an example of how context affects one's awareness of aspects of the biblical text. When he first went to Japan as a missionary he was astounded

> to discover that many things important to me were of little or no importance to Japanese: eternal life, propositional truth, individual freedom, forgiveness of sin, a personal God, history. These were things I had been trying to market [to the Japanese]. At the same time I found things important to the Japanese that were not priorities for most westerners, but I discovered, things to which Scripture speaks: approval and sense of belonging, security, relationships, feelings, honor of parents, present "salvation," obligations, loyalty, beauty, love of nature, and the value of suffering.
>
> (McQuilken 1996, 166)[15]

McQuilken's increased sensitivity to the Japanese context awakened a fresh insight into aspects of the biblical text he had not previously noticed. Context increases awareness of different aspects of the text.

Every Context Will Decrease Awareness of Aspects of the Text

While context increases awareness of certain aspects of the text, it also desensitizes interpreters to other aspects. "In all cultures there are elements which conspire against the understanding of God's Word" (Padilla 1980, 65).

---

[15] Another illustration comes from a personal letter this author recently received from a missionary colleague in Ethiopia. "I am preparing to preach the book of Ruth in a single message at [a nearby church].... I've read that book countless times and never been knocked off my feet by verse 1 (famine in the land). However, for the last month I have been reading a first hand account of the work [of a group in the province of Tigray] from 1987 - 1991. The book includes graphic descriptions of the famines in Tigray and the flight of people to the Sudan. I could taste and feel some of their experience of tearfully saying good-bye to their homes and then trudging west. Now Ruth 1:1 will never be the same to me. I'd like to think that I better understand the author's meaning and the despair of the opening scene....Because of today's beggars at my door and yesterday's history of Ethiopia, the significance and meaning of 'famine in the land' have gelled for me in a way that probably cannot happen for most North American readers" (personal letter to author from Vic Anderson).

That is, interpreters and theologians in every culture will overlook some of the traits of a text because of their context. Often systemic and personal sin that has infected their culture or individual circumstances will dull and blind them to the way the text is challenging them.[16] At other times they

> **As theologians realize the extent to which their context blinds them to certain parts of the biblical message, they can curb their tendencies to textual blindness by consciously surfacing their own cultural, theological, historical and personal preunderstandings as they study Scripture.**

will simply miss the full significance of textual details because of cultural, historical, or personal biases. In either case, they will miss the full meaning and relevance to their lives of some of the teachings of Scripture.

For example, most believers in the North American context have little or no experience of the suffering characteristic of the Christian life in the New Testament (2 Timothy 3:12). They may give texts about suffering only cursory consideration, or may substitute an understanding that trivializes the message of the New Testament writer. The prosperity and religious security of the American context "conspire against" North American theologians' full understanding of the biblical teaching on suffering.

As theologians realize the extent to which their context blinds them to certain parts of the biblical message, they can curb their tendencies to textual blindness by consciously surfacing their own cultural, theological, historical and personal preunderstandings as they study Scripture. Rather than pretending that they have eliminated these preunderstandings and are reading the text objectively, they should consciously test their understanding of the text against the subjective biases they *know* that they have. They can ask: "If my biases predisposed me to see the text in this way, how might the text be challenging my biases? What can I learn from others who come to the text with different preunderstandings?" It is against these very points of contextual bias that the Word of God must have a "corrective

---

[16] See Larkin (1988, 293-99) for an extensive biblical discussion on the effects of sin in shaping preunderstanding with the result that interpreters and theologians will be less aware of key aspects of the biblical text.

function," (Tienou 1984, 161) challenging readers with scriptural messages that may be offensive. As Conn points out, contextualized theology "must always insist on that particular element of Christianity that stands in direct conflict with the" mindset of the non-believing context (1984, 240).

Context Shapes the Questions Brought to the Text

One of the main reasons that context affects theologians' awareness of aspects of the text is that their context consciously or unconsciously shapes questions that they bring to the text. Questions shaped by context often stimulate fresh theological probing of Scripture, revealing overlooked truth that speaks to contemporary issues. "The historical situation also contributes to the interpretive process by posing questions which demand scriptural answers" (Padilla 1980, 69). It is often forgotten that the great creeds and confessions of the church did not emerge from a vacuum or a theological ivory tower. Most of them were forged in response to theological issues facing the church (Conn 1984, 241-242).[17]

But, while context can provide questions that illuminate aspects of the text not previously noticed, they can also lead theologians to (sometimes unwittingly) see "truths" in the text that God never intended and miss the message that God does intend. Larkin expresses a valid concern about this. When the concerns of the interpreter "do not correspond with the concerns of the text, the interpreter will ask questions the text cannot answer, and the interpreter will not be able to hear the answers the text is giving" (Larkin 1988, 298-99). Many contextual theologians make this very mistake. Croatto, for example, says that

> a hermeneutic reading of the biblical message occurs only when the reading supersedes the first contextual meaning (not only that of the author but also that of his first readers).

---

[17] "The Westminster Confession of Faith of the seventeenth century, for example, is more than simply a gleaning from Scriptures of what its authors believed to be faithful teaching on a wide variety of topics: it addresses those words of Scripture to its historic setting, to a world in apologetic conflict with Rome and with Anglican high-church principles. In the process, it affirms truth to its own world" (Conn 1984, 241-42).

> This happens through the unfolding of a surplus-of-meaning disclosed by a new question addressed to the text.
>
> (1981, 3)

But the purpose of asking questions is not to find answers that are not in the text, but to search for answers that are already there and understand their significance for the modern context. Croatto's mistake is identical to that of many context-based theologians: the contemporary cultural context becomes the controlling paradigm that reshapes the message of Scripture into something it was never intended to say.

Instead, when interpreters approach the text, they should expect Scripture to alter their questions, and they should build their theology around the questions reshaped by the text. Larkin emphasizes that

> through successive exposure to God's Word [interpreters] are able to bring their preunderstanding and, as a result, their interpretation and application closer and closer to alignment with Scripture's truth . . . . At the very heart of the hermeneutical process correctly undertaken is a sanctification process. The Word of God challenges, corrects, and informs the interpreter's preunderstanding, and renews the mind.   (1988, 302)

It is inevitable that theologians will bring a preunderstanding of questions and concerns to the Scriptural text. But theologians must not forget that "the text itself sets the agenda and continually reforms the questions that the observer asks of it" (Osborne 1991, 324).

The Jerusalem Council of Acts 15 provides a specific New Testament illustration of theologizing prompted by contextual questions. The theological issue at the Council was whether or not Gentiles should be required to be circumcised and obey the Law of Moses in order to be fully accepted as true followers of Jesus. In other words, would Gentiles have to become Jews in order to be Christians? After listening to testimonies of the work God had performed through Peter, Paul, and Barnabas, James reflected on Amos 9:11-12 and drew his conclusion: the Scriptures were perfectly in line with what God was doing among the Gentiles. The question at hand undoubtedly made James aware of implications of

Amos 9 that he had not previously considered. The result was a step forward in the church's emerging theology of conversion.

Context Shapes the Forms by Which Theology Is Conceptualized and Expressed

Context not only influences theologians' awareness of aspects of the biblical text. Context also shapes how they conceptualize and express truth as it emerges from the text.

Even though they seek to read Scripture as it was originally intended to be read, theologians are still influenced by their own cultural, historical, and personal contexts. "There is no such thing as a presuppositionless theology" (Tienou 1983, 89-101). People do not understand until they have conceptualized something in their own minds in terms of images, experiences, and information that are already there. As Gregory notes,

> New elements of knowledge must be brought into relation with other facts and truths already known before they themselves can be fully revealed and take their place in the widening circle of the experience of the learner....The act of knowing is in part an act of comparing and judging—of finding something in past experience that will explain and make meaningful the new experience....Knowledge cannot be passed from mind to mind like objects from one receptacle to another, but must in every case be recognized and rethought and relived by the receiving mind.
>
> (1971, 70-71, 84)

Understanding of the essential message of a passage of Scripture will come through forms and symbols with which the reader is already familiar. Even as they attempt to read a text as it was originally meant to be read, interpreters will begin to understand and express the meaning of that text through what they already know and have experienced. "Every interpretation of the text implies a world-and-life view" (Padilla 1980, 70). These worldviews "provide us with religious paradigms for 'seeing' things, pre-answers that shape our questions" (Conn 1984, 16). Theology will always be shaped by and expressed in the thought categories of the theologian.

> True theology is the attempt on the part of the church to
> explain and interpret the meaning of the gospel for its own
> life and to answer questions raised by the Christian faith, using
> the thought, values and categories of truth which are
> authentic to that place and time.   (Gilliland 1989, 10-11)

The New Testament is full of examples of theology conceptualized and expressed in the thought categories of the context. Paul's sermons in Acts 13 (to a Diaspora synagogue), Acts 14 (to an animistic crowd in a rural town), and Acts 17 (to the sophisticated intelligentsia of the Areopagus) and his testimony in Acts 22 (to a fiercely nationalistic Jewish mob) and Acts 26 (to the Roman ruling class of Syria-Palestine) vividly illustrate how he fashioned his message to his context. Each of the four gospels is a crafting of the disciples' encounter with Jesus for a different community of readers.[18] The epistles were each written as "theology in context," addressing specific situations and questions with the truths of the gospel (Fee and Stuart 1982, 44-46). In the same way, theology that is biblical and relevant will be expressed in forms that communicate to each specific context.

How much freedom do theologians have in allowing their context to shape the forms by which they express their theology? At one extreme, theologians could respond that scriptural and confessional forms are always identical with meanings and therefore are indispensable to communicate theological truth in new contexts. For example, they could insist that women cover their heads in order to obey the injunctions of 1 Corinthians 11. They could insist that the only way to express the truth of Jesus' deity and humanity is to follow the wording of the Chalcedonian creed that Christ possesses two undivided, inseparable natures in one person. On the other extreme, theologians could decide that they are free to discard the forms of Scripture or the ancient creeds of the Church and substitute new ones in communicating theology in a new context. For example, theologians in a Western context might suggest discarding the use of water in a baptismal ceremony and substitute entry into a coffin to illustrate more vividly the truth that the new believer has died and been resurrected with Christ. Or the modern church could

---

[18] See, for example, Gordon Fee and Douglas Stuart's *How to Read the Bible for All Its Worth,* 103-105.

completely ignore the Chalcedonian formula in order to produce a more contemporary expression of Christ's divinity and humanity. How are forms related to meaning in the conceptualization and expression of theological truth?

Evangelical anthropologist Paul Hiebert presents a balanced model of the relationship of form and meaning in communication (Hiebert 1989, 101-120). On the one hand, he argues that equating form and meaning reflects a naïve positivism that cannot be maintained in real life. On the other hand, he points out that it is equally dangerous and naïve to say that form and meaning can always be radically divorced from each other.

Instead of either identifying form and meaning or denying any intrinsic relationship between form and meaning, Hiebert suggests that the relationship between form and meaning be viewed as a continuum. At one end, form and meaning are sometimes *arbitrarily linked*. For example, the sounds to represent the idea of a dog may be "dog" (in English), "perro" (in Spanish),

> **Some forms in Scripture are so closely tied to meaning that they should be maintained transculturally.**

or "wesha" (in Amharic). There is nothing that inherently connects any of these sounds to the idea of a dog; the connection is purely arbitrary. Sometimes form and meaning are *loosely linked*. Some connection exists between the form and the meaning, but the link might be disconnected in cross-cultural communication. For example, many agricultural societies link land and fertility with being female and link battle and violence with being male. Theologically, the connection between a woman wearing a head-covering and expressing submission or modesty may be a loose link: a head-covering will communicate submission or modesty in one culture but may be better replaced with another form to communicate the same meaning in another culture. Sometimes form and meaning are *tightly linked*. Though the two are not completely equal, the form cannot be discarded without in some way affecting the meaning. Baptism as a symbol of death, burial, and resurrection with Christ would seem to be tightly linked. It would be difficult or impossible to communicate the full theological truths of baptism without the use of water. Finally, form and meaning are sometimes *equated*. For example, when a minister says, "I now pronounce you husband and wife," his words (the form) actually create a new relationship between a man and a woman. In certain sacramental theological systems, the use of specific words during baptism and the Lord's Supper are understood to create a new reality by actually conferring grace.

Hiebert's model of a continuum of form and meaning has many implications for understanding the contextual nature of theologizing, particularly when comparing the statements of theologians in two different cultures or two different times. While theologians do not have the freedom to ignore completely the forms of Scripture or the creeds and confessions of the church, neither should they slavishly insist on using the same exact form to express the same theological truth. Interpreters are not free to impose or discard biblical forms thoughtlessly in their theologizing. Some forms in Scripture are so closely tied to meaning that they should be maintained transculturally. Conversely, other scriptural forms are less tightly tied to meaning; a substitute form will more clearly communicate scriptural truth. Forms established by churches of one culture and period of history should not be considered the exclusive way that Christians in another time and culture can express the same theological truth. Creeds and confessions are expressions of biblical truth for specific times and places. As such, they unite the universal church around a common history and serve as examples of theology that was both biblical and relevant in the past. But the forms of creeds and confessions will rarely (if ever) be *equal to* the truth they are expressing. In certain cultures and situations a *different* form might be the only way to express the *same* confessional truth.[19]

---

[19] For an example of using different forms to express the same truth articulated in the Chalcedonian creed, see Steve Strauss, "Perspectives on the Nature of Christ in the Ethiopian Orthodox Church: A Case Study in Contextual Theology," Ph.D. Dissertation, Trinity International University, 1997, especially pp. 225-30, 236-392.

Implication of the Contextual Nature of Theology: Theologians Must Engage in Intercultural Theologizing[20]

Because no culture can understand all the traits of Scripture, and because each culture contains elements that will help it uncover what another culture might overlook, *intercultural theologizing* is essential for the universal church. Intercultural theologizing is the cross-pollination of many contextual theologies between churches of different contexts. Intercultural theologizing plays at least two key roles in the process of doing theology. First, such sharing of theologies enriches the theology of the church in each context and the theology of the universal church. Listening to theologies from other contexts opens the eyes of theologians to what they may have missed in the text and helps prevent them from being blinded by their own cultural biases and theological presuppositions. Second, intercultural theologizing helps ensure that each contextual theology remains biblical and congruent with the theology of the universal church (Conn 1984, 246-57). If theologies developed in a local context become genuinely disparate from the cross-cultural theology of the church universal—universal in time and location—it is likely that they are no longer biblical and no longer Christian theologies.

Intercultural theologizing should take place at four levels: between churches of different cultures, between individuals of different educational and social levels within the

---

[20] Because context also affects the way people learn, the methods adopted for teaching theological truth should also be adapted to the context. However, this discussion of the contextual nature of *theological education* as opposed to the contextual nature of *theologizing* is beyond the scope of this article. Interested readers are referred to the following sources: Lois McKinney, "Contextualizing Instruction: Contributions to Missiology from the Field of Education," *Missiology*, 12 (July 1984): 311-26; Peter Chang, "Steak, Potatoes, Peas and Chopsuey: Linear and Non-linear Thinking in Theological Education," *Evangelical Review of Theology*, 5 (October 1981): 279-86; Earl and Dorothy Bowen, "Contextualizing Teaching Methods in Africa," *Evangelical Missions Quarterly*, 25 (July 1989): 270-75; Ajith Fernando, "Communicating Theological Truth to the Asian Mind," *India Church Growth Quarterly*, 10 (October-December 1988): 305-316; Jim Plueddemann, "Culture, Learning, and Missionary Training," *Internationalising Missionary Training*, ed. William Taylor (Grand Rapids, MI: Baker, 1991): 217-30.

churches of each culture, between different denominations and theological traditions, and between the church of each generation and the church of past generations.

Between Churches of Different Cultures

Because the church in each culture will have some areas of special insight into scriptural truth and other areas of blindness to scriptural truth, churches in each culture must share the fruit of their theological activity. "Any monocultural perspective on truth is no more complete than the single perspective of any given individual (Kraft 1979, 292)." The gospel and its ramifications are far bigger than any one culture. There is no regional church that has a monopoly on theological truth, nor any church that has nothing to contribute to the worldwide church. Believers from each culture can learn much about God by listening to the insights of their brothers and sisters from other cultures (Tabor 1978, 10; Cf. Sundkler 1978, 510; Kraft 1979, 295).

> **Many in the Western church harbor a paternalistic attitude that their theology is "objective" and uninfluenced by Western culture.**

The importance of intercultural theologizing has generally been ignored by the Western church. Many in the Western church harbor a paternalistic attitude that their theology is "objective" and uninfluenced by Western culture. Consequently, they believe that non-Western theologians should simply accept theologies worked out in the West or that, at most, fresh non-Western theologies should be adaptations of the "objective" theology Westerners have already done.[21]

But Western theologians need to realize that their theology has also been contextually conditioned. They, too, have blind spots that can be illuminated by the insights of non-Westerners. Not only must non-Western churches be free to develop biblically-centered contextual theologies; Western

---

[21] Conn sees the feeling among Western theologians that their theology is "objective" and that other theologies are contextualized versions of Western theology as a major reason why much of Western theology has lost its evangelistic, missionary purpose and become more theoretical and esoteric (1984, 222-23).

churches must listen to these non-Western theologies to enrich their own theologies and the theology of the universal church.

> Every individual, group, discipline, and culture has much to offer the rest by way of insight and specialized understanding . . . . Theologizing by those of nonwestern cultures (if within scriptural limits) can both enrich the rest of us and alert us to deficiencies in our commonly held interpretations.
> (Kraft 1979, 298, 304; cf. 303)

Believers from every nation can enhance their understanding of God's revelation and correct their own blind spots by listening to the theology of churches from other cultures. "Every church must learn to be both learner and teacher in theologizing" (Conn 1984, 252).

Between Different Socio-Educational Levels

Not only must theologizing be done by the church in every culture; it must also be done by Christians at every social and educational level. Theology "has all too frequently been conceived as an academic discipline in which only a few intellectually qualified experts, who may or may not participate in the life of the church, are able to engage" (Padilla 1983, 81). But "reflection on truth is not an exercise of the trained elite alone" (Gilliland 1989, 26; cf. Thiselton 1992, 532).

Non-professional theologians must play an especially important part in raising relevant questions that need to be addressed from Scripture, but they should also be part of the process of reflecting on what the Scripture says to these issues. Even as believers from different cultures will see different aspects of biblical truth, so believers from different educational and social environments within the same culture will contribute different but complementary insights into the Bible's response to a particular issue. Professional theologians bring to the theologizing process exegetical tools and knowledge of the historical development

> **...believers from different educational and social environments within the same culture will contribute different but complementary insights into the Bible's response to a particular issue.**

of theology. But theologizing is the privilege of every member of the body of Christ. It is a process that must always be done in the broad community that is living out the theology.

Between Different Theological Traditions

One of the most important forms of intercultural theologizing is the sharing of theologies between denominations and churches of different theological traditions. Each theological tradition has a tendency to allow its theology to become a paradigm that controls the exegesis of biblical texts. "Mere *interpretations* of texts can themselves take on the status of controlling paradigms in our lives, which, when they become both all-powerfully directive and unchallengeably 'for-ever fixed' begin to assume a quasi-idolatrous role, as securities in which we place *absolute* trust" (Thiselton 1992, 124; cf. 379). When theology controls exegesis, the priority of the biblical text is lost.

To prevent this, Thiselton calls for a measure of "socio-critical *suspicion*" towards one's own theology and a willingness to listen to those from outside of one's reading community. Such suspicion of one's own understanding and willingness to listen to a *different* understanding of a text can initiate retrieval of the meaning of the text and open the doors for renewal and change within a theological tradition (Thiselton 1992, 344). "The point *where we feel ourselves under attack from the Scripture*, where our natural reason is offended by it, and where we are flung into tumults, is *the very point where genuine interpretation can take place and profound under-standing be reached*" (Thiselton 1992, 193, italics original). Theologians of every theological persuasion and every culture need to listen to one another, consider how others interpret the text and ask what can be learned from them.

With the Church of Past Generations

Part of the contextual nature of all theology is its historical context. "All expressions of Christian doctrine are rooted in history and are, therefore, historically and culturally conditioned" (Muller 1991, 91). The doctrinal struggles of past generations and the subsequent creeds and confessions that emerged were shaped by that context. "Creeds, as an expression of the confessional character of all theologizing, are 'historically situational.' They are human acts of confession of God's unchanging good news, addressed to specific human cultural settings" (Conn 1984, 242).

The creeds and confessions of the church are, therefore, historical and cultural theologies addressed to particular situations the church has faced. But they also reflect a desire to reach beyond the contextual and express universal truth that will unite and provide identity for the church across generations and cultures. "In the dialogue between the contextual and the universal, the fallible church *points beyond itself and its own context* to that which lies beyond it, especially to the divine promise of the future, and the universals of the cross and the resurrection"(Thiselton 1992, 592). Theology is contextual, but it is also an attempt to reflect truth that is universal.

Because creeds and confessions are both contextual and universal, the church must neither ignore them nor unthinkingly parrot them. "Contemporary systematic theology, therefore, cannot afford simply to repeat the language that it has been given—nor can it afford to ignore the past and attempt to strike out in new and innovative directions and expect to achieve any results or lasting significance" (Muller 1991, 94). Simply to repeat confessions is decidedly *not* to understand them or be faithful to them. Contextual theologians today must study and use the creeds of the past, not in slavish repetition of their words and phrases to maintain the pretension of doctrinal purity, but as past models of contextual theology seeking to express universal truth.[22] Grappling with the contextual theologies of the past is a form of intercultural theologizing which provides today's church with an outside perspective on its own theology (Conn 1984, 204).

Summary

How should evangelicals respond to the idea of contextual theology? What role do cultural and historical contexts play in shaping theology? This paper has argued that

---

[22] "Faithfulness to such doctrines does not necessarily mean repeating them; rather it requires, in the making of any new formulations, adherence to the same directives that were involved in their first formulation" (Lindbeck 1984, 81).

the Scripture can and should be the basis for all theologizing. God has written his Word so that believers of all cultures and historical periods can understand the essential message of biblical texts. Though theologians will come to the text conditioned by their own context, the commonalities among human beings of all cultures, the nature of Scripture, and the nature of human communication argue that theologians can and should seek to build their theology on the message of Scripture. But though Scripture should be the underpinnings for theology developed in any context, context will affect theologians' awareness of aspects of the biblical text, making them more or less aware of details of the text, and shaping the questions that they bring to the text. Context further shapes the forms by which theological truths are conceptualized and expressed. Because theologians' context plays such a significant role in the way their theology is shaped and expressed, theologians from every culture need to be active in intercultural theologizing—learning from theologians of different cultures, socio-educational levels, theological traditions, and periods of history.

Sources Cited

Bevans, Stephen. 1985. "Models of Contextual Theology." *Missiology* 13 (April): 197.

Bowen, Earl and Dorothy. 1989. "Contextualizing Teaching Methods in Africa." *Evangelical Missions Quarterly* (July): 270-75.

Chang, Peter. 1981. "Steak, Potatoes, Peas and Chopsuey: Linear and Non-linear Thinking in Theological Education." *Evangelical Review of Theology* (October): 279-86.

Conn, Harvey M. 1984. *Eternal Word and Changing World*. Phillipsburg, NJ: Presbyterian and Reformed Publishing.

Croatto, J. Severino. 1981. *Exodus: A Hermeneutics of Freedom*. Maryknoll, NY: Orbis.

Erickson, Millard. 1985. *Christian Theology*. Grand Rapids: Baker.

Fabella, Virginia and R. S. Sugirtharajah (Eds.). 2000. *Dictionary of Third World Theologies*. Maryknoll, NY: Orbis Books.

Fabella, Virginia. 2000. "Contextualization." In *Dictionary of Third World Theologies*, ed. Virginia Fabella and R. S. Sugirtharajah, 58-59. Maryknoll, NY: Orbis Books.

Fee, Gordon and Douglas Stuart. 1982. *How to Read the Bible for All Its Worth*. Grand Rapids: Zondervan.

Fernando, Ajith. 1988. "Communicating Theological Truth to the Asian Mind." *India Church Growth Quarterly* (October-December): 305-316.

Geertz, Clifford. 1973. *The Interpretation of Cultures*. N.P.: HarperCollins.

_____. 1983. *Local Knowledge*. N.P.: HarperCollins.

Gilliland, Dean S. 1989. "Contextual Theology as Incarnational Mission." In *The Word Among Us: Contextualizing Theology for Mission Today*, ed. Dean S. Gilliland. Dallas, TX: Word.

Gregory, John Milton. 1971. *The Seven Laws of Teaching*. Grand Rapids: Baker.

Gruden, Wayne. 1983. "Scripture's Self-Attestation and the Problem of Formulating a Doctrine of Scripture." In *Scripture and Truth*, eds. D. A. Carson and John D. Woodbridge, 19-59. Grand Rapids: Zondervan.

_____. 1994. *Systematic Theology: An Introduction to Biblical Doctrine*. Grand Rapids: Zondervan.

Hesselgrave, David J. and Edward Rommen. 1989. *Contextualization: Meanings, Methods, and Models*. Grand Rapids: Baker.

Hiebert, Paul. 1989. "Form and Meaning in the Contextualization of the Gospel." In *The Word Among Us: Contextualizing Theology for Mission Today*, ed. Dean S. Gilliland, 101-120. Dallas, TX: Word.

Hirsch, E.D. 1967. *Validity in Interpretation*. New Haven, CT: Yale University Press.

Johnson, Elliott E. 1990. *Expository Hermeneutics: An Introduction*. Grand Rapids: Zondervan.

Kaufman, Gordon. 1991. "Doing Theology From a Liberal Christian Point of View." In *Doing Theology in Today's World*, eds. John D. Woodbridge and Thomas McComiskey, 413-414. Grand Rapids: Zondervan.

Kraft, Charles. 1979. *Christianity and Culture*. Maryknoll, NY: Orbis Books.

Larkin, William. 1988. *Culture and Biblical Hermeneutics*. Grand Rapids: Baker.

Lindbeck, George A. 1984. *The Nature of Doctrine: Religion and Theology in a Postliberal Age.* Philadelphia: Westminster.

McKinney, Lois. 1984. "Contextualizing Instruction: Contributions to Missiology from the Field of Education." *Missiology* (July): 311- 26.

McQuilken, Robertson. 1996. "Use and Misuse of the Social Sciences: Interpreting the Biblical Text." In *Missiology and the Social Sciences: Contributions, Cautions and Conclusions,* eds. Edward Rommen and Gary Corwin, EMS Series Number 4, 165-183. Pasadena: William Carey Library.

Miquez, Nestor Oscar. 2000. "Hermeneutical Circle." In *Dictionary of Third World Theologies,* ed. Virginia Fabella and R. S. Sugirtharajah, 97. Maryknoll, NY: Orbis Books.

Muller, Richard A. 1991. "The Role of Church History in the Study of Systematic Theology." In *Doing Theology in Today's World: Essays in Honor of Kenneth S. Kantzer,* eds. John D. Woodbridge and Thomas Edward McComiskey. Grand Rapids: Zondervan.

Osborne, Grant. 1991. *The Hermeneutical Spiral: A Comprehensive Introduction to Biblical Interpretation.* Downers Grove, IL: InterVarsity.

Padilla, Rene. 1980. "Hermeneutics and Culture: A Theological Perspective." In *Down to Earth: Studies in Christianity and Culture,* ed. John R. W. Stott and Robert Coote. Grand Rapids: Eerdmans.

_____. 1983. "Biblical Foundations: A Latin American Study." *Evangelical Review of Theology* (April).

Plueddemann, Jim. 1991. "Culture, Learning, and Missionary Training." In *Internationalising Missionary Training,* ed. William Taylor, 217-30. Grand Rapids: Baker.

Ryan, Samuel. 2000. "Decolonizing Theology." In *Dictionary of Third World Theologies*, ed. Virginia Fabella and R. S. Sugirtharajah, 66. Maryknoll, NY: Orbis Books.

Strauss, Steve. 1997. "Perspectives on the Nature of Christ in the Ethiopian Orthodox Church: A Case Study in Contextual Theology." Ph.D. Dissertation, Trinity International University.

Sundkler, Bengt. 1978. "Towards a Christian Theology in Africa." In *Readings in Dyamic Indigeneity*, ed. Charles H. Kraft and Tom N. Wisley. Pasadena, CA: William Carey Library.

Tabor, Charles R. 1978. "Is There More Than One Way to Do Theology?" *Gospel in Context* (January): 10. Cf. Sundkler, "Towards a Christian Theology," 510; Kraft, *Christianity in Culture*, 295.

Thiselton, Anthony. 1977. "Semantics and New Testament Interpretation." In *New Testament Interpretation: Essays on Principles and Methods*, ed. I. Howard Marshall. Grand Rapids: Eerdmans.

_____. 1980. *The Two Horizons: New Testament Hermeneutics and Philosophical Description*. Grand Rapids: Eerdmans.

_____. 1992. *New Horizons in Hermeneutics*. Grand Rapids: Zondervan.

Tienou, Tite. 1983. "Biblical Foundations: An African Study." *Evangelical Review of Theology*, 7 (April): 89-101.

_____. 1984. "The Church in African Theology: Description and Analysis of Hermeneutical Presuppositions." In *Biblical Interpretation and the Church: Text and Context*, ed. D. A. Carson. Grand Rapids: Baker.

6

The Lamb and The Emperor: Theologies of Revelation Countering Syncretism

Ron Stansell

The book of Revelation is too often read for prophecy and too seldom read for its vital message to a church under pressure to accept compromise. Picture with me an account of an epic struggle between the bedraggled followers of the Lamb and the mighty Roman Empire—the powerless against the most powerful totalitarian state on earth at the time. All the Christians had to do to come to peace with their culture was a polite bow to the Emperor. In our day when once again politics and religion seem to be colliding on every hand, surely Revelation has something to teach us. How can we in the twenty-first century live in a world of hostile political powers and remain radically faithful to the Lamb?

Christ the Lamb

Of the many titles for Christ in the Apocalypse, none is more central than the metaphor of the Lamb. The vision of the throne and the Lamb in chapters four and five of Revelation is in many ways the foremost vision of the book and forms the springboard for the rest of the book. The Lamb, although looking as if he had been slain is nonetheless standing in the center of the throne (Rev, 5:6). Thus, the Lamb who both redeems and rules is the most comprehensive and pivotal image for Christ in the book (Lioy 2003, 165).

> **The Lamb opposed the gods of Rome: there is only one "Lord of Lords and King of Kings.**

Enter the Emperor

The gravest single pressure upon the churches of Asia Minor was to worship the emperor, something that was not fully declared until the time of Emperor Domitian, placing the dating of Revelation by most scholars at 94-96 AD at the end of a rather ferocious persecution. It was Domitian who first assumed the title of "Lord and God," thus declaring himself to be an absolute monarch (Angus and Renwick 1988, 208).

Acceptance of new religious forms had been a common Roman pattern and predated Domitian by centuries. Animism had easily accepted traditions from Italian, Etruscan, Greek, Egyptian and oriental sources (Angus and Renwick 1988, 212). The status of political leaders in the ancient world is a case in point, where leaders were often given a quasi-religious status. Augustus Caesar, for one, seems to have been delighted by the Eastern practice of calling their kings divine. He saw this as a "bond of union" pulling together the many political provinces conquered by Roman legions. Although Augustus Caesar's successors followed his example of expecting to be considered divine, there was never much heartfelt devotional warmth in the practice. The mystery religions tried to fill the void with devotion to spirits and lords, but were tolerated by the state because they maintained a formal observance of emperor worship (Angus and Renwick 1988, 213).

To understand fully the heavy pressure applied to Christians to worship the emperor, one must remember that Rome was basically tolerant toward "legal religions," those religions that had been officially incorporated into the Pantheon, and that even the unrecognized illicit religions usually went without much opposition because they bowed to the emperor.   The idea of persecuting an unrecognized religion existed in principle, however, and was applied to Christians because they seemed to break the bond of union with the state (Angus and Renwick 1988, 213). All that was required of Christians to avoid the hostility of the state was to acknowledge the supremacy of the Emperor. This they found impossible to do. The conflict arose between Christianity and the state, not so much because it was an "illicit" religion and not because of aggressive evangelism per se, since even some of the mystery religions actively sought converts. Rather, conflict arose because for the Christians, the Kingdom of God had come in Christ Jesus and was being established on the earth, something incompatible with emperor worship.

Even though in one sense the "kingdom was not of this world," in another sense Christians were experiencing a new earthly kingdom, a new fellowship and society under the rule of God.   Even though early Christians had no political ambitions, Rome could not tolerate the idea of a kingdom of another God upon earth.   Christians expected a new worldwide social organization in which all believers would be included. Christ, not Caesar, was Lord over the church in the world. Christ could have no rival. "To maintain their own life and mission, [Christians] had to be intolerant" of the state's demands (Angus and Renwick 1988, 214). Christians could not ignore the contest between Caesar and Christ and maintain integrity.

In the twenty-first century, many Christians across Africa and Asia are also suspected of disloyalty. The Lordship of Christ may bring harsh persecution and even death. The principle of breaking with a totalitarian political state and standing aside from a totalitarian religious culture may have similarities.   While there are certainly significant reasons to develop culturally sensitive approaches and to maintain identity with any culture (something true for first century Christians and true today in the Muslim, Hindu, Russian Orthodox and Communist Chinese worlds), the principle of the Lordship of Christ is undoubtedly a frequent stumbling block and offense, and an important dividing line between biblical orthodoxy and syncretism. How are we to deal with this huge challenge of quasi-religious political power?

The overwhelming solution to syncretism found in the Apocalypse resides deeply in the *message, mission* and *method* of Christ the Lamb. This study will conclude with a summary of guidelines to shape training for cross-cultural workers who face similar syncretistic challenges in both the West and in limited access regions where political forces resist the Lordship of Christ.

The Lamb is the Message

The word Lamb appears first in chapter 5 and then in ten of the following 17 chapters, a total of 28 times. The Greek term used in Revelation for Lamb (*arnion*) appears only once elsewhere in the New Testament, so it becomes all the more a special property of John in Revelation (Morris 1969, 96).

What does John intend by calling Jesus a Lamb? Is he simply referring to the atoning sacrifice of Jesus? That would be a good first assumption, remembering the early apostles preached Jesus was the Servant of God, sent to suffer death in fulfillment of the prophecy of Isaiah (Acts 8:32ff). The apostle Peter specifically called him "his servant Jesus" (Acts 3:13). Elsewhere the New Testament looks back to the reconciling sacrifice of Christ on the cross and proclaims that message with vigor (2 Cor. 5:11-21). Despite the theme of judgment inherent in Revelation, it is primarily a book about God's grace with an emphasis on the forgiveness available through the sacrifice of the Lamb (Walvoord 1966, 115).

The Lamb is also linked with worship and celebration ("the wedding supper of the Lamb" in Rev. 19:9), and with the cosmic destruction of the forces of evil ("the Lamb will overcome" in Rev. 17:14). This is a sovereign ruler who is not only Lamb but also Lion. Robert Mounce says it well: "In one brilliant stroke John portrays the central theme of the New Testament revelation—victory through sacrifice" (Mounce 1977, 144). This Lamb rides like the king he really is, a mixed metaphor perhaps without equal!

> **The message of the Lamb was that Christ is both an atoning sacrifice and sovereign Lord.**

The author of Revelation is deeply indebted, then, to the Isaiah 53 passage where the Servant is led "like a lamb to the slaughter," a powerful symbol of "self-giving defenselessness" (Eller 1981, 175). The redemptive nature of the Lamb is re-emphasized in the Revelation 15 vision, when the names of Moses and the Lamb are linked together in the title for the song of rejoicing over deliverance (Rev. 15:3). The redeeming works of God experienced by Israel during the Exodus are culminated in the redemptive work of the Lamb in Revelation (Mounce 1977, 287).

So it is that while the Servant of God in Isaiah 53:7 is a slaughtered Lamb, the Lamb of Revelation is a standing Lamb, symbolic of victory and sovereignty (Mounce 1977, 145). Only a standing Lamb could be worthy of praise due the sovereign deity. Only a standing Lamb could be depicted with seven horns to declare the perfection of his power, and with seven eyes to point to perfection of knowing (Morris 1969, 97). Only a standing Lamb could be proclaimed Lord, unequalled by any mere Roman emperor. He is "King of kings and Lord of lords" (Rev. 19:16), far superior to Emperor Domitian's claim of being *"deus et dominus,"* God and Lord (Summers 84).

The theme of victory comes to something of a climax in Revelation 19:11-16 when the rider on the white horse appears dressed "in a robe dipped in blood" (v. 13). What is the significance of this strange phrase? Is it the blood of the enemies soon to be vanquished, or is it the blood of the Lamb himself? Note that the bloody robe appears *before* the battle, not afterward. Various writers (along with this author) contend that this is the blood of a victory already won, a victory won on Calvary, a victory the Lamb won by giving his own life rather than by taking the lives of his enemies (Eller 1981, 185).

George Eldon Ladd takes issue with this, saying that the image of Revelation 19:11-16 is entirely that of a warrior and not a redeemer (Ladd 1972, 254). What Ladd fails to observe in the course of Revelation is the frequent play on the twin concepts of Lion and Lamb carried forward from chapter 5. The Lion-Lamb is a warrior who has been sacrificed. For the Lamb, it is a victory won not by battle but by death. He is worthy because he was slain (5:9) He freed his followers from sins by his blood (1:5). Those who overcome evil likewise follow the Lamb into hardship (2:3). This is the right side up world of Revelation where losers really win, and martyrs produce a spiritual harvest because of their willingness to suffer. The message in the face of syncretistic pressure is that Christ is Lord and earthly governments do not receive our ultimate allegiance. The redemptive Lamb is not merely working in the invisible world of supernatural powers, but is a Lamb incarnate in the world facing earthly powers to overcome them. The followers of the Lamb await the coming of the kingly Lion, but will nonetheless experience some degree of redemption in this world as they proclaim the message of the Lamb.

The Extent of Mission

The overwhelming message of the Christian mission as portrayed in Revelation, then, is that Christ is Lord, a truth that directly influences the extent or scope of the mission. By definition a sovereign deity rules over the entire universe. The seven spirits with the seven all-seeing eyes of the Lamb (Rev. 5:6) are "sent out into all the earth," a statement likely written at a time when Rome was near its zenith of geographic extension. The prostitute of Revelation 17:15 ruled over "peoples, multitudes, nations and languages" but all of creation bows not before the prostitute or before Caesar's throne but before the throne of the Lamb (Summers 1951, 90). There may be a real sense in which Revelation is the fulfillment of the theology of mission found in the Gospel of John, the so-called "universal gospel." Just as John's Gospel stresses "the universalism of salvation" (Hahn 1965 134), so Revelation declares the universalism of his reign. In the Gospel, Jesus is called the "light of the world," and the universal and rational *logos* of God. In Revelation, the Lamb and his bride work together to push back the frontiers of darkness and to establish a universal reign (Hahn 1965, 134). The warfare continues until victory comes and history draws to a close (Jones 1984, 64-65). The extent of the mission of the Lamb, then, is worldwide in a two-fold sense, one part spiritual and "not of this world," another part "worldly" and with a political dimension. The destruction of the ten kings of the earth by the Lamb surely reflects victory over the spirit of arrogance arrayed against God, but it need not be entirely spiritualized. The tone of Revelation is that all of creation, including its political systems, is coming under the dominion of the Lamb in both spirit and living social reality. The Lamb metaphor pictures Christ in a campaign to establish God's standard of justice and to redress evil in society.

For example, what would the fall of Babylon and its allied kings have meant to the original readers of Revelation? While there was great wealth in Rome as seen in the many articles of trade in luxury items listed (Rev. 18:11-15), Rome also included masses who lived in dire poverty and survived on a dole system (Summers 1951, 91). John called his readers to "choose the eternal rather than the temporal, to resist temptation, to refuse to compromise with pagan secularism ... not only in the reign of Domitian but also in every other chaotic period of world history ..." (Summers 1951, 93).

The first century church refused to retreat into an ethnic enclave where there was no evangelism and where the goal was merely to maintain political and demographic balance. To stop evangelization would have seemed a strange accommodation to the writer of Revelation who believed in a sovereign Lamb. Likewise, a prohibition against morality and faithfulness in daily living would have been impossible to obey. While the Lamb's reign in Revelation is not limited to the present world, it certainly includes the present world. The church serves the Lord in this world, not in the world to come (Dyrness 1983, 179) and the scope of the Lamb's mission includes people everywhere now. A consideration of the Lamb's reign, then, leads to a third aspect of mission related to the Lamb: the method of his ministry.

The Method of Mission

How does the Lamb accomplish his goals? Although death and suffering are implicit in the Lamb metaphor, this Lamb is like no other. He has not had the fight kicked out of him! He is an active judge who receives joy at a wedding feast. Can this regal, sovereign Lamb be called defenseless? Hardly, yet we cannot forget that the method of the Lamb to accomplish redemption was to suffer and die. Theologian Oscar Cullmann closely links the Lamb figure of Revelation with the Suffering Servant of Isaiah, saying that while the action of the Servant was completed in the earthly life of Jesus, the same concept of suffering is connected with the ongoing present work of Christ in the world (Cullmann 1963, 81). Just like the earthly Jesus was self-giving and defenseless, the Christ present with the church is also self-giving and defenseless.

The method used to gain victory in Revelation strangely contradicts the warrior metaphor. The victory over sin is won by the blood of the Lamb (Rev. 1:5). His right to be seated upon the throne and to open the seals depends upon his death (Rev. 5:9), not upon his prowess as a warrior. Even the worthiness of his followers who join him in victory depends upon his blood (Rev. 7:14). The power to overcome Satan rests upon the blood of the Lamb (Rev. 12:11, 19:13), not one's success in battle.

> **The extent of the mission of the Lamb was worldwide and reached to all cultures, transcending the barriers of nationalism and ethnicity.**

How does one resist the siren call to compromise methodology? The answer lies in following the example of the Lamb in self-giving. The Lamb and the 144,000 share the same experience of an obedient death as first-fruits (Rev. 14:4). They share in the purity of their testimony. The call to a radical brand of discipleship to oppose syncretism rings vibrantly in passages like this. One writer calls it a "perfect, uncomplaining discipleship" (Ladd 1972, 191).

Historically few individual Christians have modeled their witness after Jesus as the Suffering Servant. The institutional church in society has an even poorer record. "For the most part, the church has not been a defenseless, self-expending servant of mankind . . ." (Eller 1981, 180). Those who "did not love their lives so much as to shrink from death" (Rev. 12:11) are the true followers of the Lamb and the ones most likely to bring true honor to him.

Admittedly, this could be a revolution for mission! The Lamb metaphor cries out that conversion comes not by physical force but by people becoming convinced of the power of Jesus' sacrifice. Jesus' sacrifice proves to be ultimately victorious. Evangelism by coercion would be a syncretism of the grossest sort, a profound violation of the spirit of the Lamb. Coercion was tested and miserably failed to bring vital faith to medieval Western Europe, to Muslim lands during the Crusades and to Latin America under the Spanish and Portuguese Conquistadores. Persistent, overcoming Christians across the centuries, however, have hastened the defeat of the devil by focusing upon the sacrifice, death and resurrection of the Lamb in their proclamation and in their living examples. This is at the heart of true Christian conquest (Eller 1974, 129). Could not proclamation accompanied by unconditional love, if practiced widely, bring an end to some oppression and injustice and open doors to the evangelization of those who have resisted force (Lamoreau and Beebe 1980, 33)? Self-sacrifice is a strong weapon against syncretistic compromise, and helps explain the early church's success in evangelism despite their powerlessness in the political realm during its first 300 years of history.

> **The method of mission for the Lamb and his followers was obedient suffering and self-sacrifice.**

The worldwide evangelical mission force tends to be strongly committed to peaceful and non-coercive evangelism, but is it equally committed to aggressive love? The church is called to do battle in love alongside the Lamb, engaging Satan on every level of existence until the end of history (Jones 1984, 7). The battle will ultimately demand that a disciple be cut free from dependency upon any one political system and freed from nationalistic prejudice that builds barriers to mission. The battle requires radically obedient discipleship like the obedience of the Lamb himself.

Conclusion

In conclusion, we have seen three major theological guidelines from Revelation to shape the training and practice of mission to avoid syncretism. First, it is important to clearly define the message: it is the Lamb himself who redeems through his self-giving sacrifice and will eventually gain the victory and establish his Kingdom. That is wonderfully good news to the followers of the Lamb, but it will not be happily received by every culture or quasi-religious power. Conflicts will arise. Second, to avoid syncretism the mission cannot be limited by geography or ethnicity, but must include individuals from all people and their societies. Christians cannot be true to the universal gospel, for example, and bow to Muslim or Hindu fundamentalist complaints that to seek converts among them is cultural genocide. Third, self-giving sacrifice is the time-honored divine method always present in mission. The followers of the Lamb are marked by compassion. To employ coercion is to slip into accommodation and syncretism, never to be considered by the Lamb or his followers.

In addition, this study has discovered at least six practical and direct responses to syncretistic pressures found in Revelation that might be especially useful in regions

> **Proclamation of the Lamb accompanied by unconditional love will end much oppression and open many doors where force has failed miserably.**

dominated by Islam, Hinduism, Buddhism or Secularism but useful also in the West. The goal of the six responses that follow is to maintain faithful loyalty to the Lord Jesus while living in a hostile context that encourages syncretism.

First, Revelation calls the church to *ardent worship of the Lamb.* Readers receive repeated invitations to join with the four living creatures, the angels, the 24 elders, the gathered multitudes, or with the martyrs to proclaim the Lordship of the Lamb (Rev. 4:8, 4:11, 5:9-13, 7:10, 1:12, 7:15-17, 11:15-18, 12:10-12, 15:3-4, 16:5-7, 19:1-8). Devotion to the political state pales in comparison to this throbbing love for the Lamb.

Second, the ministry of the church is to be modeled after the *self-sacrificing work of the Lamb.* The attitude of the church, aligned with Paul's call in Philippians 2:5-11, is to take on the attitude of Christ in humility and self-giving, not taking on the methods of the world to do battle against compromise. The coercive methods of the state have no place in the ministry of the followers of the Lamb and the temptation to use them is doomed to failure and spiritual mediocrity.

Third, the church is called to cultivate a spiritual experience that leads to *moral purity.* The martyrs are dressed in white, not having defiled themselves. Closely allied to this is the need for training in "patient endurance" so frequently mentioned (Rev. 1:9, 2:2-3, 2:10, 2:12, 2:13, 6:9, chapter 7, 12 and 13, and 14:12). While persecution can at times deter insincere conversions and keep the church at a high level of purity and even toughen Christian leadership against heresy, it has at other times ripped congregations apart and produced apostasy (Bromiley 1986, 773). Persecution is never an unmixed blessing and must be dealt with carefully, lest compromise intrude.

Fourth, the church needs *discipleship programs that deal more directly with materialism.* Materialism was implicit in the Mediterranean animism that sought prosperity and fertility at every turn in the Roman world. The sin of materialism is explicit in the fall of Babylon (Rev. 18). Materialism is an issue everywhere among animists, in the emerging economies of Asia, and certainly in the secular West. Both totalitarian and democratic states around the globe regularly promote a materialism that has no sense of hope beyond health, wealth and physical comfort. Holistic mission and social concern, as meaningful and necessary as they are, are bankrupt if they fail to give a hope beyond the present world.

Fifth, teachings must be developed to address *the heresies and deceit of Satan* as they appear from within the church. There must be better discernment about the deceit of lawlessness (e.g., the Nicolaitans of Rev. 2:6); discernment on idolatry like that produced by the teachings of Balaam (Rev. 2:13-15); discernment over pagan sexual immorality and the proclamations of other false prophets (like the Jezebel of Rev. 2:2); and discernment on the Gnostic heresy of seeking Satan's "deep secrets" (like that in Thyatira of Rev. 2:24). All of these heresies are appearing again in the twenty-first century.

Sixth, teaching is needed to deal with the threat of *compromise with the state*. This needs to include facing the demands of Islamic and Hindu nationalists, African political and religious messiahs, communist bureaucrats, Latin American dictators or Western secular states. The church is weakened if, for whatever reason, the Lordship of the Lamb is replaced by the lordship of the state or culture. Western evangelicals are certainly vulnerable to this kind of syncretism as well, not only when they fail to develop positive teachings that avoid heresies, but also when they fail to develop a biblical understanding of the role of the state.

What *is* a Christian's relationship to political powers? What answers are there for brothers and sisters trying to live truly Christian lives under hostile governments? The Lordship of the Lamb is clearly the answer proclaimed in Revelation. "Worthy is the Lamb!" He is worthy, indeed, worthy to be the

> ## The Lamb Defeats Syncretism
>
> • By ardent worship of the Lamb.
>
> • By the self-giving service of the Lamb and the church.
>
> • By the moral purity of the Lamb and the Church.
>
> • By a discipleship that overcomes materialism.
>
> • By theological clarity in the face of heresy.
>
> • By surrendering to the Lordship of the Lamb, not to the lordship of political or cultural power.

great dividing line between truth and falsehood, worthy to be the positive standard of faithfulness, worthy to do battle against the titans of this world. We need to acknowledge that God has *created* the political power of the state, but also that he *transforms* the power of the state. The book of Revelation thrusts upon the reader a startling demand to seek the centrality and Lordship of the Lamb and urges his followers to understand and respond correctly to ungodly pressures from political states, be they from democratic or totalitarian governments, or from secular or quasi-religious cultures.

Sources Cited

Angus, S. and A. M. Renwick. 1988. "Roman Empire and
Christianity," *The International Standard Bible
Encyclopedia.* Ed. G. W. Bromiley. Vol. 4. Grand
Rapids: William B. Eerdmans.

Bromiley, G. W. 1986. "Persecution," *The International Standard
Bible Encyclopedia.* Ed. G. W. Bromiley. Vol. 3. Grand
Rapids: William B. Eerdmans.

Cullman, Oscar. 1963. *The Christology of the New Testament.*
Philadelphia: The Westminster Press.

Dyrness, William A. 1983. *Let the Earth Rejoice! A Biblical
Theology of Holistic Mission.* Westchester, Illinois:
Crossway Books.

Eller, Vernard. 1974. *The Most Revealing Book of the Bible.*
Grand Rapids: William B. Eerdmans.

_____ . 1981. *War and Peace from Genesis to Revelation.*
Scottdale, Pennsylvania: Herald Press.

Ellison, Stanley A. 1999. "Everyone's Question: What is God
Trying To Do?" *Perspectives on the World Christian
Movement.* Pasadena: William Carey Library.

Hahn, Ferdinand. 1965. *Mission in the New Testament.*
London: SCM Press.

Holcomb, Ron. 2004. Unpublished response paper. Evangelical
Missiological Society-Northwest Regional Meeting.
Portland, OR: April 16, 2004.

Jones, T. Canby. 1984. *George Fox's Attitude Toward War.*
Richmond, Indiana: Friends United Press.

Ladd, George Eldon. 1972. *A Commentary on the Revelation
of John.* Grand Rapids: William B. Eerdmans.

Lioy, Dan. 2003. *The Book of Revelation in Christological Perspective*. New York: Peter Lang.

Lamoreau, John and Ralph Beebe. 1980. *Waging Peace. A Study in Biblical Pacifism*. Newberg, Oregon: The Barclay Press.

Morris, Leon. 1969. *The Revelation of St. John. An Introduction and Commentary*. Grand Rapids: William B. Eerdmans.

Mounce, Robert H. 1977. *The Book of Revelation*. Grand Rapids: William B. Eerdmans.

Senior, Donald and Carroll Stuhlmueller. 1984. *The Biblical Foundations for Mission*. Maryknoll, New York: Orbis.

Summers, Ray. 1951. *Worthy is the Lamb*. Nashville: Broadman Press.

Vos, H. S. 1988. "Rome," *The International Standard Bible Encyclopedia*. Ed. G. W. Bromiley. Vol. 4. Grand Rapids: William B. Eerdmans.

Walvoord, John F. 1966. *The Revelation of Jesus Christ*. Chicago: Moody Press.

7

To the Muslim I Became a Muslim?

J. Dudley Woodberry

The Apostle Paul stated,

> To the Jews I became a Jew, in order to win the Jews. To those under the Law I became as one under the Law (though I myself was not under the Law) so that I might win those under the Law...I have become all things to all people, that I might by all means save some. I do it all for the sake of the gospel.... (1 Corinthians 9:19-20, 25)

If Paul were retracing his missionary journeys today, would he add, "To the Muslim I became a Muslim"? Or even more apropos to my assignment, would he and the Jerusalem Council endorse Muslims being free to follow Jesus while retaining, to the extent that this commitment allows, Muslim identity and practices, as these Jerusalem leaders endorsed

Jews being free to follow Jesus while retaining, to the extent that that commitment allowed, Judaic identity and practices?

To answer these questions, we shall look through the biblical lens of the incarnation. How was the gospel incarnated in Jesus and Paul, and how was it to be incarnated in the divergent congregations that make up Christ's Body the Church (Eph. 4:12-13)?

John Travis described the spectrum of Christ-centered communities of Muslim-background believers (MBBs) or Muslim believers (MBs) under six rubrics (C1 through C6) on the basis of : (1) their language of worship, (2) the cultural and religious forms they used, especially in worship, and (3) their identity, whether Muslim or Christian (1998, 407-408). C1 refers to a community that reflects the culture of foreign Christians or a minority indigenous Christian group. The continuum progresses to C4 where participants use their ethnic language or Arabic in worship, use what are considered "Muslim" forms of worship but with Christian content, and consider themselves and are considered to be "Christians."

C5 Defined (Travis 1998)

Christ-centered Communities of "Messianic Muslims" Who Have Accepted Jesus as Lord and Savior.

C5 believers remain legally and socially within the community of Islam. Somewhat similar to the Messianic Jewish movement. Aspects of Islamic theology which are incompatible with the Bible are rejected, or reinterpreted if possible. Participation in corporate Islamic worship varies from person to person and group to group. C5 believers meet regularly with other C5 believers and share their faith with unsaved Muslims. Unsaved Muslims may see C5 believers as theologically deviant and may eventually expel them from the community of Islam. Where entire villages accept Christ, C5 may result in "Messianic mosques." C5 believers are viewed as Muslims by the Muslim community and refer to themselves as Muslims who follow Isa the Messiah.

Questions to consider:
1. What might have been the results if Muslim evangelism throughout history had all been based on a C5 approach?

2. What elements of a C5 approach make you feel most comfortable? What elements make you feel least comfortable?

C5 expresses a group of persons who accept Jesus as Lord and Savior but remain within the Muslim community to lead others to follow Christ in an "insider movement" (in contrast to C6 who are secret believers). Some C5 persons continue to worship in the mosque, but virtually all in the groups with which I am most familiar have their basic worship

---

Incarnational Mission

Just as Christ was incarnated as a person, so missionaries can be said to need to incarnate themselves into a new context. They cannot come as newborns, but they can learn the language and culture in such a way that they can behave like one who was born in the culture. (Moreau, Corwin and McGee 2004, 12)

Question to consider:

1. No living person can incarnate as Jesus did—we cannot literally be born a second time in a new cultural context. With that in mind, what are the limitations of an incarnational approach to mission?

---

and Bible study in house gatherings of like-minded followers of Christ. They consider themselves to be, and are considered to be, "Muslims," at least socially and legally, but of a special kind. They are those who follow Isa (the Qur'anic word for Jesus) and believe what the Bible teaches even where it differs from the Qur'an.

In actual practice the distinctions between the six categories are often not clear or consistent, and Muslims are coming to faith in Christ in all of these categories. I have been asked to evaluate C4 and C5. Elsewhere, however, I have documented that the religious vocabulary of the Qur'an and all of the so-called five pillars of Islam, except the references to Muhammad and Mecca, were used by Jews and/or Christians before Islam (Woodberry 1989, 283-312; 1996, 171-186). Furthermore, C4 contextualization is now broadly accepted in mission circles as at least legitimate. Therefore, I shall confine my remarks to C5 communities or "insider movements."

For reasons of security and to honor commitments of confidentiality very little research on "insider movements" has been made available to the general public, but there has been research on and recording of such communities and movements in various parts of Asia and Africa. Much of this has been reported in restricted contexts of expatriate and national missionaries and missiologists – some with authorization and some without. While striving not to violate confidentiality or reasonable security, I shall try in this paper to evaluate "insider movements" by applying biblical criteria to concrete situations which I have seen first-hand.

The Incarnational Models of Jesus and Paul

With Jesus we see the divine model for incarnating the gospel among people whose world view was similar to that of most Muslims, and with Paul we see how that model was lived out in different religio-cultural contexts.

The Model of Jesus

His incarnation is announced as "The Word became flesh and dwelt among us, and we beheld his glory, the glory of the father's only son" (Jn. 1:14). He in turn gave us that same glory: "The glory which you have given me, I have given them" (Jn. 17:22). And he gave us a similar mission: "As the father has sent me, so send I you" (Jn. 20:21).

Further, God sent his Son to be incarnated under the same Law that guided the people whom he sought to redeem: "God sent forth his Son...born under the Law to redeem those under the Law" (Gal. 4:4-5). Therefore, as we follow Jesus we might go under a similar Law – or remain under that Law – for the redemption of those under that Law.

A number of observations appear relevant to our topic. First, Jesus observed the Mosaic Law, but rejected the additional traditions of the elders that nullified that Law (Mt. 15:1-9). And he internalized and deepened its meaning in the Sermon on the Mount. Therefore, his incarnational model includes following and internalizing the Mosaic Law. Second, qur'anic and Islamic Law in general draw heavily on Jewish Law with its roots in Mosaic Law (Roberts 1925; Neusner and Sonn 1999; Neusner *et al* 2000; Woodberry 1989, rev. 1996; Torrey 1933). The Qur'an even includes all of the 10 Commandments, although keeping the Sabbath is associated particularly with the Jews (20:8; 22:30; 7:180, 163; 17:23; 6:151; 24:2; 5:38; 4:112, 32). And Islamic Law did not develop the priestly and sacrificial functions and ritual in the same way as

Judaism did. Therefore, although there are some differences, much of Islamic Law is similar to Mosaic Law and can be internalized and interpreted as fulfilled in Christ. Thirdly, the leaders of the Temple and synagogues had corrupted Judaic worship and rejected Jesus, but he and his first followers continued to identify with Judaism and to participate in temple and synagogue worship. Therefore a case may be made for Muslims who follow Jesus to continue to identify with their Muslim community and participate, to the extent their consciences allow, in its religious observance.

The Model of Paul

Paul wrote to the church in Corinth where the local religion even promoted immorality:

> To the Jews I became a Jew, that I might win the Jews; to those who are under the Law, as under the Law...that I might win those who are under the law....I have become all things to all people that I might by all means save some.   *(1 Corinthians 9:20, 21)*

After showing the outworking of this in specific situations, he passes the model onto us: "Be imitators of me as I am of Christ" (11:1). The same Paul who argued in the epistles to the Romans and Galatians against bondage to the Law, had Timothy circumcised when he was going to minister among Jews (Acts 16:3) and took converts with him into the Temple to be purified (Acts 21:26). As we have noted Islamic Law is based on the Law of Judaism. Even if it were not, however, Paul teaches adaptability even to a pagan culture like Corinth as long as one is guided by conscience and the desire to glorify God and that people be saved (1 Cor. 10:23-33).

The Incarnational Model of the Jerusalem Council

In Acts 15 we see how the early church leaders dealt with a missiological problem that resulted from the gospel crossing a cultural barrier – though it was from those who followed the Law to those who did not rather than the reverse, as in our present considerations. Nevertheless we can identify and apply the criteria they used.

How God is Working

Paul and Barnabas "reported the conversion of the Gentiles... and... all that God had done with them" (vss. 3-4), how "God who knows the human heart, testified to them by giving them the Holy Spirit, just as he did us, and in cleansing their hearts by faith, he made no distinction between them and us" (vss. 8-9). And they told the "signs and wonders that God had done through them among the Gentiles" (vs. 12). Then Simeon told "how God first looked favorably on the Gentiles" (vs. 14).

There are now case studies of insider movements in a number of regions in Asia and Africa that demonstrate how God is working, with phenomenal growth in one South Asian country that we in the School of Intercultural Studies at Fuller Theological Seminary have been studying with repeated visits for years. This movement and others with which we are in contact give clear evidence that God is working in them. One Protestant denomination now directs most of its ministries among Muslims to equipping members of these movements. In the Spring of 2003 I was privileged to hear first-hand reports of those from each of their regions, and again it was clear that God was at work in these people.

There are significant movements to Christ from Islam in North Africa and Central Asia that are not insider movements nor very contextualized to Islamic culture. The contexts are different. Whether or not there was a previous national church and, if so, how much rapport it had with the Muslims are significant factors. My assignment, however, is to evaluate the insider movements.

The Call of God

At the Jerusalem Council Peter rose and said, "My brothers, you know that in the early days, God made a choice among you, that I should be the one through whom the Gentiles would hear the message of the good news and become believers" (vs. 7). And God through a vision showed him that, for the sake of the kingdom, he should break traditional dietary rules that kept Jews and Gentile apart (Acts 10).

In the case studies that we are following today, followers of Christ have likewise believed themselves called to break the traditional barriers between communities to incarnate the gospel in the Muslim community. In many cases God has confirmed the call by transforming lives through Christ.

Reason

Peter at the Jerusalem Council asks, "Why are you putting God to the test by placing on the neck of the disciples a yoke that neither our ancestors nor we have been able to bear?" (Acts 15:10). The apostles and elders, with the consent of the whole church, then sent a letter to the disciples in Antioch presenting their decision by saying, "it has seemed good to the Holy Spirit and to us..." (vss. 22, 23, 28). They used their own reasoning alongside the guidance of God's Spirit.

When we apply reason to the present discussion we see reasons for and reasons against insider movements of disciples of Christ within the Muslim community. Peoplehood in most Muslim cultures involves a mix of religion, culture, politics, nationality, ethnicity, and family. Apostasy then is an act that affects all these. Add to this the fact that the word "Christians" in these contexts often connotes Western (with its aggression and immorality) or some local ethnic group with different (often distasteful) customs.

The question then arises as to whether Muslims may accept Jesus as Savior and Lord while remaining socially and legally Muslim. In the Qur'an itself the word *islam* just means "to submit" to God (2:112), and Jesus' disciples bear witness that "we are Muslims" (literally, *those who submit*) (3:52; 5:111). The Qur'an also speaks of certain individuals who received the book before the Qur'an who said, "We were Muslims before it" (28: 52-53). Muslim qur'anic commentators say they were, or included, some Christians (McAuliffe 1991, 240-246). Thus there is at least some textual rationale for disciples of Christ from Muslim contexts to continue to include "Muslim" in their identity. However, because the word has developed in modern usage a more restrictive meaning, it would seem more transparent to use a designation such as "I submit to God (*aslamtu* in Arabic) through Isa al-Masih (the qur'anic title meaning Jesus the Messiah)."

This approach could be seen as following the historical pattern of designating groups within the Muslim community by their founder, such as the Hanbalites (after Ahmad b. Hanbal) or the Ahmadiya (after Ghulam Ahmad) though, as in the latter example, some Muslims may reject the group as heretical or non-Muslim.

Other disciples of Jesus from Muslim contexts have adopted the designation Hanif, which in the Qur'an referred to the religion of Abraham that pre-Islamic monotheists like Waraqa b. Nawfal sought. He was a cousin of Muhammad's first wife Khadija and became a Christian (Guillaume 1955, 83, 99, 103). The Qur'an says that Abraham was not a Jew nor a Christian, but a *hanif*, a *muslim* (3:67) and described him as one who submitted (*aslama*) to God. (4:125). `Umar, the second Muslim caliph, even used the term to describe himself when he met with a Christian leader (Rubin 2002, 403A). Its value is that it is generally an acceptable term which has referred to people like Ibn Nawfal who became a Christian and the apostle Paul calls those who belong to Christ "Abraham's offspring" (Gal. 3:29).

An advantage of insider movements is that they can provide an opportunity for the gospel to be incarnated into a Muslim culture with a minimum of dislocation of those elements of Muslim societies that are compatible or adaptable with the gospel. And, although they have aroused intense opposition, sometimes instigated by members of traditional churches, they have frequently allowed more opportunity and time for ordinary Muslims to hear and see the gospel lived out than when the new disciples of Christ are expelled upon conversion or join a traditional church with a different ethnic and cultural constituency and having little rapport with the Muslim majority. Likewise, it allows faith and spiritual maturity to develop in a context relevant to the new disciples' background and probable ministry.

> The whole character of the missionary's message is determined by his attitude toward the non-Christian religion that he has to wrestle with.
>
> J. H. Bavinck (1949, 109)

On the other hand there can be drawbacks. There is not a clear break with non-biblical teachings of Islam. Discipling raises greater challenges as does building bridges with traditional churches, if there are any.

Theology

Peter, before the Jerusalem Council, raised the theological argument that God "in cleansing their [the Gentiles'] hearts by faith made no distinction between them and us" (vs. 9) and went on, "we believe that we will be saved through the grace of the Lord Jesus, just as they will" (vs. 11). That is the decisive element, not whether they follow the law or not.

Theological themes that are relevant to insider movements include that of the faithful remnant, which refers to a genuine relationship of faith with God (Amos 5:15). Although it originally applied to the faithful remnant of God's people Israel (Isa. 46:3), it includes those from other nations (Isa. 45:20; 66:18). Another theme is the kingdom (or kingly rule) of God, which like yeast will quietly transform individuals and groups from within (Mt. 13:33) and salt which likewise influences its surroundings (Mt. 5:13).

The people of the kingdom who form the local churches and the universal Church are, of course, especially relevant. Even the believers who meet in houses are called churches (Rom. 16:5l; 1 Cor. 16:19), and these would correspond to the groups that meet regularly in houses for worship and Bible study that are at the core of the insider movements with which I am familiar. Expressing the universal Church becomes the great challenge for them because it is the body of Christ incarnated in the world today (1 Cor. 12:12-27).

Scripture

James before the Council then shows how the inclusion of the Gentiles also agreed with Scripture (Acts 15:15-17). When we look for scripture that is relevant to insider movements, we see that in the Old Testament God sometimes worked outside the channels of his chosen people – through Melchizedek, for example. We even observe the prophet Elisha apparently condoning Naaman going into a pagan temple with the king he served and bowing with him before an idol (2 Kings 5:17-19).

In the New Testament Jesus—in the Sermon on the Mount—internalized and deepened the Law (which, as we have noted, was similar in many ways to Islamic Law). At the same time he did not let it hinder his relating with those he came to save (Lk. 7:36-50). Paul, while arguing against the necessity of following the Law, observed it to further his ministry with the Jews as in his circumcising of Timothy (Acts 16:3), having his own hair cut when under a vow (Acts 18:18), and performing the purification rites in Jerusalem when James and the elders there encouraged him to do so because of the Jews (Acts 21:26).

On the other hand the Epistle to the Hebrews was apparently written to Jewish followers of Christ who, under persecution, were conducting themselves as a form of Judaism—perhaps because Judaism was then a recognized religion by Rome but not Christianity. They are warned of the peril of falling away (6:1-8) and are called to persevere (10:19-39; Green 1989, 233-250).

Guidance of the Holy Spirit

At the Jerusalem Council, Peter noted that God testified to the inclusion of the Gentiles in the Church by giving them the Holy Spirit (Acts 15:8), and in the joint communiqué to the church in Antioch the apostles and elders said that "it has seemed good to the Holy Spirit and to us" not to impose any further burden on the Gentiles than some essentials (vs. 28). Jesus had promised, "When the Spirit of truth comes, he will guide you into all truth" (Jn. 16:13). Many of those that I have met in insider movements have evidenced by the fruit of the spirit, wisdom, and devotion the indwelling Spirit of God. Because of the limitation of formal training opportunities for the believers in insider movements, they are highly dependent on the Bible as interpreted and applied by the Holy Spirit to them. But my questioning of numbers of them and the reports of others that I trust lead me to conclude that, although they are different from traditional Christians, they certainly evidence the guidance of the Bible and the Spirit.

The Essentials

The apostles and elders in Jerusalem, when stating that circumcision was not necessary, were dealing with *salvation*. When they added some "essentials" (vss. 28-29), they were dealing with *fellowship* and *morality*. The prohibition of fornication (vss. 20, 29) obviously had to do with the low Greco-Roman morality out of which the Gentiles came. As for food offered to idols, although Christians are free to eat it, the act might cause others to stumble (1 Cor. 8:1-13). Therefore, believers should not exercise that freedom (Act 15:20, 29). The same is true of blood and meat that contains blood. Since the Law of Moses, which forbids the eating of blood, had been so widely preached (vs. 21), eating it might hinder table fellowship with many Jews.

How does all this apply to disciples of Christ within the Muslim community? First, there is freedom to observe the Law or not to do so, since salvation does not come through the Law. But because relationships and fellowship are so important, the disciples of Christ should not use their freedom in a way that might unnecessarily hinder their relationships with Muslims or traditional Christians.

Acts 15 ends with Paul and Barnabas separating in their missionary work because they could not agree on whether to take John Mark (vss. 36-41). Here we see that when we cannot agree we can carry on God's work in separate spheres until we can agree.

Some Critical Issues

There are a number of critical issues, some of which have been treated above.

Use of the Term "Muslim"

A case has been made above for the use of the term "Muslim" by followers of Christ, but it is often best to qualify it in some way indicating that our submission is through Isa al-Masih (Jesus the Messiah). In any event we are not to deny Jesus Christ. Further, although disciples of Christ from Muslim backgrounds may legitimately retain their Muslim legal and cultural heritage, it is far more problematic for a person of

153

Christian background to attempt this. The outsider might be helpful in suggesting biblical guidelines, but those from a Muslim background are in a better position to understand the meaning of labels and identity in their contexts, hence to answer these questions.

Attending the Mosque and Using the Qur'an

Again insiders understand better what attending the mosque or using the Qur'an means in each context; so are in a better position to decide what is best. One factor to consider is the motive. Our research shows that many were first attracted to Christ through the Qur'an. One North African with a number of his family members that he had led to Christ, said that no one would listen to him if he did not continue to use the Qur'an, with the Bible, and attend the mosque. We do know that the early Jewish Christians, like many Messianic Jews today, continued to attend the synagogue (Acts 9:1-2; 23:2). And the Judaic establishment at the time was hostile to Christians (Acts 9:1-2; 23:2) even as many Muslims are today. If people continue in the mosque, however, they must not say or do anything against their conscience (Rom. 14:14). In studying Muslim followers of Christ over a number of years, I have found them less interested in the Qur'an as they read the Bible and less interested in the mosque as they worship with other believers.

Reciting the Confession of Faith

I have enquired of those in insider movements what they do with the *shahada*, the confession: "There is no god but God, and Muhammad is the Apostle of God." One answered that some say that in his polytheistic context he was like an Old Testament prophet. This reflects the ambiguity of the Nestorian Patriarch Timothy (d. 823) who responded to the Caliph al-Mahdi's question concerning what he thought of Muhammad with the words, "He walked in the path of the prophets" (Gaudeul 1990, 34-36). Most of those I asked, however, said that they kept quiet when the part about Muhammad was recited or they quietly substituted something that was both biblically and qur'anically correct like "Jesus is the Word of God."

The Unity of the Church

In the early church, as we have seen, James, Cephas and John were chosen to go to the Jews and Paul and Barnabas to the Gentiles (Gal. 2:9). Each evangelistic thrust was relatively homogeneous. The Jews and Gentiles could keep much of their own identity and follow Christ. But to express the universal Church, they needed to have fellowship, which was expressed by eating together. This required some additional adjustments. So with the insider movements, there is much freedom for them to retain their identity but over time some adjustments will need to be made for the sake of fellowship in the broader Church. The same Paul who argued for the freedom of the Jewish and Gentile churches to retain their own identity also argued that Christ had broken down the wall between Jew and Gentile so they might be one body, the Body of Christ (1 Cor. 12:12-27). The same freedom must be there for the Muslim and traditional Christian churches. This is how Christ is being incarnated on the earth today.

Sources Cited

Bavinck, Johan Herman. 1949. *The Impact of Christianity on the Non-Christian World.* Grand Rapids: William B. Eerdmans Publishing Company.

Gaudeul, Jean-Marie. 1990. *Encounters and Clashes: Islam and Christianity in History*, vol. 1. Rome: Pontificio Instituto di Studi Arabi e Islamici.

Green, Denis. 1989. "Guidelines from Hebrews for Contextualization." In *Muslims and Christians on the Emmaus Road*, ed. J. Dudley Woodberry. Monrovia, CA: MARC.

Guillaume, Alfred. 1995. *The Life of Muhammad: A Translation of [Ibn Hisham's Recension of Ibn] Ishaq's Sirat Rasul Allah.* London: Oxford University Press.

McAuliffe, Jane Dammen. 1991. *Qur'anic Christians.* Cambridge: Cambridge University Press.

Moreau, A. Scott, Gary Corwin and Gary McGee. *Introducing World Missions: A Biblical, Historical, and Practical Survey.* Grand Rapids: Baker Academic, 2004.

Neusner, Jacob and Tamara Sonn. 1999. *Comparing Religions through Law: Judaism and Islam.* New York: Routledge.

Neusner, Jacob, Tamara Sonn and Jonathan Brockopp. 2000. *Judaism and Islam in Practice: A Sourcebook.* New York: Routledge.

Roberts, Robert. 1925. *The Social Law of the Qoran.* London: William and Norgate.

Rubin, Uri. 2002. "Hanif." In *Encyclopaedia of the Qur'an*, ed. Jane Dammen McAuliffe. Vol. 2, 402-403.

Torrey, Charles Cutler. *The Jewish Foundation of Islam.* 1933. New York: Jewish Institute of Religion Press.

Travis, John. 1998. "The C1 to C6 Spectrum: A Practical Guide for Defining Six Types of 'Christ-Centered Communities' ('C') Formed in Muslim Contexts." *Evangelical Missions Quarterly* 34(4): 407-408.

Woodberry, J. Dudley. 1989. "Contextualization among Muslims: Reusing Common Pillars." In *The World among Us*. Dean Gilliland, ed. Pp. 282-312. Dallas, TX: Word Publishing. Revised 1996 with additional notes in *International Journal of Frontier Missions* 13(4): 171-186.

8

Suburban Evangelical Individualism: Syncretism or Contextualization?

J. Nelson Jennings

Towards the end of his 1994 book *The American City and the Evangelical Church: A Historical Overview*, Harvie Conn laments certain features of suburbanized evangelical Christianity in the United States, most especially what he sees as a permeating individualism. What is striking about the following block of quotations is the somewhat sudden—and from what I can tell somewhat unique among Conn's writings—appearance (three times) of the term *syncretism*, in adverbial

> The history of the evangelical church in the American city has been liberally sprinkled with a cultural pessimism toward things urban.

and adjectival forms, in reference to the bulk of contemporary U.S. evangelicalism:

> People...are now creating their own urban centers out of the destination they can reach by car in a reasonable length of time.... In this decentralized world the church loses its grip on local geographical neighborhood and is transformed into a megachurch, twenty-five minutes away by car.... Is the megachurch ... a dangerous sample of modernity in which the evangelical *syncretistically* adopts patterns for the church that will eventually destroy it? .... [Furthermore,] is [the megachurch] so controlled by a desire to satisfy the felt needs of individual concerns that it is in danger of moving its members again to yet another outer limit of choices and ecclesiastical options? Will it leave behind once more the poor as part of its mono-social constituency? .... The individualism that has been characteristic of American culture from its beginnings will continue to impact the evangelical message for and about the city. Bible-believing pulpits will continue to understand persons, sin, the gospel, and redemption in individualistic terms.... The kingdom continuity of a shalom of wholeness and justice fulfilled in Christ will be reduced to the individual assurance of peace in some inward, spiritual sense. Among suburban white and Asian "model minority" churches, this *syncretized* message will be especially strong.... The history of the evangelical church in the American city has been liberally sprinkled with a cultural pessimism toward things urban. *Syncretistically* borrowed from a predominantly middle-class white mentality, anti-urban sentiments have continually surfaced throughout the history recorded in this book (Conn 1994, 191-194).

I sat up and took notice the first time I read these pages in Conn's book several years ago. Ever since then I've been mulling over what Conn meant by his use of such a poignant, missiological term as "syncretism," usually reserved for different types of settings than U.S. suburbs.

This brief and modest paper has two objectives that I hope will help achieve an overall goal. First, I hope to unravel just a bit Harvie Conn's understanding of "syncretism" and "contextualization." The second objective is to understand, within Conn's analysis, how suburban evangelical individualism can thus be described as "syncretistic." The main goal I have in mind is a sharpening of our operative biblical notions of syncretism and of contextualization—the overarching topic of this book.

Inputs Toward Conn's View of "Syncretistic Evangelical Individualism"

We need to take a few minutes to think about Dr. Harvie M. Conn himself, to see how he came to write the kind of things we have just heard. By way of personal recollections, no doubt many reading this book could give numerous anecdotes about our missiological father and brother who went to be with Christ back in August, 1999, in his mid-60s.[1] The first time I ever heard of Harvie Conn was in the early 1980s during a conversation between two recent graduates of Westminster Theological Seminary, where Conn taught for almost three decades, from 1972 to 1999. These two young pastors giggled as they remembered Professor Conn coming into the classroom with necktie off-center and otherwise having a somewhat disheveled appearance. Reportedly his lectures were not detached, logically arranged treatises as much as they were warm, passionate appeals to service. The first and only time I met Conn was a few years later, when he and I intersected at a church missions conference, he as the main speaker and I as a newly approved, itinerating missionary. Harvie didn't disappoint my expectations based on previous reports, either as a speaker or in personal conversations.

Born a Canadian in 1933, Conn served as a church-planter in New Jersey starting in 1957, right after he had completed his undergraduate studies at Calvin College and his MDiv at Westminster Seminary. It wasn't too long before Harvie went to Korea, where he preached in various churches, taught New Testament at the General Assembly Theological Seminary in Seoul, and ministered compassionately and evangelistically among red light districts. It is this ministry among prostitutes and pimps for which Conn's service in Korea is best known.

During his long tenure at Westminster Conn taught apologetics and missions, led mission trips to India and Uganda, edited the journal *Urban Mission*, founded what became the Center for Urban Theological Studies (CUTS), and

---

[1] This and other biographical information has been taken from "Dr. Harvie Conn Home with the Lord (1933-1999)" (Information supplied by Larry Sibley: Director of Public Relations, Westminster Theological Seminary) http://www.missiology.org/EMS/bulletins/conn.htm (March 12-15, 2004).

wrote extensively. His combined evangelistic and justice-mercy zeal shines forth in the account once given to me by Rev. Edward Kasaija of Kampala, Uganda, of how Conn once organized a "garbage evangelism" activity of collecting piled-up Kampala street garbage while preaching the gospel to all bystanders. Conn was a reformed missiological pacesetter (which helps to explain my own interest in building on his work, given my

> **Without a doubt we can confirm the fact that Conn's categorization of suburban evangelical individualism as syncretistic is a negative criticism.**

reformed connections), including the way he insisted on taking an interdisciplinary approach to missiology. Perhaps his influential *Eternal Word and Changing Worlds: Theology, Anthropology, and Mission in Trialogue (1984)* exhibits Conn's interdisciplinary instincts as well as any other publication. That book also shows his fearless interaction with important, cutting-edge thinking, since, as Enoch Wan so ably points out, much of what Conn is wrestling with in that book is Charles Kraft's "dynamic equivalence" model of contextualization set forth in his still recently published book *Christianity in Culture* (Wan 1996, 128). Theologically Conn at times appeared somewhat enigmatic: while he was unquestionably evangelical and, moreover, situated at that J. Gresham Machen-founded bastion of conservative reformed theology, Westminster Theological Seminary in Philadelphia, some evangelicals saw him influenced too much by ecumenical or "liberal" theology, for example in the way the notion of "contextualization" was to be defined (Hesselgrave and Rommen 1989, 34).[2]

Categorization Problem: What is Syncretism?

Throw in Conn's emphasis on urban matters of justice, and we indeed have much upon which to chew for our overall

---

[2] The breadth of input into Conn's thinking, as well as his enigmatic style, are also evident in his writing. Note, for example, Mark Walden's comments in his review of *The American City and the Evangelical Church*: "While the book betrays some difficulty in organizing its information, and the writing has an occasional pasted-together or off-the-top-of-Conn's head feel, there is nevertheless a wealth of information here, clearly presented." http://www.cst.edu/URBANWEB/bookrvw.htm (March 25, 2004).

topic of contextualization and syncretism. In order to proceed effectively, next we need briefly to step away from direct consideration of Conn and look at the general notion of "syncretism." Conn's provocative use of that category, in reference to North American evangelicalism, was the starting point for this whole consideration. Aside from Conn, how do some selected others define "syncretism"?

We only have space here to cite a few representative examples. I will mention three general positions, moving along a scale from understanding syncretism in negative terms to seeing it as both normal and acceptable.

Evangelicals in general will resonate with the first more standard and instinctive notion of "syncretism," indicated by the very term itself as "bringing together creeds" or "mixing religions." In syncretism the Christian faith is distorted, skewed, obscured, fundamentally altered, or even obliterated by being unduly influenced by another religion, usually previously present within a particular setting. This negative view is the assumed and unstated definition in many studies.[3] Related is the understanding of syncretism as "the blending of Christian beliefs and practices with those of the dominant *culture* so that Christianity loses its distinctive nature and speaks with a voice reflective of its culture (Van Rheenen 2004)." While we are for now consciously setting aside looking at Conn's view of syncretism, we might suggest at this point that this notion of "the blending of Christian [faith with] culture" is at least close

---

[3] E.g., Clinton E. Arnold, *The Colossian Syncretism: The Interface between Christianity and Folk Belief at Colossae* (Grand Rapids, Michigan: Baker Books, 1996); R. Daniel Shaw and Charles E. Van Engen, *Communicating God's Word in a Complex World: God's Truth or Hocus Pocus?* (Lanham, Maryland: Rowman & Littlefield Publishers, Inc., 2003); Paul G. Hiebert, R. Daniel Shaw, Tite Tiénou, *Understanding Folk Religion: A Christian Response to Popular Beliefs and Practices* (Grand Rapids, Michigan: Baker Books, 1999). It is worthwhile to note that this last book at least offers a one-sentence definition: "combining elements of Christianity with folk beliefs and practices in such a way that the gospel loses its integrity and message." Interesting as well is Kraft's mention of how many scholars have equated "nativization" with syncretism. Charles H. Kraft, "Contextualizing Communication," in Dean S. Gilliland, ed., *The Word Among Us: Contextualizing Theology for Mission Today* (Dallas, TX: Word Publishing, 1989), 132.

to what he might have meant in labeling suburban Christianity as syncretistic.

A slightly more nuanced, and somewhat less negative, view of syncretism is that expressed by André Droogers as "*contested* religious interpenetration (1989, 20-21)." In part at least, Droogers suggests that syncretism is "in the eyes of the beholder." No group ever calls itself syncretistic, and in particular it is those in religious authority who make accusations of syncretism. This definition tries to avoid problems of both strictly subjectivistic and objectivistic notions of syncretism, and it seeks to incorporate the inherent controversial nature of syncretistic religious expressions.

In a way that seeks to avoid knee-jerk controversy and negativity with regards to syncretism, Robert Schreiter suggests viewing it as the necessary synthesis that occurs as part of religious identity formation. Understanding this process, which occurs most particularly in the midst of cross-cultural interaction, in a way similar to how the social sciences and postcolonial writing treat syncretistic identity formation would help achieve at least a balance between viewing religious syncretism positively and negatively. Synthesis and syncretism can thus be understood as two sides of the same coin, or even overlapping grids for evaluating the same process (Schreiter 1998, 62-83). Per this view, syncretism is not only not negative, but it is an inherent aspect of religious faith within changing contexts.

Negative religious mixing; religious interpenetration that is either negative or not depending on the position of the one pronouncing judgment; necessary synthesis of religious identity: which of these categories might best encapsulate Harvie Conn's description of suburban evangelical individualism as syncretistic?

Without a doubt we can confirm the fact that Conn's categorization of suburban evangelical individualism as syncretistic is a negative criticism. Moreover, given Conn's basic evangelical commitments, we can see clear connections between Conn's framework and what we have termed here to be a standard and instinctive notion of syncretism as religious mixing. But lest we get our categorizing cart before our horse of genuinely understanding Conn's own notion of syncretism on its own terms, we need to hear him further speak for himself.

Conn's Religious Description of Evangelicals' "Mythical" Picture of the City

Of particular relevance to the entire matter at hand is Conn's description of what he calls U.S. evangelicals' *mythical*, negative picture of the city (Conn 1987, 15-34). Calling that image "mythical" is Conn's way of placing Christians' negative instincts about the city within a specifically *religious* realm:

> Is the basic problem the failure of evangelicals to see the mythological character of their picture of the city? A myth is not a scientific creation, though it may be supported by the facts unearthed by science. It is rather a creation of the human heart designed to explain our cosmos and its relationship to God and our fellow human beings. It is intended as a rhetorical question asking, who are we, who is God, what is our world? (Conn 1987, 26-27)

Conn's explanation of myth here is further indication of just how explicit he wants to be in identifying U.S. evangelicals' view of the urban world as a *religious* view. He hardly could have been more straightforward in spelling out the five elements of what his reformed missiological predecessor, J. H. Bavinck, called "the continent of the universal religious consciousness" (Bavinck 1966, 35-106). Elsewhere Conn terms Bavinck's constellation the "five 'magnetic points'" of religion, and he practically uses the same language here in describing evangelicals' mythical vision of the city (Conn 1994, 145-46).[4] The main point for us here is that Conn sees the evangelical anti-urban bias—which will connect with how he sees evangelical suburban individualism—as religious in character.

Conn lists four roadblocks to "demythologizing" evangelicals' anti-urban myth: "our cultural reading of the Bible," equating the American dream (and Christian ideals) with a "middle-class dream," "the privatization of our faith," and racism

> *...the main elements of suburban individualism, are also for Conn explicitly religious, mythological "creations of the human heart."*

---

[4] The five 'magnetic points' are "I and the cosmos," "I and the norm," "I and destiny," "I and salvation," and "I and the Supreme Being."

(Conn 1987, 28-32). Clearly the second and third roadblocks relate directly to our objectives in this paper. What we can say with measured confidence at this point is that, given their co-conspirator status alongside an explicitly religious anti-urban mythology, evangelicals' middle-class ideology and privatization of faith, the main elements of suburban individualism, are also for Conn explicitly religious, mythological "creations of the human heart." That would explain Conn's view of syncretism—at least in terms of how he calls evangelical suburban individualism syncretistic—as the straightforward, instinctive understanding we listed as the first (and most negative) of three general views of what constitutes syncretism, namely the mixing of religions and corresponding distortion of true Christianity.

Conn on Contextualization and Syncretism

However, we should recall here that, in describing that instinctive view of syncretism, we noted the two-fold view of mixing religions and of mixing religion and culture. We also suggested that perhaps Conn's view of suburban individualism was more of the latter type. We have just seen, though, how he sees suburban individualism as religious myth, not just cultural preference. Were we just way off the mark earlier in suggesting where Conn might come down, or does this say more about the intricacy of his twin notions of syncretism and contextualization?

I believe we can begin to see more clearly here how nuanced and multi-faceted Conn's thinking is. This helps to explain as well how he has been somewhat of an enigma, whether at Westminster Seminary or within the Evangelical Missiological Society. Conn is difficult to classify neatly as a thinker, including the way in which he understood the notion of contextualization. It's not that Conn shifted around a great deal over the years. It's just that he wove together so many threads, and he did so in his own unique and fearless style.

Perhaps the clearest and most concise[5] source for Conn's nuanced view of contextualization is his 1978 *EMQ* article, "Contextualization: A New Dimension for Cross-Cultural Hermeneutic" (Conn 1978, 39-46). It is important to note first the *timing* of this article. Contextualization discussions had become increasingly prominent since Shoki Coe's 1972 introduction of the term itself, and this particular issue of *EMQ* was devoted solely to that topic. Charles Kraft's 1979 *Christianity in Culture* was set to be published, and Conn in this article is already incorporating Kraft's monumental "dynamic equivalence" thesis (Conn 1978, 42, 46).[6] It had been about six years since Conn had moved from Korea to Philadelphia to begin teaching at Westminster Theological Seminary ("Dr. Harvie Conn ..." 2004)—a period of time sufficient for fresh insights to have emerged and to have begun to crystallize within a new cultural setting.[7] The article is thus on the cutting edge of wider discussions as well as coming out of Conn's own vibrant cross-cultural experience.

At the same time, Conn's synthesizing mind incorporates much more than simply the latest trends and his own personal interests. His reformed fabric utilizes Calvin's "covenant dimension of doing theology" that unites "thought and action, truth and practice." Conn's awareness of worldwide theological emphases frees him to examine "the theology of the North Atlantic" from a certain critical distance. Together with his appreciation of what the social sciences—especially anthropology—must contribute to theological and missiological discussions, (cf. Conn 1984) these multi-faceted inputs make Conn's sense of contextualization that of "the covenant conscientization of the whole people of God to the hermeneutical obligations of the gospel in their culture (Conn 1978, 43)." For Conn, "The new dimension of covenant

---

[5] Conn's *Eternal Word and Changing Worlds* undoubtedly incorporates more material, due to having been written several years later and because it is a much larger book as opposed to a brief article. In the book, however, Conn's treatments of contextualization per se (as well as of syncretism) are relatively scattered, somewhat tangential, and offered more in reference to other issues.

[6] As indicated, Conn quotes from a 1973 prepublication draft of Kraft's 1979 book.

[7] At least this has been my experience in moving between three different continents over the past 20 years.

contextualization adds [to the traditional evangelical hermeneutic's stress on the normativity of Scripture the importance of] the concrete situation, [without which] the Christian faith runs the risk of losing itself in cultural irrelevancy or ethnocentricity (Conn 1978, 44)."[8]

Conn's holistic, interdisciplinary, and covenantal notion of contextualization is mirrored in his broadened and redefined notion of syncretism:

> Every culture, in its self-preserving and integrating capacity, carries its own 'hidden' methodologies to which man as culture bearer and covenant keeper is always liable. The danger of syncretism is always stronger when the 'translator' of biblical truth into the life of that culture is not aware of its pull, or thinks the possibility of its pull less likely in his situation. Our fullest freedom of covenant expression in culture remains in being bound by the hermeneutical methodology of God himself. The Reformation heritage of Scripture interpreting Scripture (analogia fidei) continues to provide the hermeneutical key for our struggle against cultural idols, against our repression of the divine questions, our response to contemporary answers. (Conn 1978, 45)[9]

Conn here is challenging—whether explicitly or implicitly—two assumptions. First, so-called and allegedly pristine indigenous, non-Western cultures are not prone towards rebellion against God. Second, select other cultures,

---

[8] I would suggest that what Conn labels as "contextualization" is what Shaw and Van Engen lay out, in a much more thorough and precise way, as their "four-horizon hermeneutic"—which they claim "moves beyond contextualization." Just as with "syncretism" (cf. earlier note), Shaw and Van Engen seem to be assuming a default evangelical notion of "contextualization" (Shaw and Van Engen 2003, 212). As we shall see momentarily, Conn's expanded, redefined notion of contextualization carries over into a similarly expanded and redefined notion of syncretism.

[9] As Conn indicates leading up to this quotation, he is interacting here specifically with a 1977 paper delivered by Charles Taber. There Taber suggests that, as Scripture holds sway over the total contextualizing process, indigenous [non-Western] theology can be freed not only from Western categories and methodologies, but from "considerations of methodology of any kind." Besides demonstrating once again how up-to-date Conn's thinking and writing was, Conn's taking issue with Taber shows his instinctive inclination to reshape default assumptions, in this case concerning the alleged neutral innocence of indigenous (and all) cultures.

in particular those of Western heralds of so-called and allegedly pure biblical theology and ministry methods, also are not prone towards rebellion against God. The latter point emerges explicitly in Conn's other writings as well, for example in this exhortation to practitioners of ethnographic research studies:

> Always remember that you are prone to interpret out of an ethnocentric reality, a deep-lying assumption that your own culture is significantly superior to others. A great deal has been written about the dangers of ethnocentrism in interpretation because of the assumption that the scientific method is totally objective. However, 'ethnocentric assumptions may unconsciously influence' the research process itself. (Conn and Ortix 2001, 285)

Conn could just as well have said here that ethnographic researchers are prone to interpret out of a mythical, syncretistic assumption of ethnocentric, cultural superiority. Such a manner of expression helps us see how Conn's understanding of syncretism, like his understanding of contextualization, was holistic, interdisciplinary, and covenantal—and an ongoing concern, not just a one-time event. To oversimplify the matter, but to emphasize Conn's thinking in terms of the deep, personal, conscience-rooted submission or rebellion against God inherent in what is termed contextualization and syncretism, right contextualization is obedient "conscientization," whereas wrong contextualization, or syncretism, is disobedient "conscientization." For Conn the role of human beings' ingrained religious conscience is pervasive in all areas of life, whether in so-called animistic religious beliefs and practices, so-called scientific methodologies, so-called suburbanite anti-urban mythological views, or so-called suburbanite individualistic life patterns. Insofar as any of those religious myths might combine with the Christian faith so as to alter or even nullify biblical teaching, such a resulting belief or practice should be labeled "syncretism." It should thus be no surprise to read Conn's

> **Always remember that you are prone to interpret out of an ethnocentric reality, a deep-lying assumption that your own culture is significantly superior to others.**

statements about syncretistic suburban Christianity. What is surprising is that he did not write such statements more often.

Analysis of Contextualization and Syncretism

Having just focused on Conn's twin understandings of contextualization and syncretism, and thus having noted how and why he calls suburban evangelical individualism "syncretistic," we must move explicitly towards directing our thoughts towards the overall theme of our meetings by seeking eventually to answer the question posed by the title of this paper: Is Harvie Conn right in calling suburban evangelical individualism syncretistic, or is this just an idiosyncratic view of Conn's that we might appreciate but should basically ignore in terms of how it affects our own views, or is so-called suburban evangelical individualism something altogether different in terms of how we might classify it?

My own up-front answer to this three-fold question is "for the most part," "a wee bit," and "no—with qualification." I must explain myself, of course, first by noting briefly the primary inputs into my own understanding of contextualization and syncretism. Personally and contextually, I grew up in the Southern United States, in a monolingual (English-speaking) Christian home. My neighborhood and local church were both suburban (although the church facility was located close to "downtown") and racially segregated, while the local public schools I attended through high school were racially integrated. After majoring in baseball, philosophy and mathematics at a primarily white, upper-middle-class private Southern-U.S. university, I embraced reformed theology (not necessarily to imply a causal connection) and sensed God's call into full-time gospel ministry. That led me to study at Covenant Theological Seminary in St. Louis, where, strangely enough, I now teach. Between 1986 and 1999 my family and I lived primarily in Japan, an extended sojourn that transformed us into bilingual and so-called third-culture people. Working on a Ph.D. in non-Western Christianity, based in Edinburgh, Scotland, further exposed us to much of the rest of the world.

Intellectually and academically there of course have been several influences, including examples during my high school and college years of men and women who deeply respected and followed the Bible, even when that meant thinking and living differently than one's surroundings. More recently there have been two groups of important inputs for me. One is connected with Edinburgh, at least in terms of my interaction with them, namely Andrew Walls, Lamin Sanneh and Kwame Bediako. Walls' historical picture of the universal-particular character—or pilgrim-homing instincts—of Christianity, Sanneh's explanation of some of the implications of Christianity's translatability, and Bediako's pastoral courage in pursuing implications of vernacular Scriptures have formed what for me and others has been a guiding constellation shining in the night sky of multicultural displacement. Another set—an interesting pair, actually—would be ecclesiastically and self-consciously more of a reformed persuasion. One would have to be Conn himself, as an example of a missiologist who loves the Bible and is unafraid of encouraging multidisciplinary input into theological formulations. The other would be my former colleague at Tokyo Christian University, Hisakazu Inagaki. I was privileged to co-author a book with Inagaki Sensei, consisting of my English translations of some of his Japanese material and some of my writings on Japanese theology associated with my doctoral research (Inagaki and Jennings 2000). A Christian philosopher and Reformed Church in Japan elder, Inagaki has a hybrid, Japanese-Dooyeweerdian outlook on the world and its component parts that has helped to give me an intellectual system for appreciating both the complexity and the interconnectedness of what happens throughout this sin-racked creation.

Knowing all of that should help you unravel a bit my appreciation of Conn in relation to my own understanding of Christian contextualization as the continual "particularization" of the universal[10] Christian faith within particular, multi-faceted settings. Crucial to my own use of this Wallsian universal-particular scheme for understanding contextualization (both as particular manifestations of the Christian faith, as well as the ongoing processes of adjustment to particular situations) are at least three, interrelated qualifying elements: first, the dynamic relationship between a personal covenant Lord and his responsible subjects; second, the transcendent character of this covenant Lord coupled with his immanent involvement

---

[10] Shaw and Van Engen use the intriguing term "panhuman" to point to what I call, following Walls, "universal" (Shaw and Van Engen 2003, 201).

with his world; and third, the normative and fully authoritative character of the Lord's word that, at the same time, speaks flexibly within each situation into which the Holy Spirit guides his word's translation into that language and context.

Given that operative understanding of contextualization, syncretism then becomes the loss of universal, transcendent and normative traits of the Christian faith, due to a culture's "pull" towards autonomy. Outside (etic) input becomes marginalized or even eliminated. Sins of omission, e.g., not loving one's enemies, result from this failure to pay attention to God's transcendent and normative commands; sins of commission, e.g., sexual perversions, flourish due to the lack of restraint that should be brought to bear on people's lives by God's

> **What is needed, therefore, is a framework of understanding contextualization as the universal covenant Lord speaking into and within particular, multifaceted situations with universally unified intent and purpose...**

transcendent and normative commands. There is a protection of the status quo against all critique, no matter what normative standards of justice and mercy might attempt to speak into the situation. Finally, what is genuinely local and flexible is reified into something allegedly universal and normative—which becomes problematic when other local situations are encountered.

Syncretism in this sense becomes more particular, more multifaceted, and more ongoing in its occurrences than in the instinctive "mixing of religions" sense. Because contextualization always involves a type of particular and multifaceted "mixing" of the universal-normative and the local-flexible, it would be problematic to understand syncretism only within that type of one-time religious "mixing" or "interpenetration" category—especially insofar as the Christian faith thus syncretized would be understood to enter a new situation containing a fixed and unchanging "essential core," usually understood in a conceptual, theological sense. We can recall here as well the second type of syncretism mentioned earlier, wherein "contested" religious interpenetration becomes the distinctive trait. The problem there is the lack of normativity, for the emphasis lies primarily on power in human relationships. With the third type, that of a synthesis-syncretism couplet, to be sure there is a merely semantic dimension to the discussion, i.e., what one person calls synthesis is another person's syncretism, and vice versa. Once again, however, the normative place of Scripture seems to become lost. What is needed, therefore, is a framework of understanding contextualization as the universal covenant Lord speaking into and within particular, multifaceted situations with universally unified intent and purpose, albeit using diverse languages and particular emphases and timing; syncretism in turn consists of particular perversions of these necessary processes and their outcomes.[11]

Conn's Labeling Suburban Evangelical Individualism as Syncretistic

Conn's categorization of suburban evangelical individualism as syncretistic is thus "for the most part" accurate, as I claimed above. For Conn, the anti-urban myth of suburban evangelicalism is not what the Bible teaches, nor is it in line with actual conditions in cities. One can thus see syncretistic traits of not receiving normative or etic input. Omitting duties of justice and mercy occurs; instead of those biblical values, don't many evangelicals have the same "American dream" values as anyone else: a good house (read increasing property value), a good job, and a good education? Reifying suburban lifestyles and values occurs insofar as evangelicals export their brand of the Christian faith to "less fortunate" city folks and majority-world peoples. Moreover, the individualistic Christianity Conn critiques also

---

[11] While they make a distinction between their four-horizon hermeneutic and contextualization per se (cf. Shaw and Van Engen 2003, 212), Shaw and Van Engen's approach is essentially the same as the sense of contextualization I am advocating here. Shaw and Van Engen's four horizons are the Old Testament, the New Testament, the communicator, and the receiving context. The first two have a unique normative status, while there is interplay between all four. The notion of contextualization I am advocating does not require the prominent place of "the communicator," who is an etic catalyst in the contextualizing – hermeneutical process. While I do advocate the continual need for etic input into any context, the prominent role outside communicators play in the initial stage of contextualization into a context will not continue, except in particular and exceptional instances throughout ongoing contextualization.

skews biblical teaching on community and on the importance of public truth, justice and mercy.

While I am thus in essential agreement with Conn, I would like to add a few qualifiers. For one, there are stirrings within much of U.S. evangelicalism towards directing energies "back to the city." Second, "urban" does not just mean "inner city"; entire metropolitan areas are urban areas, and the inner-city vs. suburb distinction may or may not be helpful or accurate. Third, what does proper contextualization of the Christian faith among suburbanites look like? Given the adaptability and infinite translatability of the Christian faith, so-called suburbs are also contexts within which the Christian faith will of course take on particular, local characteristics.

I also claimed earlier that Conn's view of suburban evangelical individualism is "a wee bit" idiosyncratic. By no means do I think that evangelicals should ignore Conn; on the contrary, we need to hear him thoroughly and carefully. At the same time, like anyone else Conn was in his own limited context (or set of contexts) and spoke from within it—as varied and interesting as his own life and context(s) were. Conn's active interaction with up-to-date trends of course influenced his ongoing emphases—as did his ministries in New Jersey, Korea, Philadelphia and elsewhere. While he had an amazingly wide field of vision and experience, Conn was still limited and thus local and particular in his approach to various matters, including contextualization and syncretism.

So-called suburban evangelical individualism is therefore not altogether different from other instances of syncretism—although qualification is needed. We have already seen good reasons for understanding some of its traits as syncretistic. At the same time, while religious allegiances may lie at the root of all cultural settings, there are other types of roots as well—for example social and economic—given the multi-dimensional nature of reality. Contextualization involves the Christian faith coming to terms with all spheres of a context. Hence some of the traits of suburban evangelical individualism carry a certain contextual appropriateness, one could argue. For example, Christian counseling programs dealing with individual, private hurts are entirely right. The particularities of how the Christian faith is fleshed out in each setting need to be taken seriously.

Conclusion

There is one Lord, one faith, and one baptism for the worldwide Christian Church. At the same time, the Church lives and serves in a multiplicity of contexts, into which the Christian faith must be pointedly translated. Even though there are trustworthy signposts, the path down which such ongoing contextualization processes should go is not a straightforward, given matter. Nor is there any guarantee that syncretism, or contextualization gone awry, will not occur. The dynamic relationship between the covenant Lord and his people necessarily is fleshed out in particular settings, including so-called U.S. suburban settings. God's faithfulness and commitment to redeem his world—to carry out his world mission—is our bedrock of confidence in the midst of often confusing, but necessary and given, contextualized Christian living.

Sources Cited

Arnold, Clinton E. 1996. *The Colossian Syncretism: The Interface between Christianity and Folk Belief at Colossae.* Grand Rapids: Baker.

Bavinck, J. H. 1966. *The Church Between Temple and Mosque: A Study of the Relationship Between the Christian Faith and Other Religions.* Grand Rapids: Eerdmans.

Conn, Harvie M. 1978. "Contextualization: A New Dimension for Cross-Cultural Hermeneutic." *Evangelical Missions Quarterly* (January): 39-46.

_____. 1984. *Eternal Word and Changing Worlds: Theology, Anthropology, and Mission in Trialogue.* Grand Rapids: Academie Books.

_____. 1987. *A Clarified Vision for Urban Mission: Dispelling the Urban Stereotypes.* Grand Rapids: Ministry Resources Library.

_____. 1994. *The American City and the Evangelical Church: A Historical Overview.* Grand Rapids: Baker.

_____. 1994. "Case-study 4: Korea." In *Eerdmans' Handbook to the World's Religions,* ed. Pat Alexander, rev. ed. Grand Rapids: Eerdmans.

_____ and Manuel Ortix. *Urban Ministry: The Kingdom, the City & the People of God.* Downers Grove, IL: InterVarsity Press.

"Dr. Harvie Conn Home with the Lord (1933-1999)" http://www.missiology.org/EMS/bulletins/conn.htm (March 12-15, 2004).

Droogers, André. 1989. "Syncretism: The Problem of Definition, the Definition of the Problem." In *Dialogue and Syncretism: An Interdisciplinary Approach*, eds., Jerald D. Gort, et al., Currents of Encounter Series. Grand Rapids: Eerdmans.

Hesselgrave, David J. and Edward Rommen. 1989. *Contextualization: Meanings, Methods, and Models*. Grand Rapids: Baker.

Hiebert, Paul. G., R. Daniel Shaw, Tite Tiénou. 1999. *Understanding Folk Religion: A Christian Response to Popular Beliefs and Practices*. Grand Rapids: Baker.

Inagaki, Hisakazu and J. Nelson Jennings. 2000. *Philosophical Theology in East-West Dialogue*. Encounter Series. Amsterdam: Rodopi Bv Editions.

Kraft, Charles H. 1989. "Contextualizing Communication." In *The Word Among Us: Contextualizing Theology for Mission Today*, ed. Dean S. Gilliland. Dallas, TX: Word.

Schreiter, Robert J. 1998. *The New Catholicity: Theology between the Global and the Local*. Faith and Culture Series, ed. Robert J. Schreiter, 62-83. Maryknoll, NY: Orbis Books.

Shaw, R. Daniel and Charles E. Van Engen. 2003. *Communicating God's Word in a Complex World: God's Truth or Hocus Pocus?* Lanham, MD: Rowman & Littlefield Publishers, Inc.

Van Rheenen, Gailyn. 2004. "Worldview and Syncretism" http://www.missiology.org/mongolianlectures/worldvie wandsyncretism.htm (March 16).

Wan, Enoch. 1996. "A Critique of Charles Kraft's Use/Misuse of Communication and Social Sciences in Biblical Interpretation and Missiological Formulation." In *Missiology and the Social Sciences: Contributions, Cautions, and Conclusions,* eds. Rommen, Edward, and Gary Corwin, EMS Series Number 4, 121-164. Pasadena: William Carey Library.

9

Post-Constantinian Missions: Lessons from the Resurgence of Paganism

Michael T. Cooper

Introduction

Nearly three decades ago W. A. Visser't Hooft suggested that Europe consisted of "statistical Christians who for one reason or another continue to be counted as church members though, in fact, their lives are controlled by non-Christian convictions" (Visser't Hooft 1977, 350). He observed that among these statistical Christians of Europe "neo-Pagans" were found (Visser't Hooft 1977, 350). A few years later William Edgar, in response to secularization, observed, "We are beginning to realize that Christianity is not being replaced by materialism, but by a sort of neo-[P]aganism" (Edgar 1983, 307).

A decade after Visser't Hooft, Lesslie Newbigin posed the question, "Can the West be converted?" (Newbigin 1987). After returning from nearly four decades of missionary service, he began to identify the Paganism[1] he encountered in England as more resistant to the gospel than the Hinduism he encountered in India.[2] While Newbigin suggested that Paganism, indifferent of its expression, is "born out of a rejection of Christianity, (1987, 7; cf. Willimon 1999, 3-10)"[3] Marc Spindler added that, "For a significant number of people, European neo-[P]aganism is an ideology of resistance against global systems, drawing upon mythical elements in the pre-Christian tradition of European cultures" (Spindler 1987, 10).

Consistent with Newbigin and Spindler's observations, Paul Heelas identifies a shift in contemporary Western society to witchcraft, earth goddesses and shamanism. He states, "I think that it is fair to say that [P]aganism has become the key resource for those (increasing numbers) who have counter-cultural concerns"(Heelas 1996, 88). Similarly, Peter Jones has identified a new religious left from which results a Western spiritual monism. He states, "The real enemy of the Church's

---

[1]The use of Paganism and neo-Paganism will be defined in chapter three. For now, Paganism and neo-Paganism should be understood as sharing similar religious beliefs derived from pre-Christian European religions.

[2]See Newbigin's *A Word in Season* (1994), in particular, chapters 7, 9 and 13.

[3]Newbigin understood Paganism, as encountered in Western culture, as a companionship between Enlightenment ideals and Eastern monistic culture (see Hunsberger 1998, 148-151). Even though he did not relate Paganism to the pre-Christian European traditional religion of Druidry *per se* there is a clear correlation between it and Hinduism (see Ellis 1994, 48-49). It seems that Newbigin's background in India made him aware of the resurgence of an unidentified religious tradition in response to secularization (see Newbigin 1989, 213, where he agrees with Rodney Stark's assessment for the revival of "otherworldly religious organizations"). I conclude, then, that Newbigin understood Paganism as a religious expression far more resistant to Christianity than its pre-Christian form, although he does not define it, rather than a nomenclature for a secular culture.

faith is no longer antireligious atheistic humanism but a revived [P]agan religion" (Jones 2001, 31).[4]

The question of how we arrived in a religious climate with "otherworldly" expressions of belief can be answered by a critical look at what some have called the Golden Age of Faith. This paper discusses Christianity after Constantine and the remnant Pagan belief that became a part of the church and has led to the revival of pre-Christian European Native Religions. The study concludes with a discussion of a missiological lesson to aid in the avoidance of syncretism when Christianity is brought to a new culture.

Christianization Versus Evangelization of Western Europe

After the "conversion" of Constantine the Christian church enjoyed a position of privilege unprecedented in its brief history. The religious edicts of toleration (AD 314 and AD 324) provided a milieu of religious pluralism; however, it was not long before the church began to suppress the religious beliefs of Pagans. Constantine's actions of legalizing the church bolstered the authority of the clergy. The clergy would now be exempted from certain taxes and civic duties in order to concentrate fully on the responsibilities of their office. Bishops sat as judges in civil suits and were given authority equal to law (Walker 1985, 184). Almost as a foreshadowing of Enlightenment rationalism, Constantine's heirs issued a law against superstitions and sacrifice (AD 341) (Bonner 1984, 346). Wilbert Shenk described the situation in terms of an emerging religio-political context that equated citizenship in the empire with membership in the church (Shenk 1994, 8). Rodney Stark points out that Constantine's conversion eliminated Christianity's dependence on volunteerism. It became an elite organization with state support (Stark 2001, 107).

Constantine and Christian emperors following him embarked upon a massive and spectacular building campaign to honor God just as Pagan emperors had

---

[4]In a personal correspondence with me, Jones related that he believes there are only two religions in the world, one that worships the creator and the other that worships creation. Paganism, then, is understood as a religion that worships creation.

dedicated buildings to Pagan gods. These basilicas were immense and costly. The church of St. John Lateran in Rome is but one example of the great expense of building a church according to imperial standards,

> Around 500 pounds weight of it [gold] were needed at a cost of some 36,000 solidi. This sum, which might be translated into approximately £60 million today, could have fed about 12,000 poor for a year (according to calculations from Dominic Janes' God and Gold in Late Antiquity). Another 22,200 solidi worth of silver (3,700 lbs.) was required for light fittings and another 400 pounds of gold for fifty gold vessels. (Freeman 2001, 19)

These basilicas looked more like the great audience halls of emperors and Pagan temples than the house churches of the previous centuries. Horrified by the change in Christianity, St. Jerome would write, "Parchments are dyed purple, gold is melted into lettering, manuscripts are dressed up in jewels, while Christ lies at the door naked and dying" (Jerome, *Ep.* 22, 32, in Freeman 2001, 13). By the end of the fifth century the church would accept its newfound wealth.

Priestly vestments came in line with the ornate churches and those of the deposed Pagan priests. Under Constantine, the office of bishop ultimately became the most powerful office in a city. Their influence was felt not only in religious matters, but also in social and political matters. The very fact that they were reprimanded for accepting gifts for penance, or from those desiring to be ordained for personal profit, demonstrated their power over a congregation and in a city (Percival 1956, 268). The clergy's newly attained authority negatively influenced their commitment to a disciplined Christian life (Stark 2001, 107). This was far from the Christianity in Tertullian's day: "There is no buying and selling of any sort in the things of God. Though we have our treasure chest, it is not made up of purchase-money, as of a religion that has its price" (Tertullian, *Apology* 39).

In spite of the state and church's efforts, from time to time Paganism enjoyed moments of revivals that sought to reinstate the priesthood and restore Pagan shrines.[5] It was not

---

[5] Consider the Pagan emperors Julian ca. 361 and Eugenius ca. 391.

until the Visigoth Alaric's sack of Rome (AD 410) that organized Paganism in the Roman Empire ceased. However, the writings and decrees of history from Augustine to the antiquarians of the 19th century testify to what has been called "pagan survivals" among common people (Jones and Pennick 1995, 72-73).

The privileged position that Christianity enjoyed after Constantine's conversion summarily oppressed other religions. Less than a hundred years after his conversion, Augustine sought theological justification for the use of diverse means to convert heretics.[6] Perhaps motivated by the Edict of Unity, which he viewed as an act of providence (Augustine, Ep. 185, vii, 26), his understanding of Luke 14:23[7] led him to coerce the conversion of heretics and unbelievers. He saw the justification of this type of conversion in Paul's experience with Christ on the road to Damascus.

> You also read how he who was at first Saul, and afterwards Paul, was compelled, by the great violence with which Christ coerced him, to know and to embrace the truth; for you cannot but think that the light which your eyes enjoy is more precious to men than money or any other possession. This light, lost suddenly by him when he was cast to the ground by the heavenly voice, he did not recover until he became a member of the Holy Church. *(Augustine, Ep. 93.5)*

According to Henry Kamen, "he [Augustine] established a precedent which fortified the practice of repression by the mediaeval [sic] Church" (Kamen 1967, 14).[8] Augustine regarded the punishment of Pagan practices as acceptable, "For which of us, yea, which of you, does not speak well of the laws issued by the emperors against heathen

---

[6] According to Hans von Campenhausen, it was a "theological justification of force" (1998, 239).

[7] "And the master said to the slave, 'Go out into the highways and along the hedges, and compel them to come in, so that my house may be filled.'"

[8] It is important to note that it is from Augustine that we derive *bellum justum* as well as *bellum Deo auctore*.

sacrifices? In these, assuredly, a penalty much more severe has been appointed, for the punishment of that impiety is death" (*Ep.* 93,10). He believed that the church had a responsibility to weed out the tares from the wheat.

> There is an unjust persecution which the ungodly operate against the Church of Christ; and a just persecution which the Churches of Christ make use of towards the ungodly . . . .
> The Church persecutes out of love, the ungodly out of cruelty. *(Augustine in Kamen 1967, 14)*

It was Augustine's justification that set the agenda for the advancement of Roman Christianity on the continent of Europe. According to Prudence Jones and Nigel Pennick, adherents of Pagan religions suffered the death penalty if they did not submit to baptism or if they continued their religious practices (Jones and Pennick 1995, 127). David Bosch notes that a Christian emperor could not reign over a Pagan people. Baptism was forced upon them in order for the emperor to justly rule. There was no distinction between political and religious loyalty (Bosch 1991, 224).

Thomas Aquinas believed that Augustine's justification of the use of force against those who opposed the Catholic Church was legitimate. Quoting from Augustine's *A Treatise Concerning the Correction of the Donatists* as the theological basis for the church's agenda to convert heretics, Aquinas affirms the Augustinian position,

> None of us wishes any heretic to perish. But the house of David did not deserve to have peace, unless his son Absalom had been killed in the war which he had raised against his father. Thus if the Catholic Church gathers together some to the perdition of others, she heals the sorrow of her maternal heart by the delivery of so many nations.
> *(Augustine, Ep. 185)* [9]

---

[9]Quoted in Thomas Aquinas, *Summa Theologica*, Part II-II, Q 10, A 8, Rep 4. It is important to note that the Donatists were theologically orthodox. It was their unwillingness to accept the consecration of bishops ordained by those who had fallen in sin that caused Augustine's reaction.

Conversion in Europe was often politically motivated: whether fear of death or hope for victory at war and prosperity. It was also from the top down. After a king's conversion the people would follow (Newbigin 1994, 175-76). Emma Restall Orr, joint chief of the British Druid Order, might be correct when she asserts, "The conversion of kings took place as an acknowledgement of a more powerful god of battle, not a move to a god of love" (1998, 39). The result of this method of enticing Pagans to become Christian caused Pagan folk practices to go underground.

Christianization of Pagan Practices[10]

While Christianity became the dominant belief system in the Middle Ages, it was not without having been profoundly influenced by its Pagan antagonists (Bonner 1984, 341). The Christianization of Pagan practices provided elements of continuity in the new religious lives of converts (Bonner 1984, 350). Rituals and festivals were Christianized and infused with new meaning while saints and martyrs replaced local deities; all officially sanctioned by the church only to be occasionally liberated by the Pagan masses as expressions of identity (Jones 1998, 85; Hillgarth 1987, 325-27). Christianity was not successful in eradicating the Pagan influences of the past. The discontinuity between Christianity and Paganism no longer existed as it once had. Peter Brown notes that even in the church at Hippo Augustine "felt that the quality of his own congregation had already been seriously diluted by the semi-pagans who had joined the church *en masse*, when Christianity became the established religion" (Brown 1967, 234). The Roman Church in general did not discourage mixed marriages between Pagans and Christians since they seemed to work out in its favor (Rees 1988, 18). Pagan practices had crept back into the church and many were Christian by name only.

In spite of efforts by the church to disassociate with Pagan celebrations the practices remained. Ultimately the

---

[10] Richard Fletcher, *The Barbarian Conversion: From Paganism to Christianity* (Berkeley, Cal.: University of California Press, 1999), 16.

church would concede to the practices and instill or infuse them with Christian meaning. According to Jones and Pennick, under the papal direction Gregory I, missionaries christianized Pagan religious expressions as well as holy places (1995, 75).[11] Pope Gregory, writing instructions to Mellitus, abbot to the Gauls, as he is sent to join Augustine of Canterbury in England states,

> For there is no doubt that it is impossible to efface every thing at once from their obdurate minds; because he who endeavours to ascend to the highest place, rises by degrees or steps, and not by leaps. Thus the Lord made Himself known to the people of Israel in Egypt; and yet He allowed them the use of the sacrifices which they were wont to offer to the Devil, in his own worship; so as to command them in his sacrifice to kill beasts, to the end that, changing their hearts, they might lay aside one part of the sacrifice, whilst they retained another; that whilst they offered the same beasts which they were wont to offer, they should offer them to God, and not to idols; and thus they would no longer be the same sacrifices. (Bede, Book 1, XXX)

J. M. Wallace-Hadrill comments that this letter indicates a change of papal missionary strategy in England. Gregory had become painfully aware of the ineffectiveness of the mission and accommodated as much as possible (Wallace-Hadrill 1988, 44).

Nearly three hundred years after Augustine of Hippo's *City of God*, which was written in part as a response to the desire to return to Pagan gods, the missionary bishop Boniface, also known as the apostle of Germany, expressed his concern

---

[11] In Pope Gregory's letter to Mellitus he states, "that the temples of the idols in that nation ought not to be destroyed; but let the idols that are in them be destroyed; let holy water be made and sprinkled in the said temples, let altars be erected and relics placed. For if those temples are well built, it is requisite that they be converted from the worship of devils to the service of the true God; that the nation, seeing that their temples are not destroyed, may remove error from their hearts, and knowing and adoring the true God, may the more familiarly resort to the places to which they have been accustomed" (Bede, Book 1, XXX).

regarding the continuation of Pagan practices in Rome to Pope Zacharias (ca. 742),

> Some of the ignorant common people, Alemanians, Bavarians, and Franks, hearing that many of the offenses prohibited by us are practiced in the city of Rome imagine that they are allowed by the priests there and reproach us for causing them to incur blame in their own lives.
> (Boniface, Ep. 40)

A few years afterwards, Pope Zacharias writes to Boniface in response to questions regarding re-baptism. Pope Zacharias alludes to Boniface's concern for those who had been baptized by heretics, "As to those sacrilegious priests who, you say, sacrificed bulls and goats to heathen gods, eating the offerings to the dead, defiling their own ministry ...." (Zacharias, Ep, 64). It seems apparent that the church struggled, not only in Rome, but also all over the continent, with the continuation of Pagan practices after the efforts of the early missionaries. There are at least three areas where "pagan survivals" are explicit in contemporary Christianity: 1) Christianization of pagan holidays, 2), Christianization of pagan gods as saints and 3) the subsequent legitimization of animistic practices.

Christianization of Pagan Holidays

To contemporary practitioners of pre-Christian native religion, three prominent Christian holidays are, in effect, Christianized Pagan festivals: Christmas, Easter and Halloween. Ronald Hutton, professor of history at the University of Bristol, a second generation Pagan and member of the Order of Bards, Ovates and Druids, points out that Christianity had no sacred calendar so it was developed based upon the old religions (Hutton 1993, 285). These Christian celebrations have provided a continuous reminder of the past.   For example, the traditional date of 25 December for occidental Christmas coincides with the mid-winter festival of pre-Christian Pagan Europe.   Between 17-24 December Roman Saturnalia was celebrated in honor of Saturn, a Roman god of fertility. In AD 272 emperor Aurelian declared 25 December the day or birthday of the unconquered sun.

When exactly the early church began celebrating the birth of Christ is unknown. Some like Colin Chapman suggest Pagans used 25 December in response to the Christian celebration. Others like Jones and Pennick view the date as usurped from Pagans by Christians as a recognition of the "historical conflation of Christ, Mithras and Sol" (Jones and Pennick 1995, 76). The point being made here is that there was a certain degree of borrowing going on at this time. Whether or not Christ was actually born on this date, while important, does not detract from the issue.

The mid-winter festival was celebrated in different ways all over Europe. Britain, Germany and the Scandinavian countries celebrated the Yule feast recognizing the lengthening of the day and hoping for the beginning of a fertile year (Chapman 1990, 31). While the Pagan names of these festivals died out, the celebrations surrounding them remained in tact (Jones and Pennick 1995, 76).[12]

The very English name of the western celebration of Christ's resurrection suggests its relationship to the Anglo-Saxon goddess of spring, Eastre. While what the English speaking West calls Easter has been celebrated from early on in Christian tradition the parallels in the symbolic meaning of the resurrection and new life are strikingly similar to Pagan understanding of renewal. The Easter fires, long celebrated as a Pagan festival according to Sir James Frazer (1922),[13] became incorporated in the church from an early date. In spite of synod attempts to ban the practice, Pope Zacharias affirms the catholicity of the practice when writing to Boniface in 751 (*Ep.* 71).

---

[12]Examples being "decking houses with evergreen, giving presents and feasting" and "Easter eggs, taken from Baltic Paganism and the Easter rabbit or hare, which recalls the sacred hares of the British tribes."

[13] Accessed at www.bartleby.com/196/, July 21, 2003. "The essentially pagan character of the Easter fire festival appears plainly both from the mode in which it is celebrated by the peasants and from the superstitious beliefs which they associate with it" (62.3.2). While many suggest that Frazer had presuppositions in his assertion regarding religious belief, we do know that Patrick lit fires on Easter eve and caused a scandal with the Druids since they also lit fires for their Beltane rituals.

Halloween provides the most deliberate attempt to Christianize a Pagan festival. Originally, All Saints Day in the Christian calendar was celebrated on 13 May. In 834 the date was moved to 1 November making 31 October All Hallows' Eve. These dates coincided with the calendar of Roman and Celtic people marking either the beginning of the new year or the end of the harvest season. It was a time to honor the dead as well as the spirit forces and to seek assurances for survival during the winter. The Christianization of this festival contributed to praying for the dead and honoring the saints rather than the various deities (Chapman 1990, 29).

Christianization of Pagan Gods as Saints

The third ecumenical council held at Ephesus in 431 convened to condemn Nestorius and Celestius's teaching. The Nicene-Constantinople Creed was fixed as orthodoxy (Murphy 1960, 53). While Nestorianism was defeated a new issue arose in Ephesus. Mary, the mother of Jesus, was given a place of honor. She was affirmed as the Mother of God (θεοκοτοφ) and the geographical and religious context added emphasis for the council's proclamation: Ephesus, the great city of the goddess Diana (Murphy 1960, 50). Hutton sees a direct correlation between Mary and Diana as well as goddesses of fertility with the various Black Madonnas of Italy (1993, 284).

It is here that Christianity apparently begins to adopt and adapt Pagan gods and goddesses for Christian practice. Jones and Pennick note, "The procession celebrating the beatification of Mary used smoking censers and flaring torches, as were once used in the procession of Diana" (1995, 75). Adrian Ivakhiv suggests that the veneration of Mary in the Middle Ages was simply a re-emergence of goddess worship (1996, 238). Chapman states,

> In pre-Christian days localities or cities often had their own local deity who was believed to protect and guard his or her own people. Sometimes the supposed dwelling of such a god or spirit was a natural feature, such as a well. With the coming of Christianity, however, the instinctive desire for a local protector was sometimes transferred to a local Christian of prominence – perhaps the person who first preached the Gospel in the area. And not infrequently

elements of the old pagan belief became mixed up in the tales of this local figure. (1990, 60)

Hutton posits that the western church fathers left the question of celestial deities open. Citing Augustine, Hutton suggests that his lack of explanation of the planets in effect allowed for the possibility of their recognition as deities. However, Augustine clearly had an aversion to astrology. In the *City of God* he notes, "But that all things come to pass by fate, we do not say; nay we affirm that nothing comes to pass by fate; for we demonstrate that the name of fate, as it is wont to be used by those who speak of fate, meaning thereby the position of the stars at the time of each one's conception or birth, is an unmeaning word, for astrology itself is a delusion."[14] Hutton suggests that by 1320 western intellectuals considered the planets as deities controlled by God. There was the belief that Christians could legitimately use the planets to gain understanding for their future (Hutton 2003).[15]

---

[14] Augustine, *City of God* (Book V, Chapter 2). Augustine is consistent with others e.g. Hippolytus who states, "But since, estimating the astrological art as a powerful one, and availing themselves of the testimonies adduced by its patrons, they wish to gain reliance for their own attempted conclusions, we shall at present, as it has seemed expedient, prove the astrological art to be untenable, as our intention next is to invalidate also the Peratic system, as a branch growing out of an unstable root." (*The Refutation of All Heresies*, Book IV, 2). St. Basil comments on practitioners of astrology, "You who are sound in yourselves have no need to hear more, and time does not allow us to make attacks without limit against these unhappy men" (*Homily* VI, 7).

[15] Notably, as phrased, this is an argument from silence, but it demonstrates an attempt to legitimize the practice of astrology. While it seems likely that nominal Christians continued the practices, it was clearly thought of as absurd by the Church Fathers and Apologists.

While Hutton might exaggerate the level of acceptance of astrology on the part of the church, it is without doubt that the lay people continued in their beliefs. These beliefs in the efficacy of astrology have continued in western society. Consider for example, the data from International Social Survey Programme (ISSP) Environment I. See *Table 1: Belief in Astrology as Scientific Truth (Source: International Social Survey Programme, Environment I, 1993.)*[16]

Astrology was also used as it was passed on to the Christian *literati* by the Druids. The Irish missionary monk Columba, who established his first monastery at Derry, launched his missionary journey and established some 300 churches in

% Believe Astrology – the study of star signs – has some scientific truth		
Nation	**Definitely**	**Probably**
Germany (West)	16	41
Germany (East)	15	41
Great Britain	7	39
United States	10	43
Netherlands	7	42
Italy	7	28
Ireland	13	41
Norway	12	44
Austria	--	--
New Zealand	8	40
Australia	4	32
Canada	9	36
Sweden	--	--
Spain	6	41
France	--	--
Portugal	--	--
Denmark	--	--
Switzerland	--	--

[16]Data from variable 31 Environment I, International Social Survey Programme, (Cologne, Germany: Zentralarchiv Fuer Empirische Sozialforschung, 2000). Sample size for Environment I distributed as follows: Germany (West) – 1014; Germany (East) 1092; Great Britain – 1261; United States – 1557; the Netherlands – 1852; Italy – 1000; Ireland – 957; Norway – 1414; New Zealand – 1271; Australia – 1779.

Ireland. After being exiled from Ireland in 563, Columba, with twelve disciples, established a second monastery off the coast of Scotland on the island Iona that was responsible for evangelizing the Picts and Scots. Iona evolved into a great missionary monastery evangelizing most of England and Scotland and sending *peregrinatio pro christo* (wanderers for Christ) to the continent. It was he who once claimed, "Christ is my Druid," and consulted the stars to determine the appropriate time for his foster son to begin his education (Ellis 1994, 243).

The adoption of the Celtic goddess Brigit into Christianity is suggested to be one of the most overtly Christian usurpations of a Pagan goddess. Saint Brigit was born in 452 and is known for founding the double monastery at Kildare. Her feast day on 1 February coincides with the pastoral festival of *imbolc*. Imbolc is a festival that celebrates fertility, creativity and healing. It has traditionally been associated with the goddess Brigit. Many Pagans see the life of the saint as assuming the life of the goddess and disregard the historicity of Brigit the Celtic abbess. Timothy Joyce sees the difficulty in separating the goddess and the saint (1998, 43) and Hutton seems to agree when he alludes to the notion that she was once considered divine (1993, 153).

Legitimization of Animistic Practices

Animistic practices in the use of icons appear to go back as far as the Iconoclastic controversy itself. Saint John of Damascus himself was not immune to this. He stated, "Devils have feared the saints and have fled from their shadow. The shadow is an image, and I make an image that I may scare demons . . . . Material things are endued with a divine power because they bear the names of those they represent" (Rushdoony 1968, 119). Here it appears that the icon is a source of power in order to be protected from evil. It is easy to see that one could believe that if he had more icons in his possession he could have more power against demons. Similarly, he believed that the icons were actually the power source. They in themselves possessed divine power and grace (Rushdoony 1968, 123).

Hutton suggests that Christian iconography was in essence used as a talisman. As a second generation Pagan and member of the Order of Bards, Ovates and Druids, he takes comfort in the fact that the early church did not feel any discomfort with classical Paganism. Christianity was successful due to its absorption of these ancient beliefs (Hutton 2003). The early iconophiles believed that the image possessed some type of quasi-magical power (Rushdoony 1968, 120).

According to Hutton, magic supplemented religion in folklorized Christianity. At one and the same time an individual could attend church in order to secure eternal reward and perform magic in order to secure earthly reward. Magic was separate from "the great contest between God and Satan" so the mundane issues of life could be handled by manipulating lesser forces and not bothering the Almighty God. "The fact that humans have sought the latter [magic] in addition [to religion] has been the result of modesty (not wishing to trouble deities), frustration (the deity has not responded), double insurance, pride and curiosity (the desire to work spiritual power directly) and consideration of convenience and expense" (Hutton 1993, 290). Stark comments,

> By thinly overlaying pagan festivals and sacred places with Christian interpretations, the missionaries made it easy to become a Christian – so easy that actual conversion seldom occurred. Instead, in customary pagan fashion, the people treated Christianity as an "add-on religion" and the popular Christianity that eventually emerged in northwestern Europe was a strange amalgam, including a great deal in the way of pagan celebrations and beliefs, some of them thinly Christianized, but many of them not Christianized at all. (Stark 2001, 114; cf. Davies 1996, 275-284; Jolly 1996; Milis 1998)

Implications for Contemporary Missions in Western Society

While a historically continuous link to organized pre-Christian expressions of native religions is not demonstrable, contemporary Paganism suggests that there has been a "pagan survival" in the church. Many Pagan practices were integrated into the church and were never completely extinguished. In one sense, it is incorrect to talk of a resurgence of Paganism. Philip Carr-Gomm, Chosen Chief of the Order of Bards, Ovates and Druids, suggests that Christianity, paradoxically, assisted in the survival of Druidry in its adoption of Pagan festivals and gods, use of sacred sites and documenting the folktales of Bards (2002, 31).

Since the turn of the twentieth century Paganism has increasingly gained a voice in the academy and popular culture. Consider for example the Nature Religions Scholars Network hosted on the University of Colorado-Pueblo web site. Their self description states:

> We are a group of scholars working in the area of nature-based religions -- in other words, those religious paths which do not depend upon written scripture or the words of one prophet or teacher but which take nature as their symbolic center. These religious traditions tend to be decentralized, to give primacy to individual experience, and to seek to overcome such dichotomies as 'nature-culture' and 'mind-body.' Examples include most "animistic" tribal religions, shamanism, and revived Western Paganism.[17]

The contemporary expression of Paganism recognizes the remnant of pre-Christian belief in Christianity. Andrew Greeley suggests that due to continued belief in the efficacy of astrology, fortunetellers and good luck charms we are not all that different from the medieval peasants (1993, 7). This is quite a contrast from what Keith Thomas wrote 20 years before Greeley, "Astrology, witchcraft, magical healing, divination, ancient prophecies, ghosts and fairies, are now rightly disdained by intelligent people" (1971, ix). Thomas adds, "What is certain about the various beliefs discussed in this book is that today they have either disappeared or at least greatly decayed in prestige" (1971, 668). However, the data suggests otherwise.

Greeley asserts that religion continues to play an important role in the lives of Europeans. At the same time, magic is increasing and growing in situations where religious faith is uncertain (Greely 2003, 39-53). While Greeley provisionally agreed that the belief in magic (as exemplified in the ISSP variables dealing with fortunetellers, astrology and good luck charms) measures New Age attitudes he concurs with the notion set forward in this paper. Namely, it is more

---

[17] Accessed 30 July 2003 from http://chass.colostate-pueblo.edu/natrel/.

likely that this continued fascination with what was once considered superstition is a result of the tenacity of pre-Christian popular religion.[18] According to Orr, astrology fits well within the practices of Druidry (Orr 1998, 74). Thus, the data on astrology fits just as well with Paganism as it would with New Age. Nevertheless, the point that is being made is that the data suggests congruency between the religious beliefs of Western society and contemporary Paganism.

Western society is witnessing a revival of pre-Christian native religions. With a deliberate attempt at historical continuity, Paganism, in its varied expressions, is growing at an annual growth rate that exceeds 28 percent (Cooper 2004). Some consider it to be the fastest growing religious expression in the West.

ESTIMATED NUMBER OF ADHERENTS OF PAGAN RELIGIONS			
	1961 (ESTIMATED)	**2001**[19]	**2011 (estimated)**
Druidry	**1.69**	33,000	392,650
OBOD[20]	**12**	9,000	41.56%
Wicca	**4.75**	134,000	1,736,720
Pagan	**5.1**	144,000	1,866,327
Total	**11.54**	311,000	3,995,697

[18]In a personal communication, Greeley agrees with this suggestion stating "I agree that your explanation is more likely." See Melton (1998, 133-149) and Spangler and Thompson (1991) for discussions on the decline of New Age. See my "Jesus and the Pagan West: . ."

[19]Data based on American Religious Identification Survey.

[20]Data represents a 19 year period from 1984 to 2003 and was obtained from the chosen chief of OBOD. The number 9,000 represents those who have enrolled in their training course.

Lessons from the Resurgence of Paganism

If syncretism is understood as per Scott Moreau, "Traditionally among Christians it has been used of the replacement or dilution of the essential truths of the gospel through the incorporation of non-Christian elements" (Moreau 2000, 924) then it would appear that what might have been attempts at relevant ministry methods in the medieval church were in fact syncretistic. The lesson to be learned for contemporary missiology addresses cultural practices that have religious expressions.

The study has demonstrated that the evangelistic methods of the medieval missionary endeavors often resulted in accommodating religious others rather than conversion. When "conversion" did occur it was often motivated by factors other than a desire to be in relationship with the Creator. What is learned from this study is the notion that conversion without personal conviction will often result in some form of "split-level" Christianity. When religious beliefs are simply suppressed and go underground the old beliefs emerge in a folklorized form of Christianity.

Eventually the folklorized form will desire a unique expression as it becomes disillusioned with Christianity, as we see in the resurgence of contemporary Paganism. The unique expression that emerges will have some sort of correlation to the religious beliefs prior to the arrival of Christianity. The fact of the revival of pre-Christian European religious expressions must challenge our understanding of the evangelization of Western Europe and make us aware of the impact of Christianizing indigenous religious practices in other cultures. The question remains, "How do we prevent such incidents from occurring?"

The answer to this question, I believe, is found in the ministry of St. Paul in Corinth. When asked about food sacrificed to idols (1 Cor 8:1-13) he made the distinction between those who know and those who are weak. The "knowers" must maintain a strict monotheism for the sake of those who do not have the same experiential or learned knowledge (1 Cor 8:7- γνω□σιφ) as them. Coye Still writes,

> *Thus, Paul has placed real limitations on the behavior of the knowers at two points. First, he counsels against all*

> *temple meal participation. Second, he curtails indiscriminate consumption at meals hosted by unbelievers. The practical aim of Paul's argument is to persuade the knowers to abstain completely from food identified as offered to idols. (Still 2002, 34)*

When religious expressions of a culture are adopted or even contextualized it has the potential of legitimizing the practices and eventually leading to syncretism. Paul's admonition to the Corinthian believers was one of abandoning the practices for the sake of the weak in Christ. Rather than accommodating as the medieval church did or infusing with new Christian meaning as many contemporary missionaries do, it appears that the only assurance of maintaining orthodoxy in Christian teaching and practice is abstinence from overtly non-Christian religious expressions. While the knower maintains the freedom to "eat," so to speak, due to liberty in Christ these practices should be abandoned for the sake of the immature in Christ.

To Paul, conversion meant a cognitive as well as a behavior change from former religious practices to new life in Christ. This does not mean that Paul is suggesting a break from religious others. Paul affirms his desire to relate to them in 1 Cor 9:19, "For though I am free from all, I have made myself a servant to all, that I might win more of them." His service to all, however, had boundaries to assure that the weak were not destroyed and that Christian orthodoxy was preserved.

Conclusion

Is there a principle in Paul's statement in 1 Corinthians 8 that might affect the way in which we observe cultural practices that have religious connotations? The fact of a remnant "pagan survival" in the church suggests an adoption, or at best adaptation, of religious practices while trying to infuse them with new meaning. However, the result was often syncretism rather than a "transforming ministry." Rather than resulting in a break with the former way of life, the weak who do not have the knowledge of the mature were likely to stumble and be wounded in conscience. This paper suggests that the resurgence of Paganism in contemporary Western society provides a 1500 year case study of missionary practice. The lesson to be learned is that adoption or adaptation of overt religious expressions of a host country will coalesce with Christianity and ultimately re-emerge in a new syncretized religious expression. Paul's strict emphasis on monotheism moves the missionary to abstinence for the sake of the new in Christ as well as the preservation of Christian orthodoxy.

Sources Cited

Bede. *The Ecclesiastical History of the English Nation*. Book 1, XXX.

Bonner, Gerald. 1984. "The Extinction of Paganism and the Church Historian." *Journal of Ecclesiastical History* 35, no. 3.

Bosch, David. 1991. *Transforming Mission: Paradigm Shifts in Theology of Mission*. Maryknoll, N.Y.: Orbis.

Brown, Peter. 1967. *Augustine of Hippo: A Biography*. Berkeley, CA: University of California Press.

Carr-Gomm, Philip. 2002. *Druid Mysteries: Ancient Wisdom for the 21st Century*. London: Rider.

Chapman, Colin. 1990. *Shadows of the Supernatural: A Guide to Popular Religion*. Oxford: Lion.

Cooper, Michael. 2004. "Prolegomena to a Christian Encounter with an European Native Religion: An Etic Perspective of Contemporary Druidry and Its Relationship to the Western Religious Landscape." Ph.D. dissertation, Trinity Evangelical Divinity School, Deerfield, IL.

Davies, Norman. 1996. *Europe: A History*. Oxford: Oxford University Press.

Edgar, William. 1983. "New Right -- Old Paganism: Anatomy of a French Movement." *Nederlands Theologisch Tijdschrift* 37, no. 4.

Ellis, Peter Berresford. 1994. *A Brief History of the Druids*. Grand Rapids: Eerdmans.

Fletcher, Richard. *The Barbarian Conversion: From Paganism to Christianity*. Berkeley, CA.: University of California Press.

Frazer, Sir James George. 1922. *The Golden Bough: A Study of Magic and Religion*. New York: Macmillan.

Freeman, Charles. 2001. "The Emperor's State of Grace." *History Today* 51, no. 1.

Greeley, Andrew. 1993. "Magic in the Age of Faith." *America* 169, no. 10.

_____. 2003. *Religion in Europe at the End of the Second Millennium: A Sociological Profile*. New Brunswick, NJ: Transaction.

Heelas, Paul. 1996. *The New Age Movement: The Celebration of Self and the Sacralization of Modernity*. Oxford: Blackwell.

Hillgarth, J. N. 1987. "Modes of Evangelization of Western Europe in the Seventh Century." In *Irland und die Christenheit: Bibelstudien und Mission*, ed. Proinseas Ni Chathain and Michael Richter. Stuttgart: Klett-Cotta.

Hunsberger, George R. 1998. *Bearing the Witness of the Spirit: Lesslie Newbigin's Theology of Cultural Plurality*. Grand Rapids: Eerdmans.

Hutton, Ronald. 1993. *The Pagan Religions of the Ancient British Isles: Their Nature and Legacy*. Oxford: Blackwell.

_____. 2003. "Astral Magic: The Acceptable Face of Paganism." Lecture given at the inaugural conference of the Sophia Centre, Bath Spa University College, "Astrology and the Academy." 13 June.

Ivakhiv, Adrian. 1996. "The Resurgence of Magical Religion as a Response to the Crisis of Modernity: A Postmodern Depth Psychological Perspective." In *Magical Religion and Modern Witchcraft*, ed. James R. Lewis, Albany, NY: State University of New York Press.

Jerome, *Ep.* Quoted in "The Emperor's State of Grace" by
Charles Freeman. *History Today* 51, no. 1 (2001). 22, 32.

Jolly, Karen Louise. 1996. *Popular Religion in Late Saxon
England*. Chapel Hill, NC: University of North Carolina
Press.

Jones, Peter. 2001. *Pagans in the Pews: How the New
Spirituality is Invading Your Home, Church and
Community*. Ventura, CA: Regal.

Jones, Prudence and Nigel Pennick. 1995. *A History of Pagan
Europe*. New York:Routledge.

Jones, Prudence. n.d. "The European Native Tradition." In
Nature Religion Today: Paganism in the Modern World,
eds. Joanne Pearson, Richard H. Roberts and Geoffrey
Samuel. Edinburgh: Edinburgh University.

Joyce, Timothy. 1998. *Celtic Christianity: A Sacred Tradition, a
Vision of Hope*. Maryknoll, NY: Orbis.

Kamen, Henry. 1967. *The Rise of Toleration*. London:
Weidenfeld and Nicolson.

Melton, J. Gordon. 1998. "The Future of the New Age
Movement," in Eileen Barker and Margit Warburg
(eds.), *New Religions and New Religiosity*. London:
Aarhus University Press.

Milis, Ludovicus (ed.). 1998. *The Pagan Middle Ages*.
Rochester, NY: Boydell Press.

Moreau, A. Scott. 2000. "Syncretism." In *Evangelical
Dictionary of World Missions*, ed. A. Scott Moreau,
Harold A. Netland and Charles Van Egen. Grand
Rapids: Baker.

Murphy, John L. 1960. *The General Councils of the Church*.
Milwaukee, WI: Bruce Publishing Co.

Newbigin, Lesslie. 1987. "Can the West be Converted?" *International Bulletin of Missionary Research* 11, no. 1.

_____. 1989. *The Gospel in a Pluralist Society.* Grand Rapids: Eerdmans.

_____. 1994. *A Word in Season: Perspectives on Christian World Missions.* Grand Rapids: Eerdmans.

Orr, Emma Restall. 1988. *Principles of Druidry.* London: Thorsons.

Percival, Henry (ed.). 1956. *The Seven Ecumenical Councils of the Undivided Church.* Grand Rapids: Eerdmans.

Rees, B.R. 1988. *Pelgius: A Reluctant Heretic.* Great Britain: The Boynell Press.

Rushdoony, Rousas J. 1968. *The Foundations of Social Order.* Presbyterian and Reformed Publishing Co.

Shenk, Wilbert R. 1994. "Encounters with 'Culture' Christianity." *International Bulletin of MissionaryResearch* (January).

Spangler, David and William Irwin Thompson. *Reimagination of the World: A Critic of the New Age, Science, and Popular Culture.* Santa Fe, NM: Bear & Co.

Spindler, Marc. 1987. "Europe's Neo-Paganism." *International Bulletin of Missionary Research* 11, no. 1.

Stark, Rodney. 2001. "Efforts to Christianize Europe, 400-2000." *Journal of Contemporary Religion* 16, no. 1.

Still, E. Coye III. 2002. "Paul's Aim Regarding ΕΙΔΩΛΟΘΥΤΑ: A New Proposal for Interpreting 1 Corinthians 8:1-11:1." *Novum Testamentum* 44, no. 4.

Thomas, Keith. 1971. *Religion and the Decline of Magic.* New York: Charles Scribner's Sons.

Visser't Hooft, W.A. 1977. "Evangelism among Europe's Neo-Pagans." *International Review of Mission* 66, no. 4.

von Campenhausen, Hans. 1998. *The Fathers of the Church.* Peabody, MA: Hendickson.

Walker, Williston et al. 1985. *The History of the Christian Church.* New York: Charles Scribner's Sons.

Wallace-Hadrill, J. M. 1988. *Bede's Ecclesiastical History of the English People: A Historical* Commentary. Oxford: Clarendon.

Willimon, William H. 1999. "Preaching as Missionary Encounter with North American Paganism: In Homage to Lesslie Newbigin, 1909-1998." *Journal of Preachers* 22, no. 3: 3-10.

10

Dwarves, Elves, and Vampires: An Exploration of Syncretism in Metro Manila

Cynthia A. Strong and David K. Strong

In January 1993, responding to a spate of electrical brownouts throughout the country, the director of the Philippine National Power Corporation blamed *dwende* (dwarves) for the failure of the Naga Thermal Power Plant in Cebu (*The Manila Times*, 15 January 1993). "There are gnomes living there," said Go. Several months later the director of the Manila highway department offered the blood of a chicken during an appeasement ritual aimed at easing public clamor over a new overpass. Residents feared to use the overpass following several anomalous deaths at the site, and they alleged that spirits had caused it.

These spirit beliefs illustrate the shared experience of many Filipinos. As common knowledge relevant to the context, they represent a cultural scene featuring fluid interactions between spirits, supernatural forces and human beings in the natural and supernatural worlds. By categorizing spirits and experiences, Filipinos have determined appropriate responses to a wide range of contextual phenomena that define attitudes and behaviors in day-to-day life.

Despite the prevalence of such beliefs, only rarely have they been presented in terms of shared knowledge or life experience. Rodney Henry (1986) and Fernando C. Gatan, Jr. (1983) take such beliefs seriously as indicative of spiritual realities based upon their biblical understandings of the supernatural.

More commonly, however, they are labeled as remnants of traditional folklore or as a superstitious epistemology of causality and explanation. Maximo D. Ramos, for instance, whose studies provided the initial academic investigation into Filipino spirit creatures, used Western categories to identify these spirits, interpreting them in the same genre as Western mythological beings (1990a, 1990b, 1990c). In the two-volume *Encyclopedia of Philippine Folk Beliefs and Customs*, Francisco Demetrio likewise concluded that the beliefs were mythic traditions of the Philippines, a collective symbolism, rather than shared cultural experience (1991, Introduction). Both these theoretical positions are predicated on Western anti-supernaturalist assumptions. Both use categorical understandings of reality derived from outside the context to interpret local phenomena.

The unfortunate result of this approach has been a pejorative treatment of Filipino spirit beliefs, resulting in their concealment from outsiders and church authorities under the guise of "split-level Christianity" and a "conspiracy of silence." Jaime C. Bulatao popularized the notion of split-level Christianity as:

> the coexistence within the same person of two or more thought-and-behavior systems which are inconsistent with each other. . . . At one level he professes allegiance to ideas, attitudes, and ways of behaving which are mainly borrowed from the Christian West; at another level he holds convictions which are more properly his "own" ways of living and believing which were handed down from his ancestors, which do not always find their way into an explicit philosophical system.... (1992, 22)

The "conspiracy of silence," on the other hand, refers in Henry's book to the epistemological and theological chasm that exists between clergy and laity in Filipino Roman Catholic and Protestant congregations as a result of differences in supernatural worldviews. The laity, fearing local spirits, keeps silent concerning their beliefs and resort to the mediation of herbal doctors and shamans, while the clergy ignore such beliefs and deal only with the ultimate need of eternal salvation. In this paper we attempt to demonstrate the power of an interdisciplinary approach for understanding syncretism. Taking Filipino spirit beliefs

Illustration of Split-Level Christianity

"A policeman in the downtown district of Manila goes fairly regularly to Mass and considers himself a Catholic. Nevertheless he collects 'tong' from the small stores in the district as protection money. He feels he has a right to it because he is their protector against gangsters.
(The Split: modern Catholic principles of justice vs. a feudal attitude that the lord may tax those whom he protects.)"

-- Bulatao 1992, 23-24

seriously, we endeavor to discover an emic, or insider's, perspective through an ethnographic exploration of the spirit domain. We then explore the historical process by which that domain syncretized with Christianity. Based upon anthropological and historical study, we propose specific steps to counter syncretism in the Philippines and conclude by suggesting that similar anthropological and historical studies constitute an essential methodology for avoiding syncretism and for understanding and combating it in the contexts where it now exists.

Dwarves, Elves, and Vampires

In 1993 Cindi involved five graduate students in a folk religion course at the Alliance Biblical Seminary in Manila in an investigation of Filipino spirit beliefs and practices. Since the research aimed at obtaining the insider's viewpoint with as little bias as possible, it was necessary that Filipinos conduct the interviews rather than Westerners. Not only are there taboos that prohibit Filipinos from discussing the spirits in certain locations, but also when interviewed by professionals and Westerners, the prevailing conspiracy of silence usually results in embarrassed smiles and an unwillingness to admit to such beliefs.

The students interviewed twenty-seven informants who lived and worked in Metro Manila, Quezon City, and Antipolo, Rizal. Although several informants had been born in Manila, most had migrated to the city from the outlying provinces in search of jobs and better opportunities, bringing with them a store of spirit knowledge and experience from the other islands and cultural groups. A majority was from the lower middle and upper lower class, as evidenced by their employment as janitors, carpenters and dressmakers. The lowest class was also represented in occupations such as car watcher, vendor, small time eatery, and househelper. Only one member of the professional class was represented, a clergyman. This related in some respect to the isolation of the class (concealed in cars, private homes, and offices) from conversations with people on the street and also to the cultural barriers that govern appropriate interaction between Filipino classes. Seven of the twenty-seven informants were students, along with an equal number of housewives, reflecting the greater availability and accessibility of these groups for informal on-the-street conversations. While the sample is admittedly small and fails to represent all classes, it nevertheless provides sufficient data to demonstrate the value of ethnography in understanding the emic categories and values that drive syncretism.

To guide the students in their search for cultural categories, question frames were used based upon James P. Spradley (1980, 85-99). Spradley incorporates the frames as a part of participant observation, but the questions themselves are useful in any lexical-semantic field analysis. The frames included:

1. *What kinds of spirits are there?*
2. *Where is the _____ found?*
3. *What does the _____ do?*
4. *What do people do because of the _____?*
5. *What can you do to prevent _____?*
6. *What is a _____ like?*
7. *Rank these spirits in order of danger/power.*

The frames provided organization for the interviews and a uniform sample of topics. The kinds of information elicited and the length of the interview varied based upon the informant's available time, interest and knowledge of the subject, and fear of supernatural consequences. After completing the interviews, the students transcribed, typed, and submitted their findings in the form of question frames and replies, along with comments and explanations. The conversations were then analyzed individually for key terms and folk definitions from which folk domains were constructed.

Learning about the Spirit World

Knowledge of the spirit world did not significantly relate to the age or gender of the informants, although the elderly were often said to have greater powers of discernment and their stories have great effect upon the young. Instead, the volume and kinds of information related to personal experience and to contact with others who knew.

Sources of information included family members (parents, grandparents, aunts, and maids), stories passed from person to person, and even popular media. Some, whose mothers were *spiritistas* (spirit workers), were able to give detailed and unusual information about particular spirits and their contexts. One *spiritista*, for example, would often see a spirit in the tree outside her home and warn the children to come inside. The importance of inter-generational communication was further indicated by the similar responses of a mother and her young child. The child knew, however, not only the spirits taught by her mother, but also those popularized in movies. Finally, stories about the experiences of others in the neighborhood were a source of information, illustrating not only the popularity of the topic but also the channels of *barrio* communication. Folk education thus proved to be an important source of information about the spirit world.

Personal experience, however, proved to be the most comprehensive source of spirit knowledge. Not only was the information provided by experienced informants much more specific than that given by other informants–especially with regard to spirit appearances and associated phenomena–but the interactions of spirits with each other and their relationships with humans were more detailed.

Recognizing and Responding to Anomalies

The study of cultural domains reveals the significant categories and concerns of the group. According to the informants, for instance, the ability to recognize and respond appropriately to supernatural phenomena was vital to community welfare. "Knowing what to do," "being confused," and "being ignorant" were relative states with regard to spiritual realities. The greater the confusion, the greater the likelihood of fear and danger in a situation. Those who knew the appropriate actions and had the ability to carry them out, in contrast, were considered courageous and admired by others in the group.

Thus knowing the locations of spirits, whether the spirits are good or evil, and whether or not to have relations with them was considered important to individual, family, and community well being. In some sense, ignorance of the spirit world correlated with shame, and informants who initially expressed disbelief in local spirits would inevitably respond with information once

> **This value on knowing about spirits is opposite to the Western secular position, which grants intellectual credibility to disbelief.**

rapport had been established to avoid the appearance of ignorance. This value on knowing about spirits is opposite to the Western secular position, which grants intellectual credibility to disbelief.

Of prime importance in "knowing what to do" was the ability to recognize and respond to anomalies in the context. Filipinos see spirits manifesting themselves in particular and unusual phenomena, measurable through their impact upon the natural world. Relatively harmless spirits, for instance, can be "felt," "appear and disappear," or "appear in dreams." A more disturbing and invasive spirit presence is manifested in the rustling leaves and bending branches stirred by a *kapre* (giant), or the sound of music near a forest tree inhabited by *engkantos* (elves). Unusual illnesses or diseases that cannot be healed by doctors and medicines represent more serious dangers. Swelling feet, for instance, indicate an offended *dwende*; insanity in a person who has disappeared for a time, the work of an *engkanto*. Exotic illnesses—an issue of blood or roaches exiting from the mouth—indicate the work of sorcerers, while death, at the farthest end of the spectrum, is the work of *aswang* (vampires) or witches and the *wak-wak* on which they ride. The ability to recognize these anomalies was considered basic to people participating in the cultural scene.

Locating Spirits

Along with the ability to recognize spiritual anomalies, Filipinos are expected to know where spirits reside. This enables them to know what areas to avoid or where to take special precautions. The potential of meeting some spirits on land were seemingly unlimited. The *dwende, aswang, multo* (ancestral ghost), *wak-wak*, demons, *mangbabarang* (human sorcerer), and *tikbalang* (monster with the body of a man and head of a horse) were described by informants as being "anywhere *sa lupa* (on land)." Spirits also resided "in heaven," "in the sea," "under the ground," "in the air," "in silent places," "in remote places," "on the road," "in populated places," and "in the barrio." Most commonly, however, spirits were associated with specific locations and particular times. Old, deserted houses, for instance, could always be expected to house a *multo* or *white lady*. Cemeteries, likewise, are known to be the dwelling places of *aswang*, *multo* and *dracula*. Spirits were felt to be most active after dark, between 7:00 p.m. and 3:00 a.m. and during a full moon, although experiences with spirits during the day were recounted as well. Even provinces and towns had their characteristic spirits. *Aswang* were associated with Panay Island, especially the cities of Dingle and Iloilo. In Cavite caves sheltered the *kamatayan* (angel of death), while the *maligno* (mystery spirit) lived in Marinduque. The island of Antique, according to one informant, had numerous spirits including the *dwende*, *kapre*, *mantiyo* or Caucasian *kapre*, *aswang*, *taiyo* and the *maranghig* (spirit of the living dead). These locations constituted the perceived environments where spirits are active. Anomalies within these areas were also more likely to be interpreted according to spirit schema.

Significant differences were perceived to exist between urban and rural areas with respect to spirit residences and spirit-human encounters. Remote forest and mountain areas, for instance, were more likely to result in chance encounters with all types of spirits because of the multiplicity of spirit residences. Caves in remote places house the *tikbalang*, *engkanto*, *aswang*, and *mangkukulam* (spirit sorcerer). Big forest trees and bamboo groves were residences for the *tikbalang*, *kapre*, *mantiyo*, *dwende*, and *engkanto*. A number of these same spirits were also associated with springs, rivers, or roads. A predominant number of the stories gleaned during the research, in fact, were set in provincial or rural locations, especially along deserted roadsides or in cogon-grass fields. Stories associated with the forest included losing one's way as a result of mischievous *engkanto* or outright kidnapping. *Kapre* appeared in the trees along forest trails. The *tikbalang* whistled alongside the road to get peoples' attention, and spirits in caves could be consulted for magical amulets or superhuman powers.

Some have supposed that traditional spirit beliefs would be discarded during urban migration, due to the greater availability of entertainment and education and the resulting modern outlook. The data, however, indicate a continuing concern about spirit presence among Manilaenos. In the city, spirits were associated with big, old houses, large trees, cemeteries, and places where death had occurred. Outside of *multo* and *aswang* stories, however, spirit experiences in the city were noticeably fewer in number.

Identifying Spirits

Different cultures remember essential details in different ways. Paul G. Hiebert has helpfully described how Western societies tend to categorize things according to intrinsic characteristics, that is, what a thing is in itself, whereas other societies may categorize things extrinsically in terms of their relationships to other things (1994, 107-133). In keeping with extrinsic set formation, Filipinos lean toward remembering details through experiential associations. Thus the problem in identifying spirits is that the phenomenology surrounding an encounter–the fear, sound, and movement–is often more memorable than the specific characteristics that distinguish the spirit's identity. Indeed, informants were somewhat hesitant to name the spirits and describe their physical attributes. Far more information was available for what spirits do (or are likely to do) than for what they looked like and what they were called.

The emphasis on behaviors may indicate some unfamiliarity with strict categories. In fact, throughout the interviews different names were given to spirits with similar attributes. One informant, for instance, confused *tikbalang* with *kapre*, describing the monstrous horse-headed man *tikbalang* with the term *kapre* or giant. Another informant confused the *aswang* with its companion, the *wak-wak*. Since only a few mentioned the *wak-wak* and since they share the same general features and behaviors, this is not surprising, but it does illustrate the tendency to cross-label spiritual phenomena. Moreover, when asked the initial question of the survey–What kinds of spirits are there?– six out of the 27 replied with cover terms like "good spirits," "bad spirits," and "monster-creatures" before they used specific terms. Only as an addendum did they offer individual names. This was especially true for informants who classified themselves as Protestants. Identification thus seems to be more in terms of type, behavior, and location than by detailed description of the spirit being's appearance.

Categorizing the spirits is rendered more problematic by the fact that they have been depicted popularly in terms of Western mythological categories, such as witch, dwarf, and fairy. Even the illustrations in Ramos' popular books betray

Western influence. Some transfer of attributes has undoubtedly occurred through such public portrayal. The dissimilarity of the Western and Filipino categories is great enough, however, to fuel popular jokes. When a local movie portrayed *engkantos* or fairies as ecologically concerned beings, the movie flopped, and local students remarked, "That is not how *engkantos* act."

Emic descriptions of spirits include such contrasts as "good and evil," "like a person" and "not like a person," and "half-half." Emphasis was placed on spirits being either good or evil, "only two kinds." Good spirits included angels and the *kaluluwa* (soul of a good person or a person without sin). Surprisingly, spirits included in the "good spirit" category also included the *dwende, engkanto, kapre,* and *multo,* although these were labeled as "friendly sometimes." Both the *engkanto* and the *dwende* have good and evil, male and female members. Good spirits make friends with humans and help them.

Evil or *masamang* spirits included the bad *engkanto* and the *dwende masama* or evil *dwende,* as well as spirits that are "like a person" and "not like a person." Evil spirits that are "like a person" (*parang tao*) are those that have a human appearance but an evil spirit. The male or female *tiyanak,* thus, is a child that died and has returned in bodily form. The *maligno* (mystery spirit) also has a human form, as does the *kamatayan* (angel of death). These spirits pose particular problems in that they are not readily recognized in human communities. Evil spirits that are "not like a person" are primarily "monster creatures" or "half-half," creatures that metamorphose into human and animal shapes to catch their victims and conceal their real identity. This category is composed of the *wak-wak, mananangal, aswang, sigbin,* and *mantiyo* or Caucasian *kapre.* Although separated from the half-half category, *white ladies* and *tikbalang* are also considered evil spirits that "are not like a person." They do not metamorphose and do not have human form. Finally, the category of evil spirit also includes the *mangkukulam* and *mangbabarang,* which are unusual humans with the power of witches and longevity. Evil spirits are known for scaring and harming humans. The worst live off human flesh and blood, through trickery making innocent people monsters like themselves. They are also known for their touchy and vengeful disposition.

Responding to Spirit Appearances

Knowledgeable Filipinos not only must recognize the phenomena surrounding spirits and their possible locations, but must also know the likely reasons for their appearance and appropriate responses. Informants could provide great detail about spirit behaviors. Spirits could appear "to communicate a message," "to help," "to court or have sexual relationships with people," "to scare," "to appear and cause victims to disappear to their place," "to take revenge for hurt," "to disturb, torment and make people suffer," and "to possess people or use them." They also could "cause great harm," "make people like them" and "kill people." The most feared spirits were those that "make *daut*" or cause bad things to happen. Spirits such as the *aswang, mangbabarang,* vampires, *kapre, taiyo, dwende masaama, engkanto, tikbalang, manananagal,* and *wak-wak* inflicted bruises, caused insanity and sickness, licked the behind of pregnant women, stepped on people, hypnotized, gave boils, imprisoned people, and cast spells. Not unexpectedly, these spirits were also considered the most dangerous in rank order tests. The *manananagal* and *aswang* were repeatedly the most feared, because "they ate human flesh" in contrast to those spirits who did not. These spirits were also "always vicious," unlike spirits which could be "friendly sometimes."

Responses to spirits related to their potential behavior. Most spirits were "avoided from fear." This involved avoiding their locations, contaminated food, noises and sounds at night, and travel at certain times, as well as moving to avoid a neighbor who was an *aswang.* Children, for instance, were instructed not to eat food from adult strangers and not to eat at classmates' homes for fear of eating an *aswang*'s food and becoming like them, and travelers in certain areas always asked a group of strong, armed men to accompany them.

The most common reaction to spirit appearances was simply to "fear and run away." In this regard some informants distinguished between "constant" and "non-constant" fear. "Non-constant" fear applied to situations in which people see a ghost or angel and are afraid, but then conquer their fear. "Constant" fear referred to those situations in which people could not conquer their fear and be courageous, so that even a *multo* in a dark place made them fear and run. Constant fear was especially associated with the *aswang, dracula, tiyanak, kapre,* and *masama dwende.*

The informants would also go to great lengths to "be very careful" around spirits. "Being careful" included maintaining respectful behaviors, giving offerings, and offering apologies. To avoid illness and retribution, spirits like the *dwende* were respectfully left alone in their residences. "People are not supposed to disturb them." Similarly, to avoid provoking the *dwende*, Filipinos do not step on or destroy anthills, urinate under *balete* trees, throw water out their kitchen windows or doors, or cut down trees without first asking permission. Common respectful warnings such as *"tabi tabi po"* will accompany these behaviors for fear that the spirits will be bumped and offended. In the city, where *aswang* or witches roam the residential areas, people will take care not to deny a strange neighbor's request. If the neighbor asks for a chicken, for example, the family will make every effort to get it for fear that the neighbor is an *aswang* in disguise, waiting to take revenge. Even animals will not be disturbed, because many spirits metamorphose into animal shapes in the course of their activities. *Aswang* may turn into cats to walk out of jail; the *mantiyo* may be a cat who heals sick children by licking them. Offerings were yet another means of "being careful." People gave gifts to persuade a spirit to leave a tree, to excuse themselves before proceeding with travel, and to atone for past offenses. Gifts or offerings to the spirit, consisting of a white or red chicken, wine and betel nut or tobacco, accompanied most rituals of placation. Sometimes people offered even bells and old, precious coins as gifts. Apologies were a major part of the ritual when sickness was involved, and the sick person would offer a gift along with his regrets.

Along with avoidance, escape, and careful behaviors, informants also mentioned defense as a necessary response. Although avoidance is the best defense, informants would also "ask help from Christ," "never leave a pregnant woman or child alone in the house," "give children an *anting-anting*" (charm), carry weapons like a bolo or crucifix, and follow the instructions of a dead relative to avoid a *multo's* appearance. Strong bamboo staves with pointed ends would be positioned around the house and under the stairs. Garlic and sometimes red peppers would be placed in doorways and open windows. Brave Filipinos might even try to kill vicious spirits by stabbing an *aswang* and killing its family or by throwing a *tiyanak* out the window. The house of a *marangig* (spirit of the living dead) could also be burned down. Those who were wise might try to counter one spirit by enlisting another spirit's help. The *mabait dwende*, for example, could be asked to help a person fight against the *masama dwende*. Spirits could also be driven away with the help of an *abolaryo* (herbal doctor). Some spirits like the *kapre*, however, were considered to be "*walang pangkontra*" or without defense.

Surprisingly, a number of Filipinos took advantage of spirit appearances to "make *duul*," go near them, or "relate to them." This contrasted with the majority who "will not relate" with them and who "avoid them from fear." Reasons for relating to certain spirits might include "seeking their power," "making friends with them for success" in exams and business, "seeking revenge" on enemies, and gaining "help in time of trouble." Such relationships were only sought with *mabait dwende* (good dwarves) or good *engkanto*; evil or bad spirits were avoided.

Counter-Cultural Perspectives

Among the 27 informants were several who held a counter-cultural perspective of the Filipino spirit world. These seven informants, who classified themselves as "Protestants" or "born again Catholics," were a part of the cultural scene by virtue of their recognition of the spirits but had somewhat different responses for classifying, interpreting, and responding to the supernatural.

In categorizing the spirits, two informants used different cover terms for evil spirits. One identified them as "fallen angels"; the other as "demons." Moreover, while retaining the culturally significant categories of good and evil spirits, they added Satan and demons to the list of evil spirits, and the Holy Spirit and angels to the list of good spirits.

Another major difference was their stated behaviors with respect to spirit appearances. Rather than adhering to behaviors of avoidance and placation like other members of the cultural scene, these informants relied on more powerful spirits, namely angels and the Holy Spirit, to defend and protect them "in Christ's name." The Holy Spirit, which is perceived as more powerful than all the other spirits, is also omnipresent, going with the believer everywhere, even "in the sea" and "where wicked spirits live."

In addition, while other informants listed some spirits as "friendly sometimes" and sought their friendship for success and aid, these seven informants perceived all spirits except angels and the Holy Spirit as deceptive, only appearing to be helpful and friendly so that they can destroy humans. They therefore opposed initiating friendships with them or submitting to their requirements.

Finally, in place of objects of protection, these informants used hymns, praise songs, and commands to prevent the appearance of spirits and to dismiss them when they appeared. Thus, while recognizing the reality of the spirits, this subgroup differed significantly from the culturally prescribed behaviors of avoidance and placation.

The History of Evangelization

Having examined the spirit beliefs and practices of a small sample of Filipinos, we are compelled to ask how such beliefs have continued despite the overwhelming Christianization of the country. After all, *Operation World* reports that 93.2 percent of the population is Christian: 67.1 percent Roman Catholic, 15.2 percent Independent (Aglipayan); and 6.8 percent Protestant (Johnstone and Mandryk 2001, 521). The *World Christian Encyclopedia* likewise reports that 89.7 percent profess Christianity: 82.4 percent Roman Catholic, 18.9 percent Independent (both Aglipayan and Iglesia ni Kristo), and 5.0

A Typology of Syncretism and Dual Religious Systems

Three Kinds of Syncretism

- ❑ Christianity is incorporated into the thought-world and practices of a non-Christian religion (e.g., West Africa)
- ❑ Non-Christian elements are blended with Christian elements within a Christian organizational framework (e.g., African Indigenous Churches, Rastafarians)
- ❑ Non-Christian religions selectively incorporate Christian elements (e.g., New Religions Movements in Japan)

Three Kinds of Dual Religious Systems

- ❑ Christianity operates side by side with another religious system (e.g., Roman Catholic evangelization of the Americas)
- ❑ Christianity is practiced with integrity but selected elements of another religion are also practiced (e.g., Christians sacrificing at an indigenous shrine in times of crisis)
- ❑ Double belonging in which cultural tradition and religion are inextricably linked (e.g., Taoism in Taiwan, Shinto in Japan)

Schreiter 1985, 146-149

percent Protestant, with nearly 20 percent affiliated with more than one group (Barrett, Kurian, and Johnson 2001, 594). One possible answer is that the indigenous pre-Christian beliefs have been syncretized with Christianity. Robert J. Schreiter has helpfully distinguished between syncretism and dual religious systems. In a dual religious system, as in Bulatao's split-level Christianity, the two religions are kept separate and applied to different areas of life. In true syncretism, however, the elements of two religious systems have been so mixed that at least one of the religions loses its basic structure (1985, 144-147). In reflecting upon the data, Filipinos seem to have incorporated primal religious beliefs into the Roman Catholic system or vice versa, in such a way that the basic structure of biblical Christianity, albeit not that of Iberian Catholicism, has been lost.

Continued syncretism in the Philippines, therefore, cannot be understood apart from the history of its evangelization. Iberian Catholicism had been shaped by isolation and the domination of the Moors. The clergy freely mixed Moorish legends into their sermons and sacred stories, thus preparing the way, as Frank Callcott put it, for "the great efflorescence of the supernatural" with its emphasis on miracles and magic that continued well into the 17th century (1923, 13). Moreover, despite the iconoclastic controversies, the medieval church used sculpture and art, including images of the saints, extensively, so that the cathedral became the "Bible of the Poor" (Petry 1962, 382-385). Then too during the *reconquista* the saints were perceived as protectors of the faithful against the infidels. When coupled with a Spanish temperament that has been characterized by John A. Mackay as intensely individualistic, impulsive, and passionate, blind loyalty and vows to the saints, and especially the Virgin, became the norm. In such an environment proper etiquette toward spiritual patrons was vital to life and well-being (1932, 3-16). Thus, untouched by the winds of reformation that were sweeping the Continent, the Spanish possessed a militant religiosity, but were poorly discipled. While they were deeply mystical, their religion consisted largely of external observances focused upon the local church, its festivals and pilgrimages (Poole 1992, 6).

The Spanish, with their unique form of Roman Catholicism, initially evangelized the islands in the 16th century, and the Filipinos wholeheartedly accepted many Roman Catholic beliefs and rituals. According to Jaime A. Belita, "The only thing Catholics had which the animists did not was an official hierarchy ruling the Church and regulating preaching and rituals, including the liturgy." He further suggests that the parallel between Roman Catholicism and the local religion consisted of the veneration of saints, the powerful and mysterious objects used in rituals, and miraculous images (1991, 167).

To these Teresita B. Obusan adds parallel ideas about the afterlife, reverence for spirits of the dead, belief in good and evil spirits, and the value of external rituals (1991, 81). From an indigenous point of view Roman Catholic rituals simply provided access to the supernatural and the opportunity to meet indigenous social and cultural needs. The cult of the saints was, therefore, widely accepted among the people. It suited local beliefs in the active role of the recently deceased *anito* (ancestral spirits), as well as with the Southeast Asian concept of the mother as the giver of life and nurture. The Filipinos also embraced rituals to empower amulets and other objects to ward off malevolent spirits, as well as rituals for the dead. For the indigenes praying for the dead in purgatory, for instance, could easily be understood as care for ancestral spirits, so much so that by the 17th century the rosary and Christian novenas were commonly used for ancestor placation (Rafael 1988, 192). The parallels are so striking that Obusan argues that Iberian Catholicism did not

Split-Level Christianity or Syncretism?

"According to the anthropologist Robert Fox, pre-Spanish society was already well-established, so that it played a major role in shaping outside religious influence—a position not too popular among Filipino social scientists. Though there appears to be no study proving or disproving Fox's position, studies in other societies show that the existing culture indeed shapes outside influences, especially in the area of religion. . . . The existing pre-Spanish religion shaped or "distorted" the Christian religion brought by the Spanish conquerors. This concept is important, for outside religious influences have often been thought to play a major role in shaping Filipino folk religion. If Fox's position is correct that the pre-Spanish society was already well established, then the shaping or "distortion" of outside religious influences would be marked strongly by the early Filipino religious tradition, and not vice versa."

- Obusan 1991, 84-85

shape Filipino religion, but rather that the indigenous religion shaped incoming Christianity to its contours (1991, 83-85). The placation of nature spirits, leadership by spirit mediums, and most of all, the consistency between the religious values and social behaviors all demonstrate that Filipino folk religious beliefs are not a "split-level" system at all, but a systematized indigenous faith.

In the Philippines devotion to the Iberian cult of saints, when coupled with forceful conquest, resulted in evangelization that was deficient in a number of ways. First of all, the similarities of form and function (i.e., images and placation) between the Spanish cult of the saints and the indigenous cult of ancestors, local gods, and ruling spirits easily distorted Filipino understandings, so that the more formal aspects of doctrine and faith that the priests sought to teach were less readily understood and accepted. What the official religion tried to remove, but could not, were the alternative sources to power available in the indigenous religion. These sources, which included rituals for the maintenance of cosmic and divine law, lay outside the experience of the Spanish clerics, and while not as conspicuous as the military weapons that supported the new religion, they were nevertheless considered by Filipinos to be as powerful and even more important to the exigencies of life. Filipinos simply did not understand the implications of Christianity nor the way that the new religion could answer the problems they faced under the old.

Second, Filipinos learned Christianity through Spanish language and customs rather than through their own language and thought patterns, resulting in further confusion. Confession was a case in point. The Spanish wrote that the people eagerly waited for days to confess their sins, but could not think of specifics when their turn came (Rafael 1988, 97). The clerics never understood that while the tribal people desired to avoid God's anger and curse, which the priests made clear would come if they avoided confession, they had never learned God's law well enough to know what they had done wrong.

Third, other theological deficiencies derived from the fact that Christianity was presented through ritual and drama rather than through discussions comparing biblical teachings and indigenous thought. Discussion of religious ideas was not considered essential, not only because the religious vocabulary in Latin and Spanish was difficult to translate, but also because there was no vernacular text for their study. While the first Roman Catholic missionaries arrived in the

Philippines in 1565, the first translation of any part of the Scriptures was not made until 1873 (Neill 1964, 209). As we have seen, the sensory-based presentation of Catholicism reinforced the traditional Filipino belief in the power of natural objects and supported their continued worship of the *anito*, but it did not encourage ideas without a ready root, such as sin, repentance, and atonement (Mulder 1992, 241). The emphasis upon the emotional and supernatural aspects of images and rituals ultimately distorted biblical meanings.

History offers one final word of caution. Natalie Zemon Davis, for instance, has cautioned against using doctrine alone as a means to distinguish popular and normative religion, because what one generation considers normative may be superstition to the next (1974, 307). Thus many practices shared by Latin American Indians and Filipinos, such as holidays and reciting the *pasyon* during Lent, were indicative not of folk culture but of the finest Spanish minds. These were central facets of religious life in the 16th century. "The folk cultures which exist today are not the result of 19th and 20th-century contact between western European civilization and the unlettered peoples of the world. . . . They are the result of continual contact between the centers of intellectual life and the masses, whether rural or urban" (Foster 1953, 164). Contrary to being syncretism, Foster argues, they are vestiges of the most sophisticated cultures of Europe, locked into cultural traditions today that reveal significant religious assumptions relevant to another time and place. This may be true of the placation and devotion given to Filipino Christian images as well, in which case, the charge of syncretism, though justified, is a modern Protestant reaction against medieval Roman Catholic religious phenomena. This further emphasizes the value of historical understanding. Studies of syncretism must move beyond merely a synchronic recognition of the problem to diachronic studies of how the problem originated.

Transforming Discipleship

We are left, finally, with a compelling question: How should evangelicals respond to such beliefs? Irving Hexham and Karla Poewe, in their study of new religious movements, contend that we cannot define popular religions simply on the basis of their superstitious or magical content. Popular religions have often been dismissed as irrational, but as illustrated in this study, they are rational given their assumptions. Moreover, "anyone who wants to communicate effectively with members of [these] religions must enter their thought world . . . by recognizing the logic of their beliefs" (1986, 14; cf. Worsley 1997). In the preceding ethnographic study and exploration of the history of evangelization, we have endeavored to enter into the Filipino thought world. It now remains to recommend a response characterized by transforming discipleship. That is, we must not only change the syncretistic beliefs of disciples, but we must also change discipleship methods that ignore these beliefs.

In order to address syncretism, disciple-makers must first understand the indigenous spirit world themselves. When confronted with anomalies, Filipinos go to those who know. If pastors and missionaries do not know this domain of Filipino experience, they will never be consulted, and thus will never have the opportunity to address the issues. We must appreciate that the knowledge in the domain is extensive; we must not ridicule it; we must not dismiss it as irrelevant knowledge. On the contrary, we must suspend disbelief

> **When confronted with anomalies, Filipinos go to those who know. If pastors and missionaries do not know this domain of Filipino experience, they will never be consulted, and thus will never have the opportunity to address the issues.**

and learn the domain adequately. We must become those who know. This does not mean that we need to pursue every aspect of knowledge about the spirits, but we must know well enough what people believe and practice, and why they do so, that we can respond to the domain with biblical insight.

In light of the beliefs and practices that have emerged from our anthropological and historical studies, disciple-makers must introduce Filipinos to the kingdom of God. Jesus announced the good news of the reign of God as both a present and a future reality. The kingdom will be revealed at the end of the age in the destruction of Satan, but it is present now in the binding of Satan (Ladd 1974, 57, 66-67). The kingdom of God thus provides an interpretive framework for understanding the relationship between God and spiritual powers active in the world (Van Rheenen 1991, 7). To this end disciples should be taught that the kingdom of God is theocentric, dynamic, messianic, and salvific (Guthrie 1981, 419-421).

Since the kingdom is theocentric, disciple-makers must introduce disciples to the God they serve. God must be presented in all his majestic holiness. He is to be feared far more than the spirits, for he is the awesome judge from whom all are separated by sin. A proper understanding of God inevitably leads to the recognition of sin as the central human problem rather than the spirits. As Arthur F. Glasser has observed, "Strange as it may seem, when Paul gave his most comprehensive exposition of the spiritual plight of humanity in his Epistle to the Romans, he mentioned neither Satan nor the powers. His focus was rather on the fallenness and guilt of the human race" (2003, 351). Not only that, but in light of the Filipino belief that territories are ruled by local spirits, an understanding of God's immanence is essential. Like Jacob, Filipinos must realize, "Surely the Lord is in this place, and I was not aware of it" (Gen. 28:16).

Second, due to its theocentric nature, the kingdom manifests God's power. God exercises sovereign authority over every principality and power. Filipinos therefore need not live in fear of demonic manifestations. Instead they must learn about the spirit domain in biblical perspective. As we have observed, Filipinos do not view all spirits as evil and are more open to contact with spirits. They must therefore be cautioned that even the devil disguises himself as an angel of light (2 Cor. 11:14). In light of Saul's encounter with the witch of Endor, ancestral spirits must be understood as demonic apparitions (1 Sam. 28). At the same time, they should be introduced to God's dynamic power. Dagon, for example, fell down before the ark of the Lord (1 Sam. 5), and Jesus and the apostles exorcised demons, so that Filipinos need not fear the hostile powers.

Third, the kingdom of God is messianic. It is thus inseparably related to Jesus, the Christ. He himself is the king, the image of the invisible God. Among Filipinos with their adoration of the Virgin Mary and the baby Santo Niño, a new vision of Jesus must be emphasized. When Filipinos regard him as localized within an image, especially as a baby under the control of his mother, rather than as the risen Lord of heaven and earth, their entire cosmology is skewed (cf. Farrow 1999). When they believe images are indwelled with a localized personality and power that must be placated, Jesus and Mary become no different than other local spirits. Disciple-makers must confront this with a vision of Jesus, risen from the dead, sitting alone at the right hand of the Father with authority over every spiritual power (Eph. 1:19-20).

Finally, the kingdom of God is salvific. The mission of the king was to introduce the blessings of redemption. Salvation ultimately involves future immortality and perfect fellowship with God, but it also entails present blessing. Through the Spirit disciples experience the indwelling power and life of God; they sense God's forgiveness; they enjoy God's gift of righteousness. Salvation, however, is not only spiritual but physical, and disciples enjoy a taste of the coming kingdom in healings and exorcisms as well (Ladd 1974, 70-80). Filipino disciples therefore need not fear or placate the powers of darkness to ensure safety. Their Lord Jesus Christ not only possesses authority over every demonic power, whether dwarf, elf, or vampire, but he also deeply desires to deliver his people.

Conclusion

This study has attempted to establish the vital necessity of both ethnographic and historical research into indigenous beliefs as a means of successfully countering syncretism. While insights from the study would apply to large areas of the globe touched by Iberian Catholicism, on a more general level the study emphasizes an appreciation for the shared cultural experience of disciples with a view toward sharing relevant biblical truth.

On Ascension Sunday, 1994, David had the privilege to preach at the Capitol City Alliance Church in Quezon City. He offered a simple sermon on the ascension, but as part of the application he merely observed that Jesus Christ is seated at the right hand of God, far above every power in heaven and on earth, and as a consequence we need not fear the *aswang*. As the congregation filed out the door, one wizened grandfather shook David's hand warmly and with tear-filled eyes said, "Thank you, Pastor, for letting me know that I do not have to be afraid of the *aswang*."

Sources Cited

Barrett, David B., George T. Kurian, and Todd M. Johnson, eds. 2001. *World Christian Encyclopedia: A Comparative Survey of Churches and Religions in the Modern World.* Vol. 1, *The World by Countries: Religionists, Churches, Ministries.* New York: Oxford University Press.

Belita, Jaime A. 1991. "Let Us Through": Multidisciplinary Reflections on Popular Catholicism in the Philippines." In *And God Said: Hala! Studies in Popular Religiosity in the Philippines,* ed. Jaime A. Belita, 165-183. Manila: De la Salle University Press.

Bulatao, Jaime C. 1992. "Split-Level Christianity." In *Phenomena and Their Interpretation. Landmark Essays 1957-1989,* 22-31. Manila: Ateno de Manila University Press.

Callcott, Frank. 1923. *The Supernatural in Early Spanish Literature.* New York: Instituto de las Españas.

Davis, Natalie Zemon. 1974. "Some Tasks and Themes in the Study of Popular Religion." In *The Pursuit of Holiness in Late Medieval and Renaissance Religion.* Studies in Medieval and Reformation Thought, Vol. 10, eds. Charles Trinkhaus and Heiko A. Oberman, 307-336. Leiden: E. J. Brill.

Demetrio, Francisco. 1991. *Encyclopedia of Philippine Folk Beliefs and Customs.* Vol. 1. Cagayan de Oro City: Xavier University.

Farrow, Douglas. 1999. *Ascension and Ecclesia: On the Significance of the Doctrine of the Ascension for Ecclesiology and Christian Cosmology.* Grand Rapids: Eerdmans.

Foster, George M. 1953. "What Is Folk Culture?" *American Anthropologist* 55:159-173.

Gatan, Fernando C, Jr. 1983. *Aspects of Ibanag Spirit Beliefs: A Study in Transformational Culture Change.* Quezon City: Asian Center, University of the Philippines.

Glasser, Arthur F, with Charles E. Van Engen, Dean S. Gilliland, and Shawn B. Redford. 2003. *Announcing the Kingdom: The Story of God's Mission in the Bible.* Grand Rapids: Baker Academic

Guthrie, Donald. 1981. *New Testament Theology.* Downers Grove: InterVarsity Press.

Henry, Rodney. 1986. *Filipino Spirit World.* Manila: OMF Literature.

Hexham, Irving and Karla Poewe. 1986. *Understanding Cults and New Religions.* Grand Rapids: Eerdmans.

Hiebert, Paul G. 1994. *Anthropological Reflections on Missiological Issues.* Grand Rapids: Baker.

Johnstone, Patrick, and Jason Mandryk. 2001. *Operation World: 21st Century Edition.* Waynesboro, GA: Paternoster.

Ladd, George Eldon. 1974. *A Theology of the New Testament.* Grand Rapids: Eerdmans.

Mackay, John A. 1932. *The Other Spanish Christ.* New York: The Macmillan Company.

Mulder, Niels. 1992. "Localization and Philippine Catholicism." *Philippine Studies* 40:240-254.

Neill, Stephen. 1964. *A History of Christian Missions.* New York: Viking Penguin.

Obusan, Teresita B. 1991. "*Tatlong Persona Solo Dios*: A Study of a Filipino Folk Religion." In *And God Said: Hala! Studies in Popular Religiosity in the Philippines,* ed. Jaime A. Belita, 67-96. Manila: De la Salle University Press.

Petry, Ray C. 1962. *A History of Christianity: Readings in the History of the Church.* Vol 1. *The Early and Medieval Church.* Grand Rapids: Baker.

Poole, Stafford. 1992. "Iberian Catholicism Comes to the Americas." In *Christianity Comes to the Americas: 1492-1776.* Charles H. Lippy, Robert Choquette, Stafford Poole, 1-130. New York: Paragon House.

Rafael, Vincente L. 1988. *Contracting Colonialism. Translation and Christian Conversion in Tagalog Society Under Early Spanish Rule.* Quezon City: Ateneo de Manila University Press.

Ramos, Maximo D. 1990a. *Legends of Lower Gods.* Quezon City: Phoenix Publishing.

---------. 1990b. *Tales of Long Ago in the Philippines.* Quezon City: Phoenix Publishing.

---------. 1990c. *Philippine Myths, Legends, and Folktales.* Quezon City: Phoenix Publishing.

Schreiter, Robert J. 1985. *Constructing Local Theologies.* Maryknoll: Orbis.

Spradley, James P. 1980. *Participant Observation.* New York: Holt, Reinhart and Winston.

Van Rheenen, Gailyn. 1991. "Kingdom Theology: Introducing Animists to Christian Perspectives." In *Communicating Christ in Animistic Contexts.* Pasadena: William Carey Library. (Available online http://www.missiology.org/folkreligion; accessed 20 December 2004.)

Worsley, Peter. 1997. *Knowledges: Culture, Counterculture, Subculture.* New York: New Press.

11

Revelation in the Chinese Characters: Divine or Divined?

How Chuang Chua

This short paper offers a critique of the particular methodology behind the linguistic analysis that makes the claim that the biblical truths relating to creation and redemption can be found hidden within the Chinese characters. The "Revelation in the Chinese Characters" thesis is popularized through these two books: *The Discovery of Genesis* (1979) by C.H. Kang and Ethel Nelson, and *Genesis and the Mystery Confucius Couldn't Solve* (1994) by Ethel Nelson and Richard Broadberry.

Chinese is one of the very few modern languages in the world whose writing system is not based on an alphabet.[1] Rather, it is an ideographic language, consisting of some 40,000 characters, each of which is an autonomous semantic unit denoting an aspect of reality as perceived by the

---

[1] An alphabetic language is one which contains a finite set of orthographic symbols, from which a smaller set of symbols is chosen to form individual words through a process of combination or permutation.

Chinese.[2] Put simply, each character refers to a thing or a concept. For want of documentary evidence, it is not known how these characters came about. One popular legend has it that a minister serving in the court of the Yellow Emperor, the progenitor of the Chinese people, invented the Chinese script after observing the footprints of some birds and animals (Yu 1963, 6). The earliest records we have of Chinese writing are the oracle inscriptions on tortoise shells and oxen bones, dated to the Shang Dynasty (1700-1066 B.C.)[3] As a result, it is generally accepted by scholars today that writing emerged in China around the second millennium B.C.[4]

The first complete Chinese dictionary was compiled by Xû Shèn (許慎),[5] but was only published two hundred years later around A.D. 120 during the Han Dynasty. This monumental work, known as the *Shùo Wén Jîe Zì* (説文解字), contains detailed etymological explanations of some 10,500 characters. It is noteworthy that even today practically all Chinese dictionaries claim to be based on the *Shùo Wén*. Indeed any serious etymological study of the Chinese

---

[2] About 30,000 of these characters are "monstrosities and useless doubles" (Wilder and Ingram 1974, v). To be adequately functional in the language, one needs a knowledge of only around 2000 to 2500 characters.

[3] The first bones and tortoise shells with character inscriptions were discovered in 1899 in a village in Henan Province, where the capital of the Shang Dynasty was located. Since then, more than 160,000 pieces of inscribed bones and tortoise shells with about 10,000 characters have been unearthed. Out of these characters, only about 1,000 (or 10%) have been deciphered (Xinhua News Agency, 2000, www.chinapage.com/ archeology/2000year.html).

[4] A mass burial site in Jiahu, Henan Province, that was first unearthed in 1962, recently yielded fourteen tortoise shells on which were found various inscriptions. These shells are dated to the seventh millennium B.C. Scholars are, however, divided as to the meaning and function of these inscriptions. (See Li, Xueqin, Garman Harbottle, Zhang, Juchong and Wang, Changsui. 2003. "The earliest writing? Sign use in the seventh millennium BC at Jiahu, Henan Province, China." *Antiquity* 77 (295): 31-44.

[5] The romanization used in this paper follows the standard Hanyu Pinyin system.

language must necessarily begin with it (cf. Wieger 1965,15; Wilder and Ingram 1974, vi).

Chinese characters can be classified into four types: pictographs, simple-indicatives, compound-indicatives, and semantic-phonetic characters (see John DeFrancis 1984, 84). Pictographs, as the name implies, are pictorial symbols that resemble the thing represented (e.g. the character 口 for "mouth"). Simple-indicative ideographs are symbols that each bears a simple indexical relation with the idea it represents (e.g. the characters 一, 二, 三, representing the numerals "one," "two," and "three" respectively). Compound-indicatives are complex characters made up of at least two semantic components, and their meaning is derived from the meaning of all the elements. An example of compound indicatives is the character 好 meaning "good", or "to be fond of": it is made up of 女 "woman", and 子 "child".[6] Finally, semantic-phonetic characters are those that are made up of two parts, one which has to do with the meaning, and the other with the sound *only* (e.g. the character 媽 for "mother", comprising the semantic element 女 "woman", and the phonetic element 馬 *ma*). It must be noted that although the character 馬 on its own is a simple-indicative ideograph meaning "horse," when it is combined with another element to form a semantic-phonetic character, it loses its semantic value completely, and assumes a purely phonetic one. So for example, we have these different characters, among others, all pronounced *ma* but with a different tonal value: 媽 (*mā*, meaning "mother"), 螞 (*má*, meaning "ant"), and 嗎 (*ma*, an interrogative marker). A vital point needs to be made that of the four categories, an overwhelming majority of the characters in use today are found in the semantic-phonetic category.[7]

---

[6] There are three explanations for this combination: (1) It is *good* to have a wife and children. (2) It is *good* for a woman to bear children. (3) A wife and a child are what a man is most *fond of.*

[7] John DeFrancis (1984,84) notes that 97% of the 48,641 characters in the Kang Hsi Dictionary (1716) belong to the semantic-phonetic category, while the remaining 3% accounts for the other three categories. Even in the *Shùo Wén*, semantic-phonetic characters account for nearly 80% of the 10,000 words Xû Shèn analyzed (see Wilder and Ingram 1974, vi).

Chinese Glyphomancy

Because of the ideographic nature of the Chinese writing system, one is able to generate all sorts of graphic puns in a way that one is not able to do with alphabetic languages. One could, for instance, conjecture that 李 (Li) has become the most common surname in the world because this character can be broken up into three parts, 十八子, which taken together can mean "eighteen children," implying that a person with this surname would be blessed with many offspring. In another example, an ingenious means that the Communists used to motivate the working masses was by telling them that the character for "heaven", 天 *tiēn*, is actually composed of the two characters 工人 *gōngrén*, which means "worker(s)". The implication is that there is no higher authority than the workers themselves: they are their own god.[8]

Given its graphic nature, it is not surprising to note that since earliest times, the Chinese language has been employed as a ready means of divination. Wolfgang Bauer rightly suggests that Shang oracle bones "owe their existence to divination and the belief that any character possessed a sort of magical power, a belief that has remained down to the modern age" (1979, 71). The art of divining the Chinese characters is known as glyphomancy, or popularly in Mandarin as 拆字 *chāi-zì*, meaning literally, "to dismantle the characters." There is a wealth of literature on the subject, the earliest dating from the seventh century A.D. Glyphomancy is still widely practiced today in Taiwan, Hong Kong, and Singapore.

Presuppositions Behind the "Revelation in the Chinese Characters" Thesis

In 1950, Chong Heng Kang, a Chinese pastor, published a book entitled *Genesis and the Chinese*. In it, he dissected various Chinese characters to show that they contain the stories in the early chapters of Genesis. Some years later, Ethel Nelson, an American medical missionary working in Thailand, read Kang's book, and became completely convinced that within the Chinese characters is

---

[8] This example was told to me by Professor Fenggang Yang of Purdue University.

embedded biblical revelation, not only of the Old Testament, but also the New (Kang and Nelson 1979, 118-19; Nelson and Broadberry 1994, 148). Nelson coauthored with Kang *The Discovery of Genesis* (1979), which stirred up a fair amount of interest, especially among Chinese pastors. However, numerous linguistic mistakes in this volume forced Nelson to publish a revised work with Richard Broadberry, a medical laboratory specialist working in Taiwan, entitled *Genesis and the Mystery Confucius Couldn't Solve* (1994).[9] One of the criticisms leveled against the earlier work was that the analysis was done on modern Chinese characters, and these are either late additions, or if not, they are in all probability very different from the original characters. It is interesting to note, for instance, that the commonly-used character for boat 船, which is often cited as an example to demonstrate Chinese knowledge of Noah's Ark in antiquity, is not one of the 10,500 characters in the *Shùo Wén* at all! The character cannot therefore be more than two thousand years old, and was invented to meet the newly-arisen shipping needs of the Chinese (cf. Wilder and Ingram 1974, 118-19).[10]

In Nelson and Broadberry (1994), the authors tried to analyze characters from the Shang bone oracles, and in the process, abandoned or modified the explanation of some thirty characters in the first book. In their place, they added about fifty new character analyses in the later book. A couple of years later, as a summary to the first two works, Nelson and Broadberry coauthored with Ginger Tong Chock *God's Promise to the Chinese* (1997) in which the authors analyzed the alleged biblical meaning hidden within some one hundred and fifty Chinese characters. The methodology used in these three books, however, is the same, and raises serious questions from the linguistic point of view. But before we discuss the problems with their analysis, it is helpful to understand some of the presuppositions behind their work.

Nelson acknowledges that she is not a linguist, but she makes no apologies for it, having "learned a bit about the Chinese written language during the months of ingesting the

---

[9] By this time Pastor Kang had already died, after retiring in Singapore.
[10] China developed her maritime technology under the Wu Dynasty during the period of the Three Kingdoms (A.D. 220-280), at least one hundred years after the compilation of the *Shùo Wén*.

submitted characters with their analyses" (1979, xvi). She adds, "Perhaps someone, such as myself not engrained in previously accumulated knowledge and biases of the language can be more objective and critical" (ibid). On her methodology, which she describes as the "hieroglyphic" system of analysis, Nelson admits that it is "new and unconventional" (1979, xv), but sees no problem with departing completely from established scholarship since, according to her, it uncovers the evidence of biblical revelation.

On biblical chronology, Nelson and Broadberry, citing the Irish Bishop James Ussher (1581-1651), believe that the biblical flood took place around 2348 B.C., 1656 years after the Creation (1994, 147).[11] The event of the Tower of Babel is dated 100 years after the flood. Nelson and Broadberry surmise that it took about forty years for "the great Chinese family" to move from Mesopotamia to China, and this synchronizes well with the founding of the first imperial house, the Hsia Dynasty in 2205 B.C.[12] The arguments that Nelson and Broadberry present are fraught with difficulties, not least of which relate to the dating of the Creation, let alone the flood. This notwithstanding, Nelson and Broadberry describe Ussher's dating of the Creation as "a monumental study," supposing it to be "close to correct" (ibid). The other problem, of course, is that we still have no written or archaeological records from the Hsia Dynasty. The dating in Nelson and Broadberry works out so "conveniently" to show that the early post-Babel settlers in China had a living memory of the great flood, and by implication, a direct relationship to the first ten chapters of Genesis. The dating system used by Nelson and Broadberry is not dissimilar to that used by proponents of Creation Science. It is therefore hardly surprising that the "Revelation in the

---

[11] Bishop Ussher is well known for his pronouncement that the Creation happened on Sunday, October 23, 4004 B.C.

[12] In this context, the word "Chinese" is an obvious anachronism. It is generally acknowledged that China as a unified political entity came only into existence during the reign of Yin Zheng (221-206 B.C.). Yin Zheng called himself Qinshihuang, which literally means "the first emperor of Qin (or Chin)." The title is not inappropriate considering that he unified China, built the Great Wall, and standardized the writing system.

Chinese Characters" thesis is readily endorsed in Creation Science literature.[13]

Problems With the "Revelation in the Chinese Characters" Thesis

As mentioned above, Nelson and Broadberry call their method of analyzing the Chinese characters the hieroglyphic system of analysis, from the Egyptian "hieroglyphs," meaning "sacred symbols" (1994, 133). The assumption is that the early Chinese created ideographs to preserve sacred truths, truths which are consistent with the early chapters of Genesis. An immediate comment must be made at this point. While it cannot be denied that the etymology of some Chinese characters may reflect a religious origin, the hieroglyphic method itself is alien to Chinese linguistic scholarship. Nelson herself admits that her analysis consists of "apparent innovations" (1979, xv). The hieroglyphic method is, of course, not unique to the "Revelation in the Chinese Characters" thesis. Other Chinese religions, such as the Taiwanese Unity Sect (一貫道), use a similar approach of dissecting some Chinese characters in order to justify their beliefs (see Jordan and Overmyer 1986, 231-34).

One of the problems with the hieroglyphic method is that it treats all Chinese characters as either simple-indicatives or compound-indicatives. It blatantly ignores the fact that most of the characters are of the semantic-phonetic type. Take, for example, the character for boat 船. Nelson breaks this character up into three elements: 舟 a vessel, 八 eight, and 口 mouth, and then concludes that the story of Noah's ark is embedded in this character (1979, xii).[14] The linguistic fact that

---

[13] See, for instance, these websites dedicated to the promotion of Creation Science: www.pathlights.com, www.swcp.com/creation, www.icr.org, among others. See also Ethel Nelson's article "The original 'unknown' god of China" in *Creation* 20(3): 50-53.

[14] It is even debatable whether 八 stands for "eight". According to Wieger (1965, 57), 八 is a primitive which means "to divide" or "to separate", but which *now* means "eight". This notwithstanding, evangelists love to use this character when preaching the gospel to East Asian peoples. Billy Graham, for instance, used this example in his crusade in Singapore in 1978.

船 is a semantic-phonetic character is totally ignored. While it is true that the element 舟 correctly means vessel, the element on the right 㕣 is purely a phonetic element. This phonetic element, when combined with the character for "gold" 金, yields the character 鉛 which refers to the metal "lead". Nelson and Broadberry obviously have no use for this character, since it does not fit into the biblical story. The hieroglyphic method of reading meanings into semantic-phonetic characters can yield rather ridiculous results: the character for mother 媽 has something to do with a female horse (女 "woman" + 馬 "horse").[15]

Nelson and Broadberry circumvent this potential problem easily by analyzing *selected* characters, only those which are amenable to the biblical narrative. In other words, the Bible is taken as the authoritative text which controls the outcome of the analysis. The implication of this is clear: without the Bible, the alleged meanings in the Chinese characters remain forever hidden. The character for boat remains that and nothing more, if one does not have any knowledge of the biblical flood. Nelson and Broadberry's method of analysis can therefore be described as eisegetical, rather than exegetical, i.e. they read into, rather than draw out from, the Chinese characters the meaning of the biblical narratives. This point is all the more crucial since there is nothing in Scripture to suggest that biblical meanings are embedded in the Chinese, or for that matter, any, language.

Another point can be made in relation to the so-called hieroglyphic method. It is not dissimilar with glyphomancy, the ancient art of divination. The only difference is that instead of telling the future, it tells the story of the past, a story which we can know completely from the Bible. And this is where the confusion lies. Nelson and Broadberry cannot be wrong about the biblical narratives, even though their methodology is way off the mark. An example from homiletics will demonstrate my point. A preacher can still "correctly" preach from any biblical

---

[15] It must be said that Kang and Nelson (1979, 29-30) do recognize "phonetic characters" like 媽 and how they work, but it is rather inexplicable that when it comes to analyzing the so-called biblical characters, they completely dismiss the possibility that these may in fact be semantic-phonetic characters.

text that God is love, even if the text he preaches from has nothing to say about God's love.

Some Missiological Reflections

Much more could be said about the Chinese characters. The reader interested in the etymology, classification, and signification of the Chinese characters is directed to the magisterial work of the Jesuit Sinologist, Father Wieger (1965). Wieger's work, based on the *Shùo Wén*, remains the authority in Chinese linguistic scholarship. It is unfortunate that Wieger's work is completely ignored in Nelson and Broadberry.

There are serious methodological and theological issues that cannot be ignored in an analysis that purports to demonstrate the deuterocanonicity, or revelatory nature, of the Chinese characters. The grounds on which to build such a case are shaky, linguistically and theologically (cf. Corduan 2003, 73). This is, of course, not to say that the Chinese characters cannot be used to illustrate biblical truths. In fact, there is potential in every culture to use its linguistic resources in imparting spiritual lessons. In English, for example, by showing that the word "atone" can be read as "at-one", Bible teachers often emphasize the fruit of reconciliation wrought by the atonement. The atonement has made us "at-one" with God, and with each other. Sunday school teachers often teach their charges the meaning of GRACE: God's Riches At Christ's Expense; or of FAITH: For All I Trust Him. But linguistic creativity in no way implies divine inspiration. In the same way, the Chinese characters can perhaps be used – indeed they have often been used – creatively to illustrate profound biblical truths. The classic example is the character for "righteousness" 義, written with 羊 "lamb" above the character for "I" 我. Hudson Taylor, the founder of the China Inland Mission (now OMF International), is credited with the ingenious explanation of the character for "come" 來: a man (人) hanging on the cross (人 + 十 → 木) with two persons (thieves) 人 on each side! Taylor used this character 來 as a creative graphic pun to extend an invitation to Chinese people to come to Christ. Timothy Boyle, missionary to Japan, apparently uses the Chinese characters in a similar way in his ministry. Boyle remarks, "[E]ven if the interpretation I give to a particular character does not in fact agree with the original etymology of the character (which is usually unknowable anyway), as long as it serves my purpose as a communication tool for the gospel, then I will not hesitate to use it" (1994, 15). Yet one needs to consider if there are ethical issues involved in using a method which not only runs contrary to established scholarship, but which may convey the false impression that the biblical appropriation of the characters is etymological in nature. And even if one takes the utmost care to ensure that the characters are used as nothing more than pure illustrations, one needs to ask, how significant is the point that one is making? After all, almost anything can be read into the characters if one is sufficiently creative.

Some may argue that the use of the Chinese characters in preaching the gospel constitutes a sort of "redemptive analogy," perhaps not unlike Don Richardson's *Peace Child* (1974). It certainly gives the gospel a familiar cultural feel to the people, an important principle in contextualization. But the concept of the redemptive analogy is not an unproblematic one, for it begs the question regarding the theological validity of implanted divine revelation in any language, or culture. Is the "peace child" a deliberate piece of divinely-implanted revelation, or is it simply a cultural practice that reflects what it means to be human? The point is that since God has created humans in His image, societies all over the world have cultural resources within them to express and understand biblical truths to a good extent without presupposing these cultural elements to carry divine intention. When missionaries or evangelists, consciously or otherwise, regard cultural elements as revelatory each time they can be used to teach the truths of the gospel, they are in effect conditioning people to adopt a particular mode of thinking about faith and culture that in long run can only lead to syncretism. This is where uncompromising missiological leadership is needed, not only to develop strategies for effective ministry results but to ensure that the means of gospel proclamation are sound.

Some years ago, I heard a preacher at a Chinese evangelistic meeting in Singapore. He preached with great zeal, using the Chinese characters throughout his sermon to illustrate God's promise of salvation to the Chinese people. In that same sermon, the preacher also emphasized that God loves the Chinese people more than others, because He has created more Chinese than any people, and that He has hidden His revelation in the Chinese language. He also argued that the wise men who visited the Christ Child in Bethlehem were Chinese. The warning of David Jordan (1993) could not be more timely: to claim that one's language, or for that matter, any aspect of one's culture, is divinely ordained as a vehicle of biblical revelation is a recipe for a dangerous Christian ethnocentrism.

Sources Cited

Bauer, Wolfgang. 1979. "Chinese Glyphomancy (ch'ai-tzu) and Its Uses in Present-Day Taiwan." In *Legend, Lore, and religion in China: Essays in Honor of Wolfram Eberhard on His Seventieth Birthday*, ed. Sarah Allan and Alvin P. Cohen, 71-96. San Francisco, Calif.: Chinese Materials Center.

Boyle, Timothy D. 1994. *Bible Stories Hidden in Chinese Characters: A Japanese Perspective*. Tsukuba, Chiba: Tsukuba Christian Center.

Corduan, Winfried. 2003. *A Tapestry of Faiths: The Common Threads Between Christianity and World Religions*. Downers Grove, Ill.: InterVarsity Press.

DeFrancis, John. 1984. *The Chinese Language: Fact and Fantasy*. Honolulu, HI: University of Hawaii Press.

Jordan, David K. 1993. "The Glyphomancy Factor: Observations on Chinese Conversion." In *Conversion to Christianity: Historical and Anthropological Perspectives on a Great Transformation*, ed. Robert W. Hefner. Berkeley, Calif.: University of California Press.

Jordan, David K., and Daniel L. Overmyer. 1986. *The Flying Phoenix: Aspects of Chinese Sectarianism in Taiwan*. Princeton, NJ: Princeton University Press.

Kang, Chong Heng. 1950. *Genesis and the Chinese*. Hong Kong: Independent Printing.

Kang, C.H., and Ethel R. Nelson. 1979. *The Discovery of Genesis: How the Truths of Genesis Were Found Hidden in the Chinese Language*. St. Louis, MO: Concordia.

Li, Xueqin, Garman Harbottle, Zhang, Juchong and Wang, Changsui. 2003. "The earliest writing? Sign use in the seventh millennium BC at Jiahu, Henan Province, China." *Antiquity* 77 (295): 31-44.

Nelson, Ethel. 1998. "The original 'unknown' god of China." *Creation* 20 (3): 50-53.

Nelson, Ethel R., and Richard E. Broadberry. 1994. *Genesis and the Mystery Confucius Couldn't Solve*. St. Louis, MO: Concordia.

Nelson, Ethel R., Richard E. Broadberry and Ginger Tong Chock. 1997. *God's Promise to the Chinese*. Lancaster, MA: Read Books.

Richardson, Don. 1974. *Peace Child*. Ventura, CA: Regal Books.

Wieger, L., S.J. 1965. *Chinese Characters: Their Origin, Etymology, History, Classification and Signification. A Thorough Study from Chinese Documents*. Translated by L. Davrout, S.J. New York, NY: Dover Publications.

Wilder, G.D., and J.H. Ingram. 1974. *Analysis of Chinese Characters*. New York, NY: Dover Publications.

Xinhua News Agency. 2000. "Oldest Chinese Characters Ever Found."Online: www.chinapage.com/archeology/2000year.html [cited 27 March, 2004].

Yu, Hsin Cheng. 1963. *Ancient Chinese History*. Taipei: Taiwan Commercial Press.

Acknowledgements

This paper was originally presented at the North Central Regional Conference of the Evangelical Missiological Society held at the Trinity Evangelical Divinity School on March 27, 2004. I am especially indebted to Dr. Robert Priest, Dr. Harold Netland, and Dr. Richard Cook for their most helpful comments on the paper. Any shortcoming in the paper, however, remains the sole responsibility of the author.

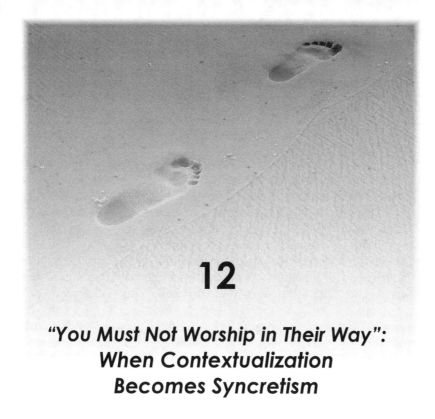

12

"You Must Not Worship in Their Way": When Contextualization Becomes Syncretism

Larry Poston

A Narrow Path

The Bible calls upon Christian evangelists, disciplemakers, and church planters to walk a very narrow path bounded by two seemingly opposed principles, one of which appears to be quite inclusivistic in implication, the other drastically exclusivistic in tone. On the one side, we find the apostle Paul's well-known words of 1 Corinthians 9:19-22:

> Though I am free and belong to no man, I make myself a slave to everyone, to win as many as possible. To the Jews I became like a Jew, to win the Jews. To those under the law I became like one under the law ... so as to win those under the law. To those not having the law I became like one not having the law ... so as to win those not having the law. To the weak I became weak, to win the weak. ***I have become all things to all men so that by all possible means I might save some*** [emphasis added].

We find in these words a profound willingness to adapt to cultural differences for the sake of winning men and women to Christ. Paul would emphasize his Jewish background when speaking to Jews (as we see him do in Acts 13:16-43). And he would set his Jewishness aside when speaking to Gentiles (as he did in Acts 17:22-31).

Now it should be obvious that Paul's use of the phrase *"all things"* cannot be taken *too* literally. There is no "blank check" here for any and all adaptive endeavors. It is certain, for instance, that the apostle would never counsel anyone to become a thief in order to win thieves, or to become a prostitute in order to win prostitutes. Concerning the prohibition of activities that are clearly pronounced by the Bible to be sinful rebellion against the laws of God, I am sure we would find little—if any—argument. But otherwise, the principle of 1 Corinthians 9—to *"become all things to all people"*—may be considered to be a biblically-approved missionary strategy. Westerners simply cannot require any and every non-Christian scattered throughout the globe to adopt Christian beliefs and practices in their Western dress. It would not be possible for such audiences to understand any more than a fraction of the meanings and purposes of such beliefs and practices. Therefore, missionary agents are called to "infiltrate" non-Christian cultures as much as they possibly can, communicating in ways that are meaningful and relevant, using such approaches as "dynamic equivalence" and the like.[1]

But once our presentation of a contextualized Gospel message has borne fruit and individuals have bowed the knee to Christ as Lord of their lives, what Biblical guidance do we have with respect to the making of disciples and to the planting of churches in other cultures? In what ways do the principles of 1 Corinthians 9 affect the Christian education of new converts and the structure of the church? In particular, what should be done with the *religious* beliefs and practices of various peoples? It is precisely at this juncture that the other side of the path we as Christians are called to walk must be

---

[1] See Eugene Nida, *Towards a Science of Translating* (Leiden: E.J. Brill, 1964), and Charles Kraft, *Christianity in Culture: A Study in Dynamic Biblical Theologizing in Cross-Cultural Perspective* (Maryknoll: Orbis, 1979).

discussed, for we find in Deuteronomy 12:1-4 a much more exclusivistic set of principles laid out for us to follow:

> These are the decrees and laws you must be careful to follow in the land that the Lord, the God of your fathers, has given you to possess—as long as you live in the land. Destroy completely all the places on the high mountains and on the hills and under every spreading tree where the nations you are dispossessing worship their gods. Break down their altars, smash their sacred stones and burn their Asherah poles in the fire; cut down the idols of their gods and wipe out their names from those places. **You must not worship the Lord your God in their way** [emphasis added].

It is clear from this command that items associated with indigenous religious systems were not only to be abandoned; they were to be obliterated. We must extend this principle, I believe, to current missiological strategy, and conclude that the importation of non-Christian religious practices into a Christian context is never to be tolerated.

It is easily demonstrated, of course, that this principle has been ignored on numerous occasions throughout the history of Christianity. For instance, it was often the case in the Middle Ages that Roman Catholic missionaries, seeking to make the conversion of European peoples to the Christian religion "easier" or to make converts feel more "comfortable" in their new faith, adopted dozens of pagan religious teachings, rituals, and practices that over time became incorporated into the Catholic faith. Loraine Boettner lists forty-five such items in his book on Catholicism. (Boettner 1962, 7-9)

Some of these items were carried over into Eastern Orthodoxy and into certain Protestant denominations as well. As a result, it is difficult for many—perhaps even most—Christians in the world today to know precisely what "Biblical Christianity" actually is. Is there in actuality a core set of beliefs and practices that are distinctly and Biblically "Christian" and form a "lowest common denominator" among Christian disciples—regardless of race, ethnicity, or nationality? Or is there no such core, and are we left with no more than an endlessly plastic and constantly changing set of beliefs and practices that are completely relative to one's historical, geographical, and cultural context?

Such questions are vital today because Christians presently appear to be in the midst of a trend which is at least partially a reaction to criticism leveled at the missionary enterprise by secular anthropologists, sociologists, and psychologists. For some time now, scholars from these academic disciplines in particular have strongly criticized what they call the "imperialistic" or "colonialistic" approaches to missions that characterized the eighteenth, nineteenth, and early twentieth centuries. While there may be some truth to these accusations in individual cases (though not nearly to the degree specified by the accusers), some contemporary Christian organizations have gone to extremes in their attempts to make amends for the past and avoid such criticism in the future.

Consequently, since the mid-twentieth century, nearly all missionary strategies have revolved around attempts to *"indigenize"* and *"contextualize"* the Christian Gospel, Christian theology, and Christian institutions. 1 Corinthians 9 has functioned as the leading Bible text for these attempts. Unfortunately, it is often the case that the principles of Deuteronomy 12 have been completely neglected, and this neglect has given rise to a number of controversial beliefs, practices, and institutions. For the purposes of this essay, I want to discuss and evaluate three such institutions that are Protestant in origin, specifically "Christian *ashrams*," "Messianic synagogues," and "Jesus mosques."

Concerning "Christian" *Ashrams*, "Messianic Synagogues," and "Jesus Mosques"

The concept of the Christian *ashram* is traced to the ministry of E. Stanley Jones (1884-1973), a missionary to India during the first half of the 20th century. Concerned that Christianity was becoming too closely identified with Western civilization and with the outcastes of the Indian subcontinent, Jones turned his attention to the upper-caste intellectuals. He began what became known as Round Table philosophical discussions with Hindu intellectuals, and adapted the Hindu communal structure known as the *ashram* to Christian purposes. Individual converts to Christianity were thus able to become part of social structures that were essentially Indian in orientation.

Jones recorded his thinking and methodologies in two books: *The Christ of the Indian Road* and *Christ at the Round Table*.

Messianic Judaism finds its origins in the Hebrew Christian Alliance, founded by Mark Levy in 1915. The movement did not gain momentum, however, until after Israel's Six-Day War in 1967, when Moishe Rosen founded the organization known as Jews for Jesus. In 1975 the Hebrew Christian Alliance changed its name to the Messianic Jewish Alliance of America, and in 1986 formed the International Alliance of Messianic Congregations and Synagogues. Although there is a wide range of practices on the part of the members of this Alliance, Messianic Jews generally will not call themselves "Christians," refuse to use the symbol of the Cross, celebrate the holidays, feasts and fasts of Old Testament Israelite religion (and do not celebrate Christian holidays such as Easter and Christmas), eat according to the Old Testament kosher laws, wear the skullcap and ritual fringes, and lead lives that to all outward appearances are indistinguishable from those of orthodox Jews. Several books have appeared regarding this movement, one of the best of which is Carol Harris-Shapiro's *Messianic Judaism* (Beacon Press, 1999).

Riding on the coattails of the Messianic Jewish Fellowships are the "Jesus mosques." "Messianic Muslims," as the adherents are referred to by some, attend what they call a mosque and pray five times daily in Arabic to Allah through 'Isa (Jesus). They continue to celebrate the fast of Ramadan, but dedicate their worship during this time period to Jesus. They eat according to the Muslim laws of *halal* (similar to the Jewish kosher laws). Advocates claim that this movement is the only viable alternative in countries where open apostasy from Islam can lead to social ostracism and even death. Articles dealing with this phenomenon include Erich Bridges' "Of 'Jesus mosques' and Muslim Christians" (*Mission Frontiers Bulletin*, July-October 1997) and Phil Parshall's "Danger! New Directions in Contextualization" (*Evangelical Missions Quarterly*, October 1998).

Generally speaking, the goal of such contextualization is to create an environment in which members of a specific culture can come to know and worship the One True God without having to cross cultural boundaries or adopt a new culture. The thinking is that if a person is allowed to keep many or even most of his or her former cultural practices after becoming a Christian, this would make Christianity much more attractive and/or "safe," and consequently the number of converts would increase dramatically. Based on 1 Corinthians 9, we can agree that this thinking is entirely valid in the case of strictly "neutral" cultural practices, by which we mean beliefs or activities about which the Bible has nothing to say. But when it comes to a convert or group of converts retaining former *religious* practices, I believe that the principles of Deuteronomy 12:1-4 forbid such an approach, for retention of religious constructs will invariably lead to syncretistic dilutions of Biblical faith. With the Deuteronomy passage in mind, let us examine more closely the three movements mentioned above.

"Christian" Ashrams

Earl Stanley Jones was variously lauded and criticized for his Round Table Conferences and for his Christian Ashrams. His philosophy of contextualization included eliminating usage of the Old Testament as generally irrelevant for Christian evangelists working in the Church Age. Christ alone should be the subject of the Gospel message, and since the Old Testament does not speak of Christ in any full or complete sense, it can with justification and without harm be laid aside.

The Round Table conferences were a venue for philosophical discussions with Hindu intellectuals, utilizing a style that was popular among casted Indians. Discussions which began with philosophy but which soon bridged over into spirituality and theology were held while seated on the floor of a room in a circle. Here we find nothing specifically religious in orientation, as no worship or formalized teaching takes place. These discussion groups can therefore be seen as a proper adaptation to a specific cultural style of learning—nothing more.

The Ashram concept, however, is more difficult to evaluate. Jones modeled his Christian Ashrams on a specifically Hindu community concept. In both, residents (called "the family") would rise at 5:30 a.m. and pursue a daily schedule that included private devotions, manual labor, group discussions, and one day per week of complete silence. Would such a structure be specifically religious in orientation and violate the principle of Deuteronomy 12? Or, since Hinduism is such a broad and diffuse religious system, could the adoption of a structure that is in many ways similar to the early Christian community as recorded in Acts be considered justifiable? Jones was criticized for his "weak" view of the institutional church, which he considered a "relative" structure. But does the New Testament give a clear enough picture of exactly what a "Christian church structure" must actually be? My own judgment is that it does not, and I would essentially side with Jones in this area. As to the ashram concept, it perhaps toes the line of appropriateness, but I would consider that of the three movements we are examining, Jones's ashrams are the least troubling.

"Messianic Synagogues"

Far more problematic, I think, are the Messianic Jewish movements that have sprung up throughout the United States, particularly since the 1970s. Contemporary converts from Judaism to Christianity who seek to preserve their "Jewishness" usually invoke the 1 Corinthians 9 passage (*"to the Jews I became like a Jew"*) and claim that missiological strategies involving indigenization and contextualization allow for—and even require—certain indigenous *cultural* characteristics to be retained by converts. They justify retention of their Jewishness by classifying their activities and customs as strictly *cultural*. But problematic is the fact that for many, "retaining Jewishness" also means retaining *religious* customs derived from the Mosaic covenant or from the rabbinic Judaism that has been developed since A.D. 70.

I would contend first of all that the practices of rabbinic Judaism have been developed by Jews in a state of unbelief, and therefore they should be treated no differently than the practices of other non-Christian religions. The development of a "portable Judaism" by Johanan ben Zakkai, his school at Jabneh, and others represents a purely humanistic religious development that retains certain elements of Old Testament Judaism but which goes beyond these and, in many cases, completely reinterprets them. Certain rituals in connection with holidays, the development of and dependence upon Talmudic commentary—all of these items have appeared completely separately from the revelation of the One True God. I believe that for Messianic Jews to retain any of these items would be a clear violation of the principles of

Deuteronomy 12. A case in point: rabbinic Judaism requires a Jewish male to wear a skullcap (yarmulke) when participating in a synagogue assembly. Prayers and other religious activities are to be carried out while wearing the cap. The New Testament, on the other hand, forbids a male to wear any kind of head covering while performing religious functions (1 Corinthians 11: 4). When forced to choose between the two conflicting traditions, which will the Messianic Jew follow? The rabbinical practice, or the New Testament principle? In every case that I am personally aware of, the rabbinical practice has been followed to the exclusion of the New Testament practice—and this I find to be enormously problematic.

As for practices derived from the Mosaic Law, the book of Hebrews pronounces such practices to be *obsolete* (Hebrews 8:13), and no more than *shadows* in comparison with the spiritual realities entrusted to the Church (Hebrews 10:1-10). Should one continue to participate in or celebrate "shadows" when real substance is available? To continue to use that which the Bible calls "obsolete" is, I believe, at best questionable, and at worst foolish. By Jesus' own command, new wine is not to be put into old wineskins, and an old garment is not to be patched with cloth from a new one (Matthew 9:16-17). Retaining Jewish, Muslim, or Hindu "wineskins" (or medieval Catholic or Orthodox "wineskins" for that matter) would be in direct violation of precepts taught by Jesus Himself.

Some would defend Messianic Judaism by claiming "special privilege" for those of a Jewish background. Given their culture's basic rootedness in Biblical revelation, coupled with their horrific experiences with Gentile Christians in the course of Church History, some have been willing to be more tolerant of their attempts to maintain a slowly dissipating culture. What harm does it really do? I can suggest three problems in particular. First is the vehement hatred for Messianic Judaism that Orthodox, Hasidic, and Conservative Jews hold. While some Messianic Jews hold that their contextualization has brought a large number of Jews to Christ, other observers have noted that an equally large or even greater number have been lost to the Gospel message due to their disgust with the adherents of the movement.

Second, there is the danger of violating the principle of Ephesians 2:11-21 and Galatians 3:28 (to be discussed in detail later). The apostle Paul makes it very clear in this context that Christians form a "third race," the members of which may no longer be distinguished as either "Jew" or "Gentile." All such earthly distinctions are no longer to be applied in the case of the members of the Body of Christ.

Finally, there is the danger of creating confusion on the part of other believers. I well remember attending the wedding of one of my students several years ago. Most of the ceremony was conducted by a Protestant minister. However, after the couple had been pronounced "husband and wife," a Messianic rabbi, in full Jewish garb, came forward from the rear of the church and blessed the couple in a very stylized and formal fashion, all in the Hebrew language. The "buzzing" that went on in the pews around me was significant: "Is he [the groom] Jewish? Or is it she [the bride]?" "I thought they were both Christians ..." "Why is an evangelical Christian marrying a Jew?" And so it went—even throughout the reception afterwards. I am sure that the couple felt that they were doing something meaningful and significant, although to me it smacked of the "trendiness" and "faddishness" into which Evangelicals seem entirely too prone to fall. To guests, however, this retention of non-Christian religious rituals was enormously confusing.

"Jesus Mosques"

Of the three movements under discussion, the most disturbing to me is the "Jesus mosque" phenomenon. Within this movement, some missionaries call themselves "Muslims," and new believers are never referred to as "Christians" or "converts." They remain "Muslims." In keeping with this policy, baptisms are often either delayed or dispensed with altogether, since this practice serves to segregate new believers from their society. Nor do new believers associate with historic Christian churches in countries where such communities exist.

Islamic forms of worship are retained, including worship in structures called "mosques." The five daily prayers are prayed, at the exact times that the Muslims pray. The main worship service is held on Friday, as is the custom of Islam, rather than on Sunday.

By all accounts, the same problems noted above in connection with Messianic Judaism are present with the "Jesus mosque" movement. Muslim leaders are outraged by such a missionary philosophy, considering it deceptive and unworthy of "spiritually-minded" persons. Other Muslims see followers of 'Isa (Jesus) as simply a new mystical, Sufi sect—one more of the many hundreds of such movements. For Muslim Christians, there is no sense of "separation," or of being "called out of darkness into light," as the New Testament so clearly directs (2 Corinthians 6:14-18). In the minds of many, there is no question but what this phenomenon is syncretistic in its very essence. The fact that some who advocate its use justify it by an appeal to "the Lord's leading" or to the fact that "it works" does not mitigate the movement's essential violation of the principles of Deuteronomy 12.

Towards a Contextualization That Avoids Syncretism

How can we as Christian ministers walk upon the fine line between the principles found in 1 Corinthians 9 and Deuteronomy 12? Let me suggest the following procedure.

First, we must *determine to the best of our ability what are the actual religious practices and religious objects of a particular culture that are purely religious in nature.* In other words, what are the items, culture by culture, that are equivalent to the prohibited items listed in Deuteronomy 12:2-4.

Generally speaking, we have here both *places* and *objects* that are identified as belonging to a particular religious system. With respect to "places," we would have to include all natural locations, as well as all humanly constructed buildings. Structures that are identified by the culture at large with a non-Christian religion (i.e., a mosque, a temple, a synagogue) would

A Closer Look At Deuteronomy 12:2-4

- **places** where false gods are served (v. 2), whether these be on "high mountains," "on hills," or "under green trees."
- **altars**
- **sacred pillars**
- **wooden images**
- **carved images of gods**
- **names of gods**

therefore be prohibited to adherents of Biblical Christianity.

"Altars" would include any piece of furniture, whether natural or manmade, that is used for sacrifices, prayer ceremonies, or the like. "Sacred pillars, wooden images, and carved representations of gods" would include any pieces of an architectural or artistic nature that would be connected by adherents of the culture at large with the worship of non-Christian deities. And the names of false deities must be carefully filtered so that neither the specific names nor the deities that such represent are retained in some "Christian" form.

Secondly, *we must identify aspects of culture which, although connected with non-Christian religious systems to some extent, are nevertheless of a general enough nature to allow use by contextualizers of the Gospel.* This step will require careful study on the part of missionary agents over a period of time, most likely several months or even years. While some may scoff at the idea of taking such a long period of time when souls are being lost, the time spent will be well worth the risk if study and subsequent strategizing will produce a church that is Biblically contextualized instead of a heretically syncretistic. The following applications might be seen as appropriate.

- Being prohibited from worshiping God in buildings that would be identified with non-Christian systems by casual observers from the general culture, we might instead opt either for a return to the house church model of the New Testament, or the establishment of a building that lacks the specific characteristics of the indigenous non-Christian religious structure. In a Muslim country, for instance, we would not meet in a building that boasts a minaret and a dome, topped by the crescent symbol of Islam. In a Jewish context, we would not meet in a building decorated with Stars of David. In a Hindu context, we would not assemble in buildings that resemble in form the towering, sweeping forms of Hindu temples, decorated with sculptures or frescoes of the various gods and goddesses. We would in each case opt for a location that would be clearly Christian (i.e., demarcated by a cross, dove, fish, or other historic symbol of the Christian faith), or in contexts where such demarcation would be clearly dangerous for believers, we would opt for a plain location with no external markers of any kind.

- If an altar is used in the Christian worship service at all, it should be constructed in such a way that no possible connections exist with altars which members of the general culture associate with indigenous religions. For instance, if the religious altars of a country are rectangular, white, and contain baskets of fruits and nuts in addition to candles and/or incense, then Christians might construct their altars of natural wood, round in shape, and unadorned save perhaps with a copy of the Bible.

- Since "graven images" are prohibited by the Christian scriptures, it would perhaps be best to dispense altogether with artistic renderings of Biblical figures. This would include popular renderings of Jesus and his disciples.

- With respect to names, we will be forced to deal with the linguistic problems inherent in Bible translation. For example, we must—when possible—make every effort to distinguish between generic and specific terms for "God." Admittedly this can be problematic. An early example from the Bible is the use of "Elohim" by the Hebrews for the supreme deity; this is a term that was perhaps more commonly used among pagans than many translators would be comfortable with today. Abraham's use of "El-Elyon" would be another instance. With respect to modern languages, we are forced either to transliterate a word from one of our own (usually Western) languages, essentially creating a new word in an existing language, or to use a word that currently exists and give it new meaning. An example of the latter is the usage of the term "Allah" when translating the Bible into Arabic, and the use of "Shang-Di" in many of the earlier translations of the Scriptures into the Chinese language. Fortunately, one is not always forced to choose between these two alternatives. A third option is sometimes available, and we are fortunate when such options exist. An example would be the early Christian's use of the Greek term "theos" as the name of the One True God, as opposed to a more specific form such as "Zeus." The latter would clearly connote to a citizen of the Roman Empire a pagan deity, while the former is a generic term to which new meaning could be given with far less difficulty.

Thirdly, *in making the kinds of decisions that I discuss above, indigenous converts to the faith must be given an active role in determining which aspects of indigenous religious practice are of a general enough nature to be retained, and those that must definitely be discarded.* This is important for the reason that those who are enculturated in a specific context will better be able to say what certain religious forms might connote to the typical member of a culture. It is doubtful that expatriates will be able to discern the finer points within a reasonable amount of time.

At the same time, care must be exercised here. It is well-known that new converts often react to their former life context in ways more extreme than what the Bible actually warrants. In their desire to make as complete a break as possible with their former lives, they will often discard things that would not necessarily be essential to discard, if we use Deuteronomy 12 as our template. In such cases, missionary agents must gently but firmly introduce the principles of Romans 14 and 1 Corinthians 8 to these new believers. As Paul indicates in 1 Corinthians 8, eating meat offered to idols is a nonsensical concept, because idols are meaningless pieces of stone or wood. During the elementary stages of the Christian life, eating such meat might be problematic because of the left-over conditioning of an individual's conscience, but growing maturity would require that one abandon such squeamishness.

Finally, *we must trust that the Holy Spirit is quite capable of preserving the integrity of new Christian movements and preventing syncretistic developments.* There is always risk when engaging in missionary activity in the way that conservative Evangelicals generally do. This is so because we are in favor of endlessly *translating* our message, rather than insisting that outsiders conform to a single imperialistically imposed model of the Christian faith and life. But such a missionary philosophy means that we will never have the amount of control over our undertakings that we might naturally like to have—and we will need to be prepared to entrust our new disciples to the Holy Spirit's care.

A "Christian Culture"?

Most good parents eventually learn the psychological principle of substitution: it is infinitely easier to forbid a child to do something if one can offer an attractive alternative in place of the undesirable item. I believe that we can use this same principle in the context of our current discussion, and I would like therefore to propose the following "substitution" for forms of contextualization that have involved the retention of indigenous religious practices.

First we must gain the special perspective found in Paul's letter to the Ephesians. In speaking of some of the implications of conversion, Paul offers a marvelous portrait of what new members of the Body of Christ have actually become.

> For he himself is our peace, who has made the two one and has destroyed the barrier, the dividing wall of hostility, by abolishing in his flesh the law with its commandments and regulations. **His purpose was to create in himself one new man out of the two**, thus making peace… (Ephesians 2:14-15) [emphasis added].

In this passage we find that a new "man" has been created in Christ (verse 15). What Paul is referring to here is a new race; a "third race," if you will, that is to be distinguished from the two "Biblical" categories of humankind: Jew and Gentile. Members of the third race do not bear the characteristics of either category. Paul extends this idea when he says to the Galatians: "*You are all sons of God through faith in Christ Jesus, for all of you who were baptized into Christ have clothed yourselves with Christ. There is neither Jew nor Greek, slave nor free, male nor female, for you are all one in Christ Jesus*" (Galatians 3:26-28).

I contend that the New Testament gives us guidelines and parameters for how this "third race" should be characterized, at both the individual and the collective levels. In other words, I believe that there are enough principles sprinkled throughout the New Testament writings for us to determine what might be called the "culture" of this new race; a specifically "Christian culture."

Let me propose that before we begin thinking about *adapting* to specific cultures, we instead make it our goal to think in terms of a *global* or *universal* "Christian culture." Each of us needs first to define *an individual Christian lifestyle* for himself/herself and, second, to determine an appropriate *social structure through which several individuals can together hone and sharpen their beliefs and practices as well as organize for specific activities.* The centuries-long debate regarding the relation of "Christ" to "culture" (Niebuhr 1956) reveals the difficulties of arriving at a consensus regarding either lifestyle or structure, but the point at which Christians divide is easy to ascertain: *the authority and interpretation of the Bible.* Only those believers who share the conviction that the Bible is the inspired Word of God, that it must be interpreted according to a grammatical-historical hermeneutic, and that it must function as their chief—if not sole—authority in matters of belief and practice will have an adequate foundation for the construction of a truly Christian culture.

Given a strong commitment to the Bible, we find abundant directives—such as those listed above—for the development of both an individual lifestyle and a local social structure. But we will need to:

1. collect and systematize these directives;
2. develop a generic model or pattern for believers to follow in the areas of individual discipleship and social interaction;
3. communicate and teach both the above-mentioned directives and model; and
4. develop an authority structure and means of accountability agreed to by and binding upon all.

If the above procedure is followed by properly motivated Christian individuals, the resulting Christian "culture" will not be specifically "Western," "Semitic," "patriarchal" or the like. At the same time, we should not be troubled by or apologize for the fact that "Christian culture" may well contain characteristics which some would identify as "Western," "Semitic," or "patriarchal," mainly because many aspects of such orientations are rooted in Biblical revelation.

At what levels of human society should we seek to implement our directives and model? If we posit a scale of all the "levels" of human concern that are possible, we can suggest the following five: individual, nuclear and extended family, local community, national (or tribal), and international (global). I contend that a universal "Christian culture" can truly exist *only* at the first three of the above-mentioned levels, namely the *individual*, the *family*, and the *local community*. I do not believe that it is possible to find practical ways in which New Testament Christianity can be implemented at either the *national* or *global* levels of humanity. I realize that such has not been the conviction of a large number of Christians within the history of the Church, but I believe that all attempts to establish Christendom at the national or global levels have resulted in the establishment of structures which are not only alien to the teachings of the New Testament, but which are in most cases fundamentally opposed to and even destructive of New Testament Christianity.

Having said as much let me give several examples of what I would consider to be foundational aspects of "Christian culture."

- With respect to *politics*, New Testament Christian culture is informed by the teachings of Paul and Peter as found in Romans 13:1-7 and 1 Peter 2:13-14. Generally speaking, these passages require submission and obedience to "kings," "governors," and in general, "every authority instituted among men." Christians are called to function within whatever political structure is in place in their country of residence, and are to consider that structure as in some sense instituted by God Himself. While some would object that totalitarian or dictatorial regimes should not be included here, it should be remembered that the words of Paul and Peter were penned to persons residing under the Roman Emporium. Even in such cases, rebellion against constituted authority is not permissible for a Christian.

- With respect to *economics*, New Testament Christian culture requires one to pay his or her taxes to the governmental structure that exists (Romans 13:6-7). Christians are to "work with their hands" (1 Thessalonians 4:11-12), and are never to be found in a state of idleness (2 Thessalonians 3:6-12). Those who have pursued unethical or criminal activities are to abandon them for honest work (Ephesians 4:28). Insofar as possible, Christians are not to be dependent upon others for their material support (1 Thessalonians 4:12). At the same time, believers are to care for other believers who are less fortunate than they in terms of material blessings (James 1:27, 2:14-17).

- With respect to the *judiciary*, New Testament Christian culture requires Christians to obey the laws of the land in which they live (Romans 13:1-7) and to settle legal disputes between each other without going to secular courts of law (1 Corinthians 6:1-8).

- *Anthropologically*, New Testament Christian culture is endogamous, requiring that marriage arrangements be made between believers only (2 Corinthians 6:14-18).

- *Morally*, New Testament Christian culture requires a strict sexual ethic and forbids premarital, extramarital, and homosexual relations (1 Thessalonians 4:3-8, Galatians 5:19, Romans 1:26-27). A Christian is not permitted to marry, partner with, or deeply befriend a non-Christian (2 Corinthians 6:14-18).

- *Ethically*, New Testament Christian culture requires strict adherence to truth-telling, and forsaking of all forms of lying (Ephesians 4:25).

While several more examples could be suggested in addition to those mentioned above, I want to turn our attention to specifically *religious* practices, which from the standpoint of our essay are perhaps the most vital to discuss. We find several passages in the New Testament that give us the *religious* essentials of our "Christian culture."

- With respect to ritual worship practices, we find that the New Testament Christians engaged in the following:

    1. A service commemorating the death, burial, and resurrection of Christ, consisting of "drinking from the cup" and "breaking the bread" (1 Corinthians 10:14-17; 11:17-34).
    2. Water baptisms, which were performed for new converts to the Christian faith (1 Corinthians 13-16).

3. The singing of "psalms, hymns and spiritual songs," to be sung to the Lord (Ephesians 5:19).

4. The "assembling of Christians together," not as an option, but in obedience to a clear command (Hebrews 10:24-25).

5. Giving ample opportunity to a variety of congregants to participate; each coming to the assembly with a "hymn, a word of instruction, a revelation, a tongue or an interpretation" (1 Corinthians 14:26).

6. Worship practices that were kept orderly, both in terms of the number of participants and the ways in which their contributions are to be expressed (1 Corinthians 14:26-33).

7. Participation by both genders in worship assemblies, in accordance with New Testament directives (i.e., 1 Corinthians 11:5, 14:34-35).

- With respect to *leadership*, the New Testament speaks of two official positions: an overseer (*episkopos,* or *presbuteros*) and a deacon/deaconess. Qualifications for these offices, as well as at least some of the functions of both, are found in 1 Timothy 3:1-13, and Titus1:6-9. These offices may be "desired" by any and all (1 Timothy 3:1); no other requirements existed for them other than conformity to the standards contained in the passages listed above.

- With respect to a *meeting place*, the New Testament shows the earliest Christians meeting daily "in the Temple courts" and "from house to house" (Acts 2:46). The former was, of course, never an option for anyone living outside of Jerusalem, and after AD 70 was not an option for anyone. "House churches" were the norm almost until the time when Christianity was made a legal religion in the Empire under Constantine in AD 313. We find Paul meeting with Christians in a "lecture hall of Tyrannus" in Acts 19:9, and it is likely that spontaneous "open air" meetings by rivers, seashores, or other places where people regularly gathered were a common occurrence. There is never, however, any mention of a "temple-like" structure for meetings of members of "the third race." The "temple of God" is always spoken of as either the individual Christian physical self (1 Corinthians 6:19-20), or the sum total of the living members of the Body of Christ (Ephesians 2:19-22).

Beyond the items noted above, little else is said in the way of religious accoutrements. Nothing is mentioned, for instance, about the need for specialized clothing or a uniform. Nothing is said regarding particular pieces of furniture (i.e., an altar), or implements to be used in worship (i.e., brass offering plates). We are left, then, with a somewhat skeletal description of practices in the earliest days, and the question we must answer is whether or not we are permitted to go beyond what the New Testament contains. If the answer to this question is "yes" (and the majority of Christians in the history of the Church have so answered), the next question becomes "how far can we go?"

I would like to propose that for our disciple-making and church planting in any culture, we *begin* with the items outlined above. These can serve as a foundation for the establishment of Christianity in a new culture. We should be careful *not* to insist upon the importation of any other item into a new culture beyond the ones mentioned above. Discipling and church planting should involve studies of the passages listed above, and the development of these generic practices within each cultural setting. Christians should seek to impress upon new members of the Body of Christ the same idea reflected by Paul in 1 Corinthians 11:16: "*If anyone wants to be contentious about this, we have no other practice, nor do the churches of God.*" In other words, this is what we *all* do.

Simultaneously, from the beginning of our work within a new culture we must teach the precepts of Deuteronomy 12:1-4, and exhort new converts to designate very carefully what items from their former religion(s) must be completely avoided. Pursuing the two of these lines of thinking and teaching, we will have established a foundation on which to build, and at the same time will have established parameters and limitations with respect to how that foundation is built upon and adapted to a new culture. A series of statements such as the following could form the basis of a working model for missiological implementation:

1. We will meet together in a building—but it will not be a building like thus and so that would be clearly recognizable as a temple, or a mosque, etc.
2. We will develop a worship style that suits our own temperament and personalities—but this style will be distinct from the worship styles of our indigenous religions, so that no participant in Christian worship will be reminded of previous activities.
3. We will compose and sing "psalms, hymns, and spiritual songs" that utilize our own forms of music—but they will have no relation to music utilized in our former religious practices.

Once these Christian cultural aspects have been defined and have become operational in specific situations, missionary agents will be able to develop concrete goals for the contextualization of their evangelism, disciplemaking, and church planting among adherents of a non-Christian religious grouping. Rather than Christians finding it necessary to adapt themselves and their message in a haphazard fashion to a multiplicity of cultures, they will instead be able to extend an invitation and call for conversion to an alternative cultural structure and lifestyle that at its most fundamental level will be valid for any and all peoples. In such a way the Church can return to its Biblical mandate to be "salt and light" to the cultures of the world, while simultaneously avoiding the dangers of syncretism.

Sources Cited

Boettner, Loraine. 1962. *Roman Catholicism*. Philadelphia: Presbyterian and Reformed Publishing Company.

Bridges, Erich. 1997. "Of 'Jesus Mosques' and Muslim Christians." *Mission Frontiers Bulletin*. July-October.

Harris-Shapiro, Carol. 1999. *Messianic Judaism*. Boston: Beacon Press.

Jones, E. Stanley. 1928. *Christ at the Round Table*. London: Hodder and Stoughton.

_____. 1930. *The Christ of the Indian Road*. London: Hodder and Stoughton.

Kraft, Charles. 1979. *Christianity in Culture: A Study in Dynamic Biblical Theologizing in Cross-Cultural Perspective*. Maryknoll: Orbis.

Nida, Eugene. 1964. *Towards a Science of Translating*. Leiden: E.J. Brill.

Niebuhr, H. Richard. 1956. *Christ and Culture*. New York: Harper-Colophon Books.

Parshall, Phil. 1998. "Danger! New Directions in Contextualization." *Evangelical Missions Quarterly*. October.

13

Legalism – Syncretism from Within: A Challenge in the Romanian Church

Cristian Barbosu

Syncretism has been generally defined as the "replacement or dilution of the essential truths of the Gospel through the incorporation of non-Christian elements" (Moreau 2000, 924). This definition describes syncretism in terms of its results, but limits its means solely to non-Christian elements adulterating and weakening the Gospel truth. Is syncretism exclusively generated by heathen agents or do Christians unknowingly sink into syncretism by declaring human customs to be the will of God, thus polluting or replacing the essential core of the Gospel? Is there a syncretism from within

> **"One of the lessons of history is that no Christian community is exempt from the perils of legalism, and Christians need to be continually reminded of its roots, masks and consequences"**
>
> Wayne Boulton (1982, 113)

(the Christian faith) rather than only from without (other religions or cultures)? This chapter is an attempt to present legalism, as a Christian element having the potential of leading believers into syncretism and affecting the very heart of the Gospel. It draws on the legalistic beliefs and practices found in some of the Romanian Evangelical Churches as supportive illustrations of the thesis proposed.

Description of the Study

Legalism[1] is the old "in-house" danger of the Christian church. I define it[2] as the *ethical-religious theory that prescribes an excessive conformity to an external religious code by which one may earn or secure his salvation.*[3] This type of syncretism is widespread not only among Evangelical churches in Eastern Europe[4] but also in many churches throughout the world. This study focuses on legalistic beliefs and practices found in some of the Baptist churches of Western Romania, in the province of Crişana,[5] the "cradle of

---

[1] The term "legalist" is argued to have been first used by Edward Fisher in a tract entitled "The Marrow of Modern Divinity" published in 1645 to designate the person who "bringeth the Law into the case of Justification" (Jackson 1979, 1-22).

[2] I do not define it as in the monistic New Testament scholarship debates, where it has to do with the interpretations of the Mosaic Law (Dunn 1985; Gundry 1996; Moo 1983; and Schreiner 1993). Neither do I define it as my compatriot Mircea Eliade does, as the ancient Chinese school of political philosophy (1987, 8:497-99) nor like Joseph Fletcher uses it in his "Situation Ethics" (1966, 27).

[3] This is a combination of several definitions: (Clark 1973, 385), (Macquarrie 1967, 195), (Smith 1921, 257) and (Merriam-Webster Collegiate Dictionary 1993, 664). Legalism is "the theory that moral conduct consists in following the rules" according to Judith Shklar, (1964, 1). A similar usage of legalism can be found in a number of works discussing similar topics from South and Central America (Alves 1985), (Baker 1999), (Padilla 1986).

[4] Legalism became the "label" used by various worldwide missionary and theological circles to describe one of the major weaknesses of the evangelical church in Eastern Europe (Ukraine, Romania, Russia, Moldova, etc.). This state of being is rather strange for the church in Eastern Europe, which has become a stronghold of faith on a deeply secular European continent (Kuzmic 1983, 503). One needs to be careful, however, of the tendency that exists in many Western churches (especially those propagating an antinomianistic faith and practice) to abuse this term, labeling anyone who upholds to certain standards of Christian living as a legalist.

[5] Currently Romania has the third-highest number of evangelicals in Europe (Johnstone 2001, 536). Crişana is the Western part of Transylvania alongside the Hungarian border and has the highest conglomeration of evangelical believers

the Romanian Baptists" (Stanculescu 2002, 90). This chapter is a work in process, intended to lay the groundwork for further more careful research. It is based on some exploratory qualitative research, including interviews, questionnaires, participant observation and experiences gathered from my years of pastoral ministry in this part of Romania. It is motivated by the love[6] and deep concern I have for my own Romanian brothers (Rom.9:1-4) of whom some are either entangled or struggling with legalism in their churches.[7] My heart bleeds for Romania and for God's churches and His servants of Eastern Europe, and although at risk, I took the initiative to expose this danger.

> **"The naked word severed from its context, is to have the same status which a statement of law has for a lawyer. In other words, this way of dealing with Scripture which treats it and its contents as a code of so-and-so-many established propositions which people must believe because it is the Word of God is legalism."**
>
> J.P. Koehler (1969, 140)

This study describes examples, possible roots and consequences of legalism. It is a descriptive study with brief prescriptive insights. The purpose of the presentation is to reveal the syncretistic danger of legalism using my own personal interactions in Romania as a realistic example of this issue. As a secondary purpose I urge anyone interested or involved in Eastern Europe (particularly Romania), to pray and help those churches that propagate legalistic beliefs to understand its severe consequences and preserve the essentials of the Gospel.

Since legalism as syncretism is broad topic, I chose to focus my presentation on what I call *Scripture-justified syncretism*. Bible-justified syncretism is a form of legalism that is

---

(particularly Baptists and Pentecostals) in Romania. According to the 2002 Census, in the city of Arad (172,000 people) there are approximately 17,000 adult baptized evangelicals (without the youth and children) including almost 8,000 Baptists.

[6] The Romanian church alone gave several hundred martyrs during the Communist regime (http://www.orthodoxnews.netfirms.com/Romanian, "Romanian Christian Churches Prepare List of Communist-Era Martyrs," *Orthodox News*, February, 3rd 2004).

[7] "Although Romania has one of the largest evangelical Christian communities in Europe, years of persecution, despair, legalism and internal division have generally left the church weakened and lacking in vision" (OM report 2002).

birthed in and by the church, accompanied by an intense religious zeal and based on sets of biblical proof-texts used to form and justify an ethical-religious external code by which the church judges one's salvation.[8]

This particular type of legalism tends to change the church's focus from the Christological conversion to a cultural/ecclesiastical conversion; from a grace-led commitment to our Lord and Savior to a law-enforced commitment to the non-written Ecclesiastical Code; from the fruit of the Spirit that needs to accompany one's salvation to lists of external rules; from preaching the Gospel for salvation to preaching a set of rules for salvation. The seeker or Christian is led to believe that his salvation is theoretically by "grace through faith" but practically achieved by his works of obedience to a strict ethical and religious code focused on externals, taught and sometimes imposed by the church. Therefore it is dangerous because of its serious soteriological implications. It is deceitful because it uses the Scripture to justify its ends. Hence, I call this type of legalism *syncretism from within,* or Scripture-justified syncretism, because it affects the very heart of the Gospel.

SIDEBAR 1

EXAMPLES AND "PROOF TEXTS" OF LEGALISTIC RULES USED TO JUDGE ONE'S SALVATION ("POCĂINŢĂ")

- Wearing of head coverings – 1 Cor. 11 (hats, scarves, head bands, or the classic *batic/ babushka*)
- No jewelry – 1Pet. 3:3, 1Tim. 2:9
- Total abstinence from smoking - 1Cor. 6:12
- Total abstinence from alcohol – Rom. 14:21
- Listening or playing contemporary Christian music (drums, electric guitars, etc.) - Ephes. 5:19

---

[8] I find it necessary to mention here that I personally know believers and churches who adopt high moral codes and traditions that border or are based on legalistic beliefs and practices but who do not condition someone's salvation on these rules. I personally respect their convictions in this regard.

SIDEBAR 2

"PROOF TEXT" LEGALISTIC RULES OFTEN USED TO JUDGE SOMEONE'S SANCTIFICATION

- No long hair for men – 1 Cor. 11:14
- No pants for women – Deut. 22:5
- No moving of feet, hands or body in the church when music plays – Eccl. 5:1
- No communion when women are menstruating Lev. 15:19-33
- A mother cannot come to church or take communion for six to eight weeks after she has given birth - Lev. 12:1-8
- No smiles or jokes from the pulpit – the Bible never specifies that Jesus smiled; also in 2 Cor. 7:9 repentance is associated with sorrow
- Women are not allowed to speak or teach in the church – 1 Cor. 14:34; 1Tim. 2:11-12
- The preachers must wear a suit and a tie when they stand in the pulpit – Exod.39

The examples presented in Sidebars 1 and 2 are just a few, to give an idea of the issues at hand. They are spread in various churches, but not in all of them. If until a few years ago, such practices and many others have been widely spread, today, in Romania, there are more and more Baptist and other Evangelical churches that want to come out of legalism. Many of these practices have been inherited from a cultural framework, therefore a discussion on contextualization is necessary at this point.

Context: origins and practices

I am a true believer in contextualization.[9] I strongly

---

[9] The process of accommodating the gospel to local situations (cultures) helps the message be relevant and impact the lives of the people from that culture. In other words, the worldview of that people provides a framework for communication. The questions and needs of that people are a guide to the emphasis of the message. It should be noticed, however, that while the form in which the message is presented may be ever-changing (accommodating), the content of biblical revelation is unchanging (Gilliland 2000, 225-27; Osborne 1991).

believe that Jesus and the apostles, proclaimed and practiced contextualization, understanding the integrative aspect of biblical truth into one's culture. They properly accommodated themselves and their presentations of the biblical message to the cultural context of those to whom they ministered, without altering the essence of the Christian message.[10]

Paul's trip to Jerusalem is one of the greatest examples of this kind. Paul—the apostle of freedom, the proclaimer of grace, the one who had courage to speak against the Law, the land and the Jews (Acts 21:28), who was willing to suffer even to the point of near-death by the hands of the Judaizers for not compromising his convictions and message—contextualized himself when he arrived in Jerusalem (Acts 21). Why? Because the church of Jerusalem was very "Jewish" in its life-style and ecclesiology,[11] perpetuating a high view of the Torah, dietary laws and even circumcision.[12] On the advice of James (the leader of the church), Paul joined four other Jews, performed ritual purifications in the Temple for seven days, (some argue that he even took a Nazarite vow), and paid for the sacrifices required, thus conforming to the normal Jewish practices of his day.[13]

Paul exemplifies the process of contextualization at its best. The culture and its norms are significant for Christian

---

[10] See Marshall 1980; Priest 1994; Priest 1997; Nicholls 1979; Kraft 1979; Hesselgrave 1979.

[11] The literature on the existence and of a Jerusalem-Jewish (Petrine) form and a Gentile (Pauline) form of Christianity is extensive and the debates abound. I recommend few books on this subject: James D.G. Dunn, *The Parting of the Ways: Between Christianity and Judaism and Their Significance for the Character of Christianity* (London: SCM Press, 1991), Vincent Martin, *A House Divided: The Parting of the Ways between Synagogue and Church*, Studies in Judaism and Christianity (New York: Paulist Press, 1995)., SCHNABEL Terence V. Smith, *Petrine Controversies in Early Christianity*, Wissenschaftliche Untersuchungen Zum Neuen Testament 2. Reihe, ed. Martin Hengel (Tubingen: J.C.B. Mohr, 1985), Nicholas Taylor, *Paul, Antioch and Jerusalem*, Journal for the Study of the New Testament Supplement Series 66 (Shefield, UK: JSOT Press, 1992).

[12] It is important to notice, however, that they did not compromise in their soteriology, the "pillars" (James, John and Peter) agreed with Paul in those matters (Gal.2:2,9; Acts 15), with the exception of the Judaizers with whom they disassociated (Acts 15:24).

[13] In Acts 16:3 Paul circumcised Timothy in Philippi for the sake of his ministry among the Jews.

outreach and way of life. That is why it is important to understand that the legalistic *framework* and its *tendencies* have their possible origins and causes in the geographical and historical mold of the Romanian evangelical faith. Many of them are influenced by and inherited from various sources.

The Romanian Orthodox Church

Many evangelical believers have been converted out of an Orthodox background that is soteriologically based on works and therefore places high and diverse demands on people (church duties, scale of virtues, specific behaviors and apparel). Some of the evangelical churches have basically converted the Orthodox principle of works into high Protestant ethics, which act more or less the same way. You can please God and inherit the kingdom not by obeying the Orthodox canons, but by conforming to the ecclesiastical code imposed by the specific Baptist church you attend. As a culture embedded in Orthodoxy for 2,000 years, Romania has its central core rooted in moral discourse defined by claims of righteousness manifested in external behavior. This is clearly seen in the evangelical sub-culture. An Orthodox influence is also present in the traditions "rânduielile bisericii" of the church. The Orthodox Church is known for its high view of the rituals and un-altered conservation of its traditions (their prominent liturgy is still the one practiced by Chrysostom in the fourth century A.D.). In many instances, when asked why he keeps "x" tradition, some Baptist believers will respond with a distorted quotation of 1 Cor. 14:33: "God is a God of order – un Dumnezeul al rânduielilor." Such "rânduieli" (rules and traditions) have become the "sacred cows" (as a Romanian pastor put it) of some of the Romanian Baptists. Based on them some believers and even some churches are accepted or rejected from some Evangelical communities.

Romanian cultural norms

Romania is a traditionalistic society where the inherited customs, "datini stramosesti," play an important role. Its primary focus is on the values of the "past," on what "has been," and as a result there is a suspicious and reluctant attitude toward what's new. Anything that comes from the West or is new in form or content is labeled "lumesc" (worldly) or "liberal" (liberal).[14] In addition, the Romanians have historically been known to be very religious[15] and focused on the external behaviors while neglecting the internals in church as well as in society. A historical collection of written impressions from foreign emissaries to Romania between 1500-1700s shows that Romanians were seen by the outsiders as very superstitious and religious people, who strictly kept numerous rules and traditions while at the same time covered multitudes of sins (Franco Sivori – 1588; Marco Bandini – 1648; Paul de Alep – 1653; Erasmus Schneider von Weismantel – 1713; Giovani Frontalo – 1764) (quoted in Barbu 2000, 15-34).

Balkanization

Romania's geographical position, which inevitably places us in the Balkanic group (although we are Latin), is an influential factor. But *balkanization* never had a positive connotation. For example, Balkanic misogynism undoubtedly influences the church (i.e. women have little say in decision making at home or in society, therefore not much say in the church either). The Balkanic attitude is also characterized by quarrels, accusations, and fights over any little issues (i.e. the annual congregational meeting of many Baptist churches). Balkanism is a culture of shame and intimidation, which is vividly seen in the way church leaders impose rules and handle deviant cases (church discipline). Vulnerability is seen as a weakness. For example, I was personally rebuked by a well-intended church member for illustrating my sermons with personal struggles because pastors should show no weakness.

---

[14] There is a common view among some Baptist leaders that the evangelical churches in the West "degraded" or "polluted" the true faith and practice, embracing liberalism and libertinism.

[15] Strabo and Herodot mentioned in their writings the "religious zeal" of the *Geti*, the Romanian ancestors (quoted in Simion Mehedinti, *Crestinismul Romanesc*, (Bucuresti: Editura Anastasia, 1995).

The Baptist founders

The Baptist belief and practice is a result of the merger of three conservative movements: (1) the German Baptists[16] that were pietistic, (2) the Romanian Baptist immigrants from Hungary, and (3) by the Anabaptists known for their rigorous ethical code (Stanculescu 2002, 144). Much of the teaching in the church was transferred from generation to generation, thus perpetuating the founders' values. As Alexander writes, "Many older pastors mentored younger men, helping them learn through the experience of church ministry in village churches without pastors. Leaders simply rose through the avenue of faithfulness, developing non-traditionally, without significant resources. Seminaries trained a handful a year" (1994, 1). Especially under the Communist regime, theological resources and training were almost nonexistent (Bohn 1997, 4), the faith being passed on especially through the traditions of the church. Although the academic situation is changing and many more Christian workers are benefiting from seminary training, the focus on the traditions of the church, "as we inherited them" is still prominent among Christian workers.

> "In teaching social sciences under Ceausescu, the word indoctrination has very often an apt description... Kept under the control of the government, the institution of higher learning had a clear tendency towards homogeneity, to function the same ways, and to produce the same outcomes. The creation of Communism, ideally and philosophically, was the creation of 'new men,' people with the same characteristics, goals and desires."
>
> (Ban 2001, 3)

Communism

Forty-five years of Communism have also greatly influenced the church. Totalitarianism, a strong legacy of Communism, based on rules and regulations, has formatted the leadership and institutions (the church included), affecting

---

[16] The first Baptist church in Romania was established in Bucharest by German carpenter Karl Scharschmidt in 1856. See Alexa Popovici, *Istoria Baptistilor Din Romania 1856-1919*, vol. 1 (Chicago, IL: Editura Bisericii Baptiste Romane, 1980), 14.

the way of thinking and acting by imposing convictions in a rather dictatorial manner. These rules were to be taught (indoctrination) and obeyed by conformity (uniformity rather than diversity), thus formatting rigid standards and fixed criteria to distinguish those in a right relationship with the church from those rebellious, liberal or wrong. Furthermore, totalitarianism affected the people in the congregations who live and think according to the authoritative structure above them, which they were made to depend on and therefore fear to question or challenge. Remnants of Communist legacies among the people in the pews are clearly seen in various forms: their deliberate choice to suffer rather than challenge the ecclesiastical authorities, and their worldview influenced by duplicity[17] where the public (external appearance) is what matters to the neglect of the private (real transformation).

Lack of theological education

In the past years the theological education in Romania developed substantially. Nevertheless, there are still many Romanian Baptist workers who have little or no theological education. Their lack of hermeneutical skills and discernment, as well as the lack of a proper understanding of Scriptural authority, led many believers to view Scripture as an end and not as a means. Because they have a high respect for Scripture,[18] many regard it with an almost superstitious reverence. In some churches people are not encouraged to exegete the passage but rather to memorize it and use it as a proof-text. There are Christian workers who will not accept the idea that hermeneutical tools can be helpful and even necessary to interpret the Scriptures. Rather the text should be

---

[17] There was a sharp distinction between the public and private spheres of the individual's life/identity under Romanian communism, which as a consequence of totalitarianism engendered the split spheres and selves. The people were manipulated by the system, but they also manipulated the system, creating an entire edifice based on false reports, false statistics, and deliberate disinformation in order to survive. This duplicity emanated from the quotidian existence of the average citizen faced with the imperative of constantly negotiating with the structures of a totalitarian regime. See Gail Kligman, *The Politics of Duplicity: Controlling Reproduction in Ceausescu's Romania* (Berkeley: University of California Press, 1988), p.15; also Denise Roman, *Fragmented Identities: Popular Culture, Sex and Everyday Life in Postcommunist Romania* (Lanham: Lexington Books, 2003).

[18] It is a major sin in some circles to put your Bible on the floor or treat it casually.

taken literally and "as it says." To quote someone, "the Bible should only be read and not interpreted," which is in itself an interpretation (Fish 1980). I was also part of a discussion where Christian teachers told me I was wrong to ask them to discern between cultural and supra-cultural truths in the book of Acts. The Bible, in their view, has no cultural elements. Everything that is written is applicable for today and to deny this is to deny inerrancy and inspiration.

In most legalistic contexts, therefore, the Bible is used as an end in itself. It is applied judicially to condemn and kill, rather than to bring life. In most legalistic encounters, Scripture is used as a means of condemnation. Zealous people search

SIDEBAR 3

BIBLICAL PASSAGES QUOTED FOR "READY-DEFENSE" BY THE LEGALISTS

1 Cor. 14:33 *"God is a God of order - Dumnezeul al rinduielilor."* The expression is used to defend the "randuieli" (rules) of the church.

Col. 2:6 *"So that just as you received Him continue to live in Him."* This passage is often used to justify the unwillingness to change one's ways, habits or rules. As I recall the famous saying, the seven last words of a dying church are: "We've always done it that way!"

Eph. 4:5 *"There is one Lord, one faith, one baptism."* Like the classical phrase of Louis the XIV ("one king, one faith, one law"), many take this verse to oppose new teaching on certain subjects, especially the taboo ones, considering them part of the "teaching of a new faith."

1 Cor. 9:21 *"I am not free from God's law, but am under Christ's law."* Many use this verse to show that zeal for Christ's law is biblical. However, they define Christ's law in their terms.

1 Cor. 7:20 *"Each one should remain in the same condition which he was in when God called him."* The verse is used to justify unwillingness to change old traditions, personal habits or worship style. One is called to "remain" in the same condition/tradition as when converted.

1 Cor. 8-10; Rom. 14 *"Do not be a stumbling block for your weak brother."* This is one of the most quoted passages in defense of any attempt to address a sensitive subject, to biblically approach it or to try to engage in dialogue on the biblical, theological or cultural basis for a specific belief or practice.

1 Cor. 11:2 *"I praise you because you... hold firmly to the traditions, just as I delivered them to you."* This verse is used to support traditions and argue against anyone who might dare to challenge or change such traditions.

and find the right verses to prove their points or justify their beliefs. The letter rules while the spirit that gives life and seeks beyond the letter is suppressed.[19] There are a number of such passages that are twisted out of their contextual meaning and quoted for ready-defense by many legalists when questioned or challenged in their beliefs. Sidebar 3 lists some examples.

Reaction to "cheap grace" influences

Many churches react to various foreign ecclesiastical beliefs and practices brought to Romania by Western missionaries.[20] In a context loaded with tradition and focused on repentance as ontological salvation, the reductionistic, simplistic and anti-nomianistic versions of the gospel presented by some believers and teachers have determined a negative response (and rightly so!) and stereotyping of the Western church, which became to be seen as *liberal* and *worldly*. The lack of contextual awareness and lack of discerning and separating supra-cultural biblical truths from Western cultural ones, was a negative factor in producing some of the reactions found in the Romanian evangelical circles.[21] I personally condemn such beliefs, encouraging those missionaries who come and preach the full Gospel, where Christ is Lord and Saviour!

---

[19] As John Stott notices, a similar situation happened in the time of Jesus: "the quarrel Jesus had with the Jews (John 5:39-40) was not over their view of Scripture, but over their use of it.... the complaint of Jesus is expressed not so much in the words 'you search' as in the words 'you think.' He does not reproach them because they searched the Scriptures, but because they regarded their search as an end in itself. They misunderstood Scripture's God-intended function, which is to point beyond itself to Christ" (Stott, *Christ*, 95-97).

[20] For example, proponents and teachers influenced by the "Free grace" movement, came to Romania even under the Communist regime, some working under the umbrella of a known mission organization. Others, such as hyper-calvinists, "seeker sensitive," also brought with them elements characteristic to their own indigenous theology but not fitted, and thus not well received, by the Romanian evangelicals. After the Anti-Communist Revolution of 1989, there was an "invasion" of such missionaries and short term groups.

[21] To balance my approach, I have to say that a similar study can be done showing the other extreme of contextualization (license, libertinism, carnality, tolerance, relativism) which characterizes many churches in the Western Hemisphere of our world, where the anti-nomianistic tendencies dilute so much so the salvific message that it becomes "another" Gospel.

CULTURALLY BASED LEGALISTIC BELIEFS AND PRACTICES (I)

- The seating in the church - men on one side, the women on the other side

- The music on the church - there are church instruments and worldly instruments: church instruments (brass instruments, mandolins, violin, organ, piano) vs. worldly instruments (guitars – classic, electric, bass – drums, tambourines, accordion). Interestingly enough there are exceptions: the big/bass drum which plays in the brass band is accepted, all other percussion are not, because they are generally taught of having voodoo or Satanic origin.

- The rhythm in the church: the accepted sacred rhythm (march, valse, gospel, country, German folk music, romantza, canzonets) and worldly rhythm (especially syncopated)

- The singing style: no raising up of hands when singing (charismatic!), no moves (dance!), little or no expression (not performance or spectacle!)

- The style of clothing: the one who preaches from the pulpit must wear coat and tie regardless of the temperature or social context or in some churches men are not allowed to wear ties, though they are required to wear long sleeved shirts buttoned to the neck.

- The type of clothing: women must wear nylon stockings and are forbidden to wear sleeveless blouses. This is an extract from a Western missionary report: "In Romania, women are rebuked for wearing nylon stockings while I heard a brother in Australia rebuking sisters for not wearing stockings."

The church, therefore, has been influenced from within and without by the culture, as with anywhere else in the world over the history of mankind. The cultural roots "are value systems that operate as hidden axioms in their interpretation," (Loader 2001, 141) influencing the way people think, act and behave even in the church (see Sidebar 4 for some cultural examples imbedded in the church). Consequently, I truly believe that anyone deciding to minister in the Romanian culture should be aware of the specific issues of the evangelical subculture in Romania that are still present in some churches. One needs to contextualize himself in order to be effective. If I may say, in the case of Romania, one needs to go through a double contextualizatization – accommodating not only to the secular culture but also to the church subculture.[22] This twofold aspect is important to be noticed.

---

[22] In some churches that manifest legalistic tendencies, the church rules are "the standard." "Real" contextualization is completely forbidden, sometimes by oral or

The Romanian secular culture is rather *different* than the Romanian evangelical subculture. They do not have any rules or restrictions on wearing jewelry, make-up, head-coverings, dress-code, dancing, etc., as the evangelicals do. Some of the Baptist churches have built their own subculture, based on Niebuhr's paradigm "Christ against culture," drawing the lines and building the walls in opposition to many Romanian secular customs. That is why, I repeat, the missionary needs to be aware of the two-fold cultural aspect, not compromising but double contextualizing himself, if he wants to be effective in those churches. They need to respect the national's biblical convictions (Rom. 14) and in many cases live with them. I recognize that this is rather difficult, but I see it as a biblical mandate (1 Cor. 8-10; Rom. 14).[23]

My personal experience in contextualization

When we started our ministry in Romania, my wife and I tried to integrate ourselves in the double-layered culture. We tried to abide by many "ecclesiastical/cultural rules" as I pastored a Baptist church in Romania. We did not have a problem with soft legalism (cultural or biblical practices that do not alter the essence of salvation). For example, although we had a different conviction, my wife covered her head, wore skirts, no earrings, even though none of these items was problematic in the church setting she grew up in, *Bonne Nouvelle* (similar to the Evangelical Free Church) in Strasbourg, France. We considered our decision as a biblical mandate in light of 1 Cor. 9:20 and Rom. 14. We also appreciated and embraced many of the ecclesiastical customs, seeing true value and positive meaning in them (sacredness of baptism and communion). Nevertheless, we did not compromise when it came to what I describe in this presentation as syncretistic-legalism but rather encouraged the believers to not elevate their convictions to the level of absolutes, warning them of the danger of syncretism. For this we paid a price.

---

written church decrees similar in form and authority to the bull Omnium sollicitudinum of Pope Benedict XIV, by which in 1744 he forbid any concessions of his Catholic missionaries to the local culture in China.

[23] The younger generation (younger than 40) tends to have a different perspective toward the church subculture. Many neglect it, and some openly reject it. This is a positive paradigm shift toward tradition and legalism in Eastern. Europe.

On the other hand, I have always been opposed to antinomistic presentations of the gospel, and I believe that a Christian is under Christ's law – the teachings of Jesus and the apostles. I believe also that a person is saved based on repentance and faith, making Christ not only Saviour but Lord of his life. I believe what Luther said, that we are justified by faith alone, but the faith that justifies does not stand alone, that is, your saving faith must be expressed by the good works and fruits of your salvation/repentance (Acts 27:20), that prove a change in your ethics, morality, essence of your behavior. Nevertheless, the emphasis of such transformation is internal (1Pet.3:3-4), the focus of God is in changing your character and your heart and not gaining salvation by following a set of external rules. That is to say, I am against smoking or drunkenness, and I consider both as sins, but I would not judge someone's salvation based on the fact that he smokes or sometimes drinks alcohol, as some legalists do. Decency, simplicity, modesty, are important themes in Scripture, but I cannot judge a woman's salvation or repentance based on the fact that she wears or not wears a head covering, which is a sign of modesty, decency, submission for many. I am not against the law, when it is used as it was intended by Jesus and Paul to be used. Jesus and Paul established many "rules," an ethical code to live by in the Christian faith (the sermon on the Mount is a clear example of that) but such rules do not save you - they need to become a reality in your life, as the outpouring of the Spirit filled life not as a scale of virtues that you need to climb or obey in order to make sure you are saved.

My main focus in doing ministry in a legalistic context was to center myself on the Word of God, trying to contextualize my theology, attempting to avoid some Western theological debates,[24] and being sensitive to the specific spiritual needs and understandings of people in this part of the world. I truly believe contextualization is essential for the ministry, and therefore I tried to do so until I reached a point where I've seen that contextualization turned into syncretism.

And here lies the main argument of my thesis. *It is one thing to contextualize yourself to cultural norms and a*

---

[24] For example, Calvinism, eschatological debates, dispensationalism vs. covenant theology, free grace vs. lordship, etc.

completely different thing to compromise the supra-cultural truths of Scripture, especially those related to the matters of salvation. In other words, when the cultural norms, traditions, church teachings or even Bible verses are used to convey a DIFFERENT way of redemption than the one and only vicarious sacrifice of our Lord Jesus Christ, then soft legalism embraces or becomes syncretism. In these cases a legalistic interpretation of Scripture becomes an obstacle of redemption instead of being used to help one toward salvation (see Sidebar 1).

SIDEBAR 5
PAUL'S WARNING AGAINST THE DANGER OF LEGALISM

In the exordium of his letter to the Galatians, Paul writes: Gal.1:6 "I am amazed that you are so quickly deserting the One who called you by the grace of Christ, to a different gospel, which is really no Gospel at all" (Gal. 1:6). Notice the tone and the terms used. As Ben Witherington points out, Paul's tone is not the one for "merely mouthing clichés" (1998, 81). The term "you are ... deserting" was used in military desertion, which was punishable by death in those times, and also used in the Inter-Testamental literature of those who turned apostate (Macc. 7:24; Sir. 6.9; Josephus Ant. 20.38, Matera 1992, 45), or (in its substantive form) of a person who left one philosophical school of thought for another (Diogene Laertius 7.1.37; 4.166). The verb used in the Greek is reflexive, indicating that the act is voluntary (they themselves are deserting) and in process, thus putting a strong emphasis on their personal responsibility (Matera 1992, 45). They have been influenced by the teachings of the Judaizers. These were Christians engaged in Jewish practices ("those of the circumcision" Gal.2:12), believers who argued that certain aspects of the Jewish law should be obeyed and thus play a role in salvation (the term Judaizer originates as a transliteration via the Latin of the Greek verb ioudaizein, which has the meaning "to live as a Jew in accordance with Jewish customs" (Campbell 1993). The Judaizers influenced the believers in Galatia to desert, not a man, a teacher or a church, but "the one who called them"—God! (Longenecker 1990, 15). They have not only turned from God, but especially relevant for our topic, they have also turned from "grace" to what the apostle will later describe as the works of law ("You have been severed from Christ, you who are seeking to be justified by law; you have fallen from grace" Gal. 5:4). *(Continued on next page.)*

(Sidebar 5 Continued...)

And here is the important point of this passage, the direct parallel to our topic. They <u>did not deny</u> Christ or his grace, but tried to improve it by <u>adding</u> requirements (same as the contemporary legalists in Eastern Europe), which in their case meant ceremonies and standards from the OT. And this is a very important detail to notice. In Acts 15:1, we have a clear example of this problem. People from the same group Paul is addressing here, the Judaizers, teach the church in Antioch that "unless you are circumcised according to the customs (Law) taught by Moses, you cannot be saved!" They based their deviant teaching on portions of Scripture, as many of the legalists in the history of the church have done. Richard Baxter, writing in 1651, says: "To make salvation the end of duty, is to be a legalist, and act under a covenant of works" (1962, 8). This is similar to the legalists in Romania today. Paul was not impressed; on the contrary, he saw it as a major problem. Why? Because when anything else, even God's law, is added to His grace, grace ceases to be grace (cf. Rom. 11:6). As F.F. Bruce writes: "The message which the Galatian Christians are disposed to accept in place of that which they received from Paul is so different from Paul's message that it constitutes ετερον ευαγγελιον – something more than another version of the same gospel, a **different** gospel (the context suggests a "qualitative difference" [Longenecker 1990, 15]), and therefore, in fact, no gospel at all, since there can be no 'other gospel' (αλλο ευαγγελιον) than the proclamation of justification by faith, apart from the works of the law, or any other works" (Bruce 1982, 82).

This was Paul's problem and the problem I face in the context where I minister. It is not just a contextualized gospel, it is "another gospel" – syncretism! As in the Galatian church, it was syncretism from within – some of the Judaizers are described to be "men who came from James" (Gal.2:12), arguing their beliefs based on biblical passages from the Old Testament! In the Romanian church, the case is similar; syncretism from within is generated by zealous church members, supported in many cases by the leadership. It is often based on Scriptural text-proofs that are derived not only from the Old Testament (Mosaic Law) but also from the New Testament. That is why I call this type of legalism Scripture-justified legalism, because it embodies the whole biblical spectrum. Consequently, I personally consider it the most dangerous type of legalism because it leads to syncretism.

(Continued on next page.)

(Sidebar 5 Continued...)

I command your attention back to the first chapter of Galatians. The results of legalism in the church of Galatia in the first century are very similar to the results of legalism in the Romanian church of the twenty-first century: *"Evidently some people are disturbing/confusing you and are trying to pervert the gospel of Christ"* (v. 7b). The Galatian believers were disturbed and confused (ταρασσειν – "mental and spiritual agitation and confusion" cf. BAGD, 990), and so are many of the Romanian believers today. In Galatia, the legalists were "disturbing, confusing" others, because they presented a distorted/perverted form of the gospel. The text specifies this problem: they are *"trying to pervert the gospel of Christ."* The term *pervert* or *distort* is a Greek word that begins with *meta* (μεταστρεφαι), indicating a change from one thing or state to another, or turning something into its opposite, thereby perverting it (BAGD, 640) – see the similarities with Moreau definition of syncretism (2000, 924). The reader can feel Paul's anger in the ironical declaration that follows: *But even if we or an angel from heaven should preach contrary to what we preached to you, be anathema!"* (v. 8) This is a conditional clause that functions as a rhetorical device to highlight the singular message of the gospel and to drastically warn them. It is translated "Let him be anathema," in some Bible versions, eternally condemned (NIV), or accursed (NASB), is the LXX rendering of Heb. *herem* (ban) (*TDNT* 1:354. *BAGD*, 63. Lev. 27:28-29; Deut. 7:26; Josh. 6:17-18.). In a holy war the *herem* involved the destruction of everyone and everything that fell under it. In Paul's case it always denotes the object of a curse delivered up "to the judicial wrath of God" (Rom .9:3; 1Cor. 12:3; 16:22; Gal.1:8,9). He repeats the warning twice, as a device of emphasizing its importance: *"As we have already said, so now I say again: if anybody is preaching to you a gospel other than what you accepted, let him be anathema!"* (v. 9).

Consequences

Legalism brings consequences. I have listed some of them in the Appendix. Below I will expand on two specific consequences that have a direct relevance to our present study on syncretistic-legalism.[25]

---

[25] I found many similarities in my interaction with pastors from Russia, Ukraine, Moldova, Central and South America.

The example of Paul, presented above, is eloquent to our argument. Paul the same apostle who gave up all to become Jew for the Jews and Greek for the Greeks ("all men to all people"-- 1 Cor. 9) in order to save them (true contextualization), faced with the problem of the Galatian church, where legalism (in their case – Mosaic nomism) became more than just a cultural norm (a salvific requirement), took a strong stand against it! Although he was strongly devoted to preaching righteousness, repentance, good works, transformation, he nevertheless opposed any teachings or practices that crossed the line into legalism. A careful reading of Galatians 1:6-9 (see Sidebar 5) allows one to see Paul's serious concern for the believers in Galatia. It is my own concern for the evangelical believers in Eastern Europe, particularly Romania. In their zeal to pursue holiness and to guard the doctrine of salvation, some believers, including Christian workers, tend to neglect the biblical warning and the necessary discernment (Rom. 10:2) when they engage these theological concepts.

Consequences of Legalistic Syncretism

As a result of that neglect, various consequences arise that do not bring glory and honor to the name of Christ, nor spiritual edification to the body of Christ. There are two specific consequences that have a direct relevance to our present study on syncretistic-legalism.

Rejection of God and of the Evangelical Church by the Unbelievers and Seekers

"The Repenters are also hostile to the bearers of the gospel. They can actually be worse than the Orthodox because of their legalism," (Prochau 2001) said an outsider who ministered in Romania. And in some cases this is true. I personally know of many unbelievers who do not want to have anything to do with some evangelical churches because they see them as spiritual ghettos that impose on their people a burdensome yoke. The ghetto mentality is presented as "biblical separation" and justified by scriptural passages such as 2 Cor. 6:17 and 1 Jn. 2:15. As Mark Baker rightly says, based on his experience in South America, these legalistic churches are "communities of exclusion." Their legalistic approach separates the church members from the outsiders and makes them afraid to come in (Baker 1999, 30).

The word by which the evangelical Christians are known, "pocait-repenter," is losing, in some circles, its deep meaning ("those who turned, dedicated themselves to God") and today often carries more of a negative connotation that is associated with legalism. Although I believe that "whoever chooses to be a friend of the world becomes an enemy of God" (Jam. 4:4), I am concerned with society's negative reaction against the evangelical church not because of Christ but because of some of its members and churches who propagate such legalistic rules.[26] One of the most frequent comments of friends and family toward those recently converted is a shocking one: "Te-ai prostit?! Te-ai pocait?!" or

> **"Woe to you scribes and Pharisees, you hypocrites! You shut the kingdom of heaven in men's faces. You yourselves do not enter, nor will you let those enter who are trying to."**
> **Matthew 23:13**

"Did you lose your mind (lit. stupid)? Did you become a repenter?" And that should not be shocking if we read Paul's affirmation of becoming "fools" for Christ. However, it is shocking when such words are used to convey the meaning of conversion, which unbelievers see as a willingness to join a sectarian group characterized by rules and regulations and not by Christ! Paul condemned the legalistic Jews of his day, arguing that "the name of God is blasphemed among the Gentiles through you" (Rom. 2:24). Such practices do not bring glory to God and people into His kingdom. On the contrary, they create repulsion in them, distancing them from Him. Like the party of the Pharisees, some of these churches are drawing the lines in the wrong places, portraying a false image of God and His church. Instead of engaging and transforming the culture as Paul and Jesus did, they oppose the culture and in turn the culture opposes them. In the process many are lost because of labels and rules. It resembles so well the Second Temple

---

[26] In a survey done in 2000 among 30 unbelievers, 21 associated the word with rules, 11 with religious hypocrisy, nine with strictness, six with narrow-mindedness, 13 with a sect or cult, one with behavioral policemen, and one with rule-obsessed people. In many cases these labels overlapped.

Judaism mentality, when the acceptance in the community of the faithful was based on numerous criteria, conditions, rituals and lifestyle rules (McKnight 1991, 79), mentality against which Jesus fervently spoke.

Rejection of God and of the Evangelical Church by the Believers[27]

A woman in her early twenties made a complete break with the church and avoided all church people and contact for ten years. This was the result of an encounter with a legalist who rebuked her one Sunday for wearing blue jeans to church, alluding to 1 Tim. 2. She ended up seeking happiness in all the things that had been forbidden before, and became addicted to smoking, drinking, parties and other such activities. She believed that she would find in these what the church failed to provide.

> *"After joining the church (after baptism), every other week I heard judgmental sermons on 'no drinking,' 'head coverings,' 'no jewelry or fancy clothes,' 'no smoking or listening to worldly music.' Dancing was out of the question. Maybe that's why I love to dance now and enjoy a glass of beer and a good cigar!"*
>
> **- A woman in her 30s**

Confusion and Deceit in Regards to Conversion

Although many churches preach the doctrine of grace in salvation, some of them practice a doctrine of works to attain righteousness. Most of the Baptist churches require catechism before baptism for all who either make a decision for Christ or are seeking to make one. It is a healthy custom, going back to the second century of the Christian church. Catechism lasts from several weeks to several months, and it is a time of biblical initiation for the recently converted person. However, in some cases it is more of a process of selection of

---

[27] Stefan Ulstein (1985) gives numerous cases (interviews) of former churchgoers who left the 'faith" as a result of the legalistic pressures found in their churches.

those who are "prepared" to "truly repent" and thus be saved from those who are not "ready." In the legalistic churches, the major lessons the candidates are taught during catechism link ecclesiastical rules to soteriology. The seeker or new believer is taught 'repentance," (Acts 17:31), which should entail a renunciation of the worldly lifestyle (1 Jn. 2:15), but is instead expressed in obedience to the ecclesiastical rules.[28] Rom.12:1-2 is a classic passage used to enforce this "turn from the world," not so much by the "renewing of your mind" as by the "renewing of your wardrobe" (i.e. getting rid of jewelry, make-up, certain types of clothing, secular music, separation from unbelieving friends, restrictions to attend movie theaters, cultural events, etc.). The person needs to convert not only to the lordship of Christ but also to the ecclesiastical code.

> *"We are possessed by an obsessional desire to justify ourselves, to declare that we are righteous, to be righteous in our own eyes, to seem to be righteous in the eyes of others. ... Saying that God loves us grants us no reassurance. We would prefer it if he gave us 50 things to do, so that when we had done them we could be at peace. We do not want an ongoing relationship with God. We prefer a rule."*
>
> **Ellul 1986, 159-61**

Confusion and Deceit in Regards to the Assurance of Salvation

In such churches, the believer's identity and security is not in Christ but in his own works of repentance, that have nothing to do with changes of heart/mind but rather keeping list of external rules. Most believers know they were saved by grace but they strongly believe that "staying in salvation" is based on their "obedience" to such ecclesiastical rules "supported" by biblical text-proofs.[29] A young active believer (14 yr. old) was sharply rebuked by a so-called "spiritually minded" person in the church for his hairstyle, and was warned that his behavior would send him to hell. The child was deeply affected. In a

---

[28] It is very similar with the Second Temple Judaism and their requirements for salvation.

[29] Similar view as in Judaism, according to E. P. Sanders (1977, 419-28).

survey done in the church, about 50 adult believers were asked what they believe it means to be a true repenter (truly saved), and what they think are some of the signs of "testing whether you are in the faith or not" (2 Cor. 13:5). More than half of them listed a series of "signs of repentance" and "fruits of repentance," which had to do with the ecclesiastical norms already mentioned (dress code, head-coverings, traditions, etc.) and not with spiritual "fruits" from Gal.5.

Conclusion

Legalism is a gangrene that slowly paralyses numerous evangelical churches around the world and sometime leads them into syncretism, replacing or diluting the core truths of the Gospel. This chapter focused primarily on legalistic practices and beliefs present in some Baptist churches in the Crisana province of Romania as a critical illustration of this dangerous trend. Although more and more churches reject legalism in Romania, in some cases, the humble and sincere attitude of the suffering Eastern European church, has been replaced by spiritual pride and fundamentalist superiority. In those circles, legalism

> **"Syncretism from within" or "Bible-justified syncretism" is the most dangerous syncretism the church may encounter.**

has become a surrogate for holiness and inward transformation and in various churches a condition for genuine salvation. Grace is labeled "liberalism," freedom in Christ "worldly living," in-depth exegesis "vain philosophy," and relevance "Westernization" or "Americanization." And it is sad knowing that some of these churches and their leaders fought to protect the Scriptures during Communist persecution, but now distort them, in many cases unconsciously, being deceived to believe they do the right thing. The present study exposed some of the possible origins of these beliefs. Although anti-nomianism was rejected and contextualization was upheld and encouraged, legalistic beliefs and practices often cross over the border of contextualization and obedience to Christ's commands, into syncretism and conditioning someone's earning or remaining in salvation upon the obedience to ecclesiastical rules and traditions. As a result, legalism causes numerous people, particularly unbelievers, to create a false image about God, the evangelical faith and the church, and to reject all. It dilutes the essence and goal of Scripture, either by submitting it to the authority of ecclesiastical tradition or by transforming it into an end rather than a means, as intended by God. The two most dangerous outcomes are: (1) this reduces grace to a merely theoretical (soteriological) matter and enthrones the works of righteousness as the means by which one may receive or maintain his salvation; and (2) it uses the Bible to justify its beliefs and practices. It is my opinion that this teaching is no different in principle than the one

> **"The issue in regard to the law was not getting in, but staying in. The Jews did not teach that obeying the law was a means to earn salvation; obedience kept one within the covenant."**
>
> **Sanders 1977, 419**

Paul fought in Galatia, where Scripture was used to proclaim "another" gospel. This is "syncretism from within" or Bible justified syncretism," a dangerous warning for any church in any culture. This type of syncretism is based on a wrong/cultural usage of biblical texts and stems out of a passionate religious zeal for purity and holiness. But it misses the target and deceives many in the process, endangering the existence of the Christian church and the essence of the Gospel truth,[30] thus destroying the foundations of the Christian faith. And, as the Psalmist rhetorically asked, "If the foundations are destroyed, what can the righteous do?" (Ps.11:3), what should we, the pastors, teachers, missionaries do, in our encounter with legalism, particularly in Eastern Europe? Here are some prescriptive insights.

First of all, let's be aware of this Christianized aspect of syncretism – syncretism from within. We cannot afford to focus exclusively on the "left wing" of syncretism (the liberal

---

[30] If one studies the life of the Jerusalem church /Jewish Christianity in the first two centuries, one would notice the gradual disappearance of this faction of Christianity. The only Christian Jewish groups that survived in the history of the church were rather small, isolated and ephemeral in time, some of which were considered cultic or heretical by the early church fathers (the Ebionites, Elkesaites, Cerinthians; see also Ignatius, *Phil*.6, *Mag*.8ff; in AD 190, Victor, the bishop of Rome and Polycrates, the bishop of Ephesus, as well as Irenaeus do not recognize these groups as part of the Christendom, cf. Eusebius *Ecc. Hist*.5.23).

encounter with culture). We need to recognize the existence of the "right wing," a more subtle, chameleonic and similarly destructive branch of syncretism. It's been there for centuries, hidden in the pews and sometime in the pulpits, using religious zeal, biblical law and the wrap of purity and separation to cover its diabolic intent: to replace, neglect or dilute the essential truths of the Gospel, in biblical terms μεταστρεφαι, changing from one state to another/ turning something into its opposite, thereby perverting it (Gal.1:7).

Secondly, I encourage you to continue the research on this topic and find solutions to the problem. The focus of this study was qualitative/descriptive. However, there is much need for a quantitative and also a prescriptive study seeking solutions to this major problem. I encourage the Eastern European Christian leaders or students who read this chapter, to do more research and engage the problems with wisdom and love and also any other Christians who fight the legalistic battles.

Thirdly, pray for many sincere believers and church leaders in Romania and Eastern Europe, who see the danger of this trend and are trying to do something about it. Some of them suffer because of their stand. Many are afraid to even engage it. I praise God for my own "conversion" out of legalism and for His grace that sustained me in very difficult circumstances when I tried to engage the legalists in dialogue. Pray for me too, as this chapter goes to press – there will be many reactions. Pastors like me and church leaders who try to take a stand against legalism need your prayers and encouragement. Pray also for the other pastors, teachers and leaders, who are still blinded by legalism. Most of them are sincere believers who have great zeal for the Scriptures but lack the necessary wisdom and hermeneutical understanding. They love the Lord but are unable to see the danger of the legalism they promote or defend. Please pray for them and engage them with gentleness and Christ-like spirit.

> *...teach them to discern what matters from what seems to matter.*

Fourthly, address these issues and challenge others to pray and help the church in Eastern Europe face this major challenge. If you have a chance to teach in Eastern Europe, help the pastors learn how to discern between what matters and what seems to matter. Try to address these issues without reacting but rather responding in wisdom and discernment, blending biblical hermeneutics with cultural sensitiveness (emic and etic perspectives). Most of the churches and Christian workers caught in legalistic bondage are rather reactionary regarding these issues. If you have an opportunity to teach, help the believers and especially the pastors discern between absolutes and convictions, cultural and supracultural truths in Scripture. Help them understand the danger of using Scripture as an end or as a means to justify their practices. They have a high view of Scripture, which is a positive platform one may use to address the issues. Let them see that you respect their opinions and convictions, even their ecclesiastical rules. However, teach them not to elevate these convictions to the level of the absolutes, judging others' salvation by them. It is vitally important that the believers understand the dangers of syncretistic legalism and when their practices cross the border of contextualization into syncretism. They must not be afraid of grace, but instead rejoice in their salvation. They must grow in the faith out of love, not fear; based on God's all-sufficient sacrifice, not on any works of righteousness, focusing first of all on heart changes, wisely choosing their battles for the Lord.

This was Paul's concern for the church in Galatia and his battle against the syncretistic–legalists of his day, the Judaizers. His warning of anathema should lead us to take a stand and warn against the great and subtle dangers of this form of legalism that has attempted to pervert the Christian church throughout history by attacking its very foundation – the doctrine of salvation in Christ alone.

"If the foundations are destroyed, what can the righteous do?"

APPENDIX

Other consequences of legalistic practices and beliefs:

1) Discrimination that results in pain and apathy among the church members.

Ruben Alves rightly observes, "The Christian is confronted with the terrible certainty that he or she will be accepted by the community only if he or she does not transgress the limits of the permissible." (1985, 147)

a) Pain.

In a church four godly couples were asked by the pastor to read portions of Scripture at a special event in the church. After the service was over, several church members criticized two of the women for daring to read Scripture with their heads uncovered (1 Cor. 11). Some criticized the pastor who called on them. The two women were deeply hurt, and to this day one refuses to be involved in anything public at the church.

A newly baptized older lady in her 80s committed herself to attend a women's prayer group. The first meeting took place on a very cold January evening at someone's home. She came full of enthusiasm but was greeted with a rebuke because she came wearing pants instead of a skirt (Deut. 22:5). This person came to me crying and confused, afraid that she could not be involved in any church activity in the winter since she had health problems requiring her to wear pants.

b) Apathy.

In some churches, even if you are modestly and decently dressed, unless you abide by the church dress code (1Cor. 11, 1 Pet. 3, Deut. 22:5), you cannot actively participate in the service by singing in the choir, playing in the orchestra, reciting a poem, reading Scripture, sharing a testimony or teaching.

The sadness of the matter is that some Christians who are in teaching positions choose, as Kirk Kenneth says, "to use the teaching of the Bible ... penally." (Kirk 1966) By this, they seek to maintain rigid forms of legalism by either reminding the members on a regular basis of the rules or by frequently preaching on them.

2) Confusion in regards to holiness/sanctification.[31]

a) Holiness = "Thou shall not..."

Many of the churches that cultivate legalistic tendencies are "Thou shall not" communities.[32] They cultivate a system that displays itself as moral, with strong claims of righteousness for external behavior and judgmental attitude toward other individuals or churches that do not hold to similar beliefs. They are militant and reactionary in their zeal to "preserve purity of the doctrine and of the church," usually invoking 2 Tim. 4:3. In the process, they confuse many new believers and deceive themselves by fighting the wrong battles with the right motives. Sometimes they closely resemble the Pharisees.[33] Asked if he believed there could be various interpretations of 1 Cor. 11, a leader in a large church answered no. Asked if he considered not wearing a head covering a sin, he answered yes. Asked if he considered that the other believers from around the world who do not hold to this conviction are sinning, he answered yes.

A group of couples attended a marriage seminar and in their quest for genuine holiness, they specifically asked the teacher to explain his own position on the head covering. The pastor explained the various valid interpretations of 1 Cor. 11 and allowed them to build their own convictions about the matter. After returning to their church, a church leader heard about the "heresy" and started to do house visitations to some of these couples, questioning and rebuking them about their convictions on this matter and others discussed in the seminar. One of the couples commented that it resembled a communist interrogation of a self-thinking dissident.

b) Holiness = "Thou shall..."

There are churches where spirituality is measured by what women wear on their heads. The most holy are those who wear a *batic* (babushka) and cover their entire head, followed by those who wear a scarf (10-20 cm wide), then a hat (in some circles hats are

---

[31] Stanculescu describes the Romanian evangelicals' pursuit for purity as "channeled toward the observance of a strict moral code, rejecting alcohol and tobacco, or the wearing of jewelry, observing strictly the Lord's Day and practicing severe church discipline" (*2002*, 369).

[32] As John Stott rightly says, "Our 'touch not; taste not; handle not' (Col. 2) has often been 'smoke not, drink not, dance not'" (1970, 86).

[33] The Pharisaic community was built on the "Thou shall" and "Thou shall not" commandments. They calculated that the law contained 248 commandments (thou shall) and 365 prohibitions (thou shall not), adding on top of those their own "preventive laws." For Sabbath alone they had more than 1,500 extra-commands!

forbidden), then a *cordeluta* (bandana). 1 Cor. 11 is the text employed in such practices. Nevertheless, in most cases, the text is never exegetically or theologically analyzed just preached "as it is."

Although some church leaders use legalism to maintain their power and draw spheres of influence, other Christian workers have sincere motives. They want to preserve ecclesiastical purity. However, their means and methods are wrong. By focusing on the external marks of a changed life, they neglect the very life that produces those marks. As Kirk says, "The fruit of the Spirit is not acts themselves but the qualities of the heart that produces acts" (1980, 436). When the church leader confuses these two elements of truth, the old proverb comes true: "A little dew in the pulpit produces a big fog in the pew." Or, on a more serious tone, "When the pastor as a teacher sows legalism to the wind, he and his successors need expect nothing but a whirlwind of ethical confusion in their counseling ministries" (Oates 1973, 38).

3) **Misunderstanding of spiritual values and priorities.**

a) Over-emphasis on the externals but neglecting the internal transformation.[34]

"They are more interested with what I wear than who I am as a person." – A new female believer

In some churches where legalism is prevalent, the term "fundamentalism" is a matter of pride. In most instances people in these churches are known for their rules but not for their virtues. As David Malone writes:

> For Fundamentalists the virtues are imperiled by the tendency towards legalism, that is, the attempt to earn God's approval through good works, as exemplified by the Pharisees in Jesus' day. Legalism emphasizes action, as do the virtues, but it can focus too easily on a list of proper and improper activities and beliefs detached from the virtues. (2001, 503)

Edward Dobson acknowledged the same danger in the Fundamentalist Journal:

> We often spend our time and resources arguing over the length of a person's hair, the content of his music, or the style of his clothes, and

---

[34] "For he is not a Jew, which is one outwardly; neither is that circumcision, which is outward in the flesh: but he is a Jew, which is one inwardly" (Rom. 2:28-29). A great work that studies how Jesus dealt with such issues in the Gospels is William Loader, *Jesus and the Fundamentalism of His Day* (Grand Rapids, MI: Eerdmans, 2001).

we ignore the real issues of Christianity, such as loving God, which just happens to be the greatest commandment in the entire Bible."(1987, 12)

In the adult Sunday school class (40-60 years old) of a large church, the question was asked on the last Sunday of the year, "What is the most important lesson you learned during the year?" Most people did not answer the question, but took the opportunity to speak against the liberalism and worldliness that had attacked their church that year, which was exemplified by several women who started to wear jewelry, others pants and still others who removed their head covering as they worshipped in church. This demonstrated what they considered the "most important" thing in their Christian life.

Many legalists rightly stress correctness of faith, but the emphasis shifts from *faith* to *correctness*. And correctness, and thus the faith, is measured according to the standard of traditionalism.[35] This is not different from the Pharisaic codes of do's and don'ts found in the Mishna and Talmud. Christ rebukes the Pharisees for the same problem: "And in so doing they 'strained out a gnat but swallowed the camel.'" This is more or less what the legalists do. They ignore the most important issues for the less important ones (Mat. 23:23-24). As John Stott says, bridging this passage to our contemporary situation, the existing legalistic churches "are the 'mint, dill and cumin' of our day, the herbs of the evangelical's back garden" (1970, 156).

Stott continues,

We have seen that the Pharisaic view of morality was superficial because it was external. Therefore any attempt to externalize either religion or morality today, or to reduce it to a few shallow rules, is a form of modern Pharisaism. Evangelicals are by no means always free from this tendency. Yet it is a hallmark of true evangelical religion to emphasize that sin and morality are inward rather than outward, that what defiles us in God's sight is what emanates form the heart, that a new birth is indispensable to a new life, and that therefore what pleases God is heart-religion and heart-morality. (1970, 159)

b) Making the form absolute and the function relative.

A final form of persecution comes from the evangelical church itself. It comes from teachers, church leaders and traditional types who confuse form and function. It comes in the form of requiring Christians to have acceptable dress standards, sing certain hymns, and require attendance in various church services each week. It is an insidious form of legalism that is nothing but persecution. Such leaders and forms of "church" are forcing younger people who want to find Christ to reject the Gospel--wrongly so--because it is too closely

---

[35] Tradition is the living faith of the dead, and traditionalism is the dead faith of the living - Jaroslav Pelikan

identified with the archaic forms of the past (which do not communicate any longer) and with their proponents. These pastors and church leaders do not release people, but control them, along with their budgets and building. I see this in every country, but especially in Hungary, Romania, Russia and Ukraine. (Vander Geissen-Reits 2004)

Authoritarianism that characterizes many legalistic Christian workers imposes uniformity and conformity. As David Miller argues, "Every legalist is a conformist" (1992, 156). The form and conformity is much more important than the function of that form. In some of these churches, divorced women are still required to wear a head covering, which is the sign of submission even though they no longer live under the authority of their husband they might have divorced years ago! The fact that I questioned this issue got several leaders quite upset, and I was accused of disturbing the peace in their church.

c) Obedience motivated by fear rather than love

Members of legalist churches find it hard to express their struggles or convictions honestly because of fear of what others may think of them and for fear of losing their standing in the church. As a result many fall into hypocrisy (duplicity) and stagnation in their Christian walk. Because of this fear, "the community shares complicity in never speaking of what may disturb or transform, only of what will comfort and secure" (Edwards 1980, 15). "The Christian allows the threats of the law to serve as motivation for obedience... fear lies at the root of his activity" (Koehler 1969). In contrast the Christian "activity that flows from faith, love and hope is natural, immediate, unprejudiced, pure and true, because it flows from the proper source of life (the Spirit). Legalistic activity shows itself to be mechanical, external, burdened with ulterior and mixed motives, opportunistic, counterfeit and insincere" (Koehler 1969, 135).

I have personally counseled and received emails from young believers strongly tempted by the homosexual lifestyle. Some of them describe themselves as sons of church leaders. They were very tormented by two issues: (1) They were not sure that homosexuality was really a sin (some American "missionaries" taught them that way!); (2) They were afraid to talk to anyone or confess their struggles because they were afraid to be excommunicated from their church family! They decide to hide their sin rather than speak about it.

In many churches there are those who are part of the "morality police." They are similar to the examples David Miller gives in his studies of legalism in the United States. Such people "are scattered throughout the Christian community and informally are encouraged to keep an eye on alumni, church members, and other preachers and speakers, then to report back to 'headquarters'" (1992, 11).

Those caught suffered consequences, which generally included restrictions in their church involvement, penalties, interdictions, church discipline, and excommunication. People live in fear of a system manipulated by intimidation.

4) Regression in the believer's walk with God.

The legalists and their communities are characterized by gracelessness, conditional acceptance, fear, hypocrisy, and self-righteous line-drawing. After his resignation, a pastor of one of these churches confessed that the process regressed when they started emphasizing legalistic rules. As J.P. Koehler noticed in his case study of the Lutheran church, when legalism steps in, "retrogression develops in the ecclesiastical life" (1969, 131).

As the history of the evangelical church unfolds, we can learn from the examples of our forerunners, such as Quakers and Anabaptists. [36] As John Audland, a Friend said: "Force and compulsion may make some men conform to that outwardly, which otherwise they would not do, but that is nothing of weight, their hearts are never better, but rather worse and more hypocritical than ever" (Kirk 1980, 436).

5) The rule of tradition in Bible interpretation.

In some of the evangelical circles, the church tradition decides which biblical interpretation is the correct one. The traditional rules themselves are deduced mostly from scriptural premises (text-proofs without exegesis) and then applied mechanically. The problematic passages are considered taboo.

---

[36] This "worldliness" was not accepted in the Quaker's Society of Friends. The following are examples of "worldliness" from the women's meeting of York in 1718: "We desire an alteration in these things... as follows: Friends' gowns made indecently, one part over long the other too short, with lead in the sleeves; and that Friends should come to a stability, and be satisfied in the shape and compass that Truth leads into, without changing as the world changes; also black and coloured silk and muslin aprons, as likewise hood or scarves not too long or broad." Another example deals with the headstones in the cemeteries: Should Friends even have them? Should they lie flat or stand upright? What, if anything, should be engraved on them: name only, or life dates as well? "What was happening during this period in Friend's history was a change from bold expectations of conquering the world for Christ to fear of being infiltrated by the world and its spirit – a mood shift form the offensive to the defensive" (Kirk 1980, 434-38).

The Anabaptists began in the sixteenth century with the same pattern of distinctive style of life, evangelistic fervor, warmth, unity of devotion, persecution and success. Early in their history, however, there arose the fear of contamination by the world, to this day embodied in the Amish and Hutterian Mennonites (Kirk 1980, 435).

A testimony from an ordained Christian worker:

> I had been teaching the gospel at a Repenter house church. They insisted that I state my opinion about head covering for women. I avoided giving my conviction for some time but eventually presented a research paper stating that it was a personal issue. I invited a Scripture-based response but they declined. Instead I was told that I could no longer take communion or speak in the church.
>
> (La Brie 2001)

This reminds me of what Jean-Jacques Rousseau said: "The Romans had been content to practice virtue; all was lost when they began to study it."

In another church a group of believers engaged the taboo passages and began to study them. In the process they changed their legalistic views on certain issues. A teacher in the church rebuked them and imposed a rule in the church against such practices. When they asked him on what basis he believed he was right, the answer was sharp and short: "Because I say so."

Sources Cited

Alexander, Ralph H. 1994. "Assessment of Leadership Development in Post-Communist Europe, 1994." unpublished paper. Consultation on Theological Education and Leadership Development in Post-Communist Europe, Oradea, Romania.

Alves, Ruben. 1985. *Protestantism and Repression: A Brazilian Case Study*. Maryknoll, NY: Orbis, 1985.

Baker, Mark D. 1999. *Religious No More*. Downers Grove, IL: InterVarsity, 1999.

Ban, Adrian. 2001. "Reform of Romanian Higher Education from 1990: Perceptions, Intentions and Procedures Affecting Leadership Development." Trinity International University, 2001.

Barbu, Daniel. 2000. *Firea Romanilor*. Bucuresti: Editura Nemira.

Baxter, Richard. 1962. *The Saint's Everlasting Rest*. Westwood, NJ: Revell, 1962.

Bohn, David P. 1997. "The Perspectives on Theological Education Evident among Evangelicals Church Leaders in Bulgaria, Hungary, Romania and Russia." Trinity International University, 1997.

Boulton, Wayne G. 1982. *Is Legalism a Heresy?* New York, NY: Paulist, 1982.

Bruce, F.F. 1982. *The Epistle to the Galatians*. The New International Greek Testament Commentary, ed. H.I. Marshall. Grand Rapids, MI: Eerdmans, 1982.

Campbell, W. S. 1993. "Judaizers." In *Dictionary of Paul and His Letters*, ed. Gerald F. Hawthorne, 512-16. Downers Grove, IL: InterVarsity, 1993.

Clark, Gordon H. 1973. "Legalism." In *Baker's Dictionary of Christian Ethics*, ed. Carl F. H. Henry, 385. Grand Rapids, MI: Baker, 1973.

Dobson, Edward. 1987. "Seven Characteristics of Legalism." *Fundamentalist Journal* 1987.

Dunn, James D. G. 1985. "Works of the Law and the Curse of the Law." *New Testament Studies* 31 1985: 523-42.

Dunn, James D.G. 1991. *The Parting of the Ways: Between Christianity and Judaism and Their Significance for the Character of Christianity*. London: SCM, 1991.

Edwards, Tilden. 1980. *Spiritual Friend*. New York, NY: Paulist.

Eliade, Mircea, ed. 1987. *Encyclopedia of Religion*, vol. 8. New York, NY: Macmillan, 1987.

Ellul, Jacques. 1983. *Living Faith*. San Francisco, CA: Harper & Row, 1983.

_____. 1986. *The Subversion of Christianity*. Grand rapids: Eerdmans, 1986.

Fish, Stanley. 1980. *Is There a Text in This Class?: The Authority of Interpretive Communities*. Cambridge, Mass: Harvard, 1980.

Fletcher, Joseph. 1966. *Situational Ethics*. London: SCM.

Gilliland, Dean. 2000. "Contextualization." In *Evangelical Dictionary of World Missions*, ed. Scott Moreau, 225-27. Grand Rapids, MI: Baker Books, 2000.

Gundry, Stanley N., ed. 1996. *Five Views on Law and Gospel*. Grand Rapids, MI: Zondervan, 1996.

http://www.orthodoxnews.netfirms.com/Romanian. "Romanian Christian Churches Prepare List of Communist-Era Martyrs." *Orthodox News*, February, 3rd 2004, 1.

Jackson, Bernard S. 1979. "Legalism.". *Journal for Jewish Studies* 1 (1979): 1-22.

Johnstone, Patrick. 2001. *Operation World*. Colorado Springs, CO: Global Mapping International, 2001.

Kirk, Kenneth. 1966. *The Vision of God*. New York, NY: Harper & Row, 1966.

Kirk, L.A. 1980. "Legalism or Permisiveness: An Inescapable Dillema." *The Christian Century* 97 (1980): 434-38.

Kittel, Gerhard, ed. 1987. *Theological Dictionary of New Testament*. Translated by Geoffrey Bromiley, vol. 1. Grand Rapids, MI: Eerdmans, 1987.

Koehler, J.P. 1969. "Legalism in an Evangelical Church." *Concordia Theological Monthly* 15, no. 3 (1969).

Kuzmic, Peter. 1983. "Why Romania Has Become the Korea of Europe."*Global Church Growth Magazine* 20 (1983): 12.

La Brie, Laurent J. 2001. "The Cost of Legalism." *Vox Domini Church Bulletin*, July 15 2001.

Loader, William. 2001. *Jesus and the Fundamentalism of His Day*. Grand Rapids, MI: Eerdmans, 2001.

Longenecker, Richard N. 1990. *Galatians*. Vol. 41. Word Biblical Commentary, ed. David Hubbard. Dallas, TX: Word, 1990.

Macquarrie, John, ed. 1967. *Dictionary of Christian Ethics*. Philadelphia, PA: The Westminster, 1967.

Malone, David. "Virtue." In *Encyclopedia of Fundamentalism*, ed. Brenda E. Brasher. New York, NY: Routledge, 2001.

Marshall, H.I. "Culture in the New Testament." In *Down to Earth: Studies in Christianity and Culture*, ed. John R.W. and Robert Coote Stott. Grand Rapids, MI: Eerdmans, 1980.

Martin, Vincent. 1995. *A House Divided: The Parting of the Ways between Synagogue and Church*. Studies in Judaism and Christianity. New York: Paulist Press, 1995.

Matera, Frank J. 1992. *Galatians*. Vol. 9. Sacra Pagina, ed. Daniel Harrington. Collegeville, MN: Liturgical, 1992.

McKnight, Scott. 1991. *A Light among the Gentiles. Jewish Missionary Activity in the Second Temple Period*. Minneapolis, MN: Fortress, 1991.

Mehedinti, Simion. 1995. *Crestinismul Romanesc*. Bucuresti: Editura Anastasia, 1995.

Miller, David R. 1992. *Breaking Free: Rescuing Families from the Clutches of Legalism*. Grand Rapids, MI: Baker.

Moo, D. J. 1983. "'Law,' 'Works of the Law,' and Legalism in Paul."*Westminster Theological Journal* 45 (1983): 73-100.

Moreau, A. Scott ed., 2000. *Evangelical Dictionary of World Missions*. Grand Rapids, MI: Baker, 2000.

Niebuhr, Richard. 2001. *Christ & Culture*. San Francisco, CA: Harper, 2001.

Oates, Wayne. 1973. "Legalism and the Use of the Bible." *Pastoral Psychology* (1973).

Osborne, Grant. 1991. *The Hermeneutical Spiral*. Downers Grove, IL: InterVarsity, 1991.

Padilla, Rene C., ed. 1986. *Conflict and Context*. Grand Rapids, MI: Eerdmans, 1986.

Popovici, Alexa. 1976. *Istora Anabaptistilor Din Romania 1527-1768*. Chicago: Editura Bisericii Baptiste Romane.

_____. 1980. *Istoria Baptistilor Din Romania 1856-1919*. Vol. 1. Chicago, IL: Editura Bisericii Baptiste Romane.

_____. 1989. *Istoria Baptistilor Din Romania 1919-1944*. Vol. 2. Chicago, IL: Editura Bisericii Baptiste Romane.

Priest, Robert J. 1994. "Missionary Elenctics: Conscience and Culture." *Missiology: An International Review* 22, no. 3 (1994): 291-315.

_____. 1997. "Cultural Factors in Victorious Living." In *Free and Fulfilled: Victorious Living in the Twenty-First Century*, ed. Robertson McQuilkin, 129-42. Nashville, TN: Thomas Nelson, 1997.

Prochau, Tim. 2001. *Romania: State of the Church.* www.ibiblitoteca.ro/stateof the church.html, 2001. Accessed.

Sanders, E. P. 1977. *Paul and Palestinian Judaism*. Philadelphia, PA: Fortress, 1977.

Schreiner, T. R. 1993. "Works of the Law." In *Dictionary of Paul and His Letters*, ed. Gerald Hawthorne, 976-79. Downers Grove, IL: Intervarsity, 1993.

Shklar, Judith. 1964. *Legalism*. Cambridge, Mass: Harvard.

Smith, Gerald B. "Legalism." In *A Dictionary of Religion and Ethics*, ed. Shailer and Smith Mathews, Gerald B., 257. New York, NY: Macmillan, 1921.

Smith, Terence V. 1921. *Petrine Controversies in Early Christianity*. Wissenschaftliche Untersuchungen Zum Neuen Testament 2. Reihe, ed. Martin Hengel. Tubingen: J.C.B. Mohr, 1985.

Stanculescu, Adrian. 2002. "Romanian Evangelical Christianity: Historical Origins and Development Prior to the Communist Period." Thesis, Trinity International University, 2002.

Stott, John R.W. 1970. *Christ the Controversialist*. Downers Grove, IL: InterVarsity, 1970.

Taylor, Nicholas. 1992. *Paul, Antioch and Jerusalem*. Journal for the Study of the New Testament Supplement Series 66. Shefield, UK: JSOT, 1992.

Ulstein, Stefan. 1995. *Growing up Fundamentalist: Journeys in Legalism & Grace*. Downers Grove, IL: Intervarsity, 1995.

Vander Giessen-Reits, Kirstin. 2004. "Blessed Are Those Who Are Persecuted."*Catapult* 3, no. 3 (2004).

Witherington III, Ben. 1998. *Grace in Galatia*. Grand Rapids, MI: Eerdmans, 1998.

14

Syncretism and Identity Among The Bayano Kuna

Eric J. Moeller

There is growing recognition in both the social sciences and missiology of the critical importance of the phenomenon of ethnicity in our world. When we think about ethnicity in missiological context, we should think of it in terms of the human quest for meaning and belonging. Meaning and belonging are found in community. While many early 20th century thinkers predicted that the salience of ethnic identity would diminish in the modern world, world events seem to have proven otherwise. Ethnicity is often a critical component in people's sense of identity. Rather than proving to be a residue of traditional society destined to diminish in importance in the modern world, ethnic identity is proving to be at the heart of human affairs. Christians cannot escape wrestling

> **Ethnic identity is proving to be at the heart of human affairs.**

with the power of ethnicity because ethnic conflicts are some of the most intractable problems facing the church and world. Issues of ethnic identity also powerfully impact mission outreach. Relations between ethnic groups often determine people's receptivity to the Gospel and alter and transform their understanding of it. Charles Taber (1991) has pointed out how mid-20th century missiology was shaped by functionalism in its understanding of culture. One of the results of exploring new theoretical paradigms for the missiological task ought to be a greater focus on ethnic identity and boundaries. Fredrik Barth (1969), in what could be called a Copernican revolution in the understanding of ethnicity, suggested that rather than anthropology focusing on the cultural "stuff" contained *within* ethnic groups, it is also the task of anthropology to focus on the problematic and socially constructed boundary *between* ethnic groups. As we try to understand the processes of religious syncretism we do well to heed Barth's advice. One of the factors that shapes the adoption and transformation of religious symbols and practices is that of struggles to shape and retain ethnic identity and to define ethnic boundaries. Also, rather than viewing cultures as isolated, independent systems that are inherently conservative, we should understand that ethnic groups exist in interaction and tension with one another. They exist in a framework of domination and subordination, resistance and accommodation. The relationships and conflicts between and within groups will inevitably shape religious processes and will consequently have a profound impact on the success and outcome of mission endeavor. Robert Montgomery, in his work, *The Sociology of Missions*, has given considerable attention to these matters. He suggests that: "In light of the importance of domination and resistance to domination in religious movements and diffusion of religions, structural or power relations *between* groups become especially important in the sociology of mission" (Montgomery 1999, 83).

My own study of millenarianism among the Bayano Kuna Indians of Panama conducted while I served as a missionary there in the early 1990's, provides a test case for the importance of focusing on ethnic boundaries and ethnic interaction in the understanding of processes of religious syncretism. Millenarianism amongst the Kuna of the Bayano region of Eastern Panama is best understood in terms of the processes of ethnic opposition. It provides an argument for continued ethnic separatism and collectivism against blending into a more individualistic *mestizo* society. The wider relevance of this case for understanding syncretistic religious systems is to focus on the importance of ethnic identity and boundaries in the social construction, incorporation and utilization of religious symbols and ideas.

Brief Ethnographic and Historical Sketch of the Kuna

It is difficult to trace the history of the Kuna back before the period of Spanish colonialism. The historical record indicates that the societies of the indigenous peoples of Panama were profoundly altered by the Spanish conquest. It would appear that previous stratified, chiefdom societies were replaced by more egalitarian social groups that existed in conflict with the power of Spain. The institutions and beliefs of the Kuna were powerfully shaped by their conscious opposition to Spanish power as well as by their interaction with other ethnic groups. The first appearance of a group in the historical record that can clearly be identified with the Kuna occurs in the early 17th century. From that point on, the Kuna engaged the Spanish-speaking peoples of the region in warfare until the late 1700's. During this time, the Kuna learned to use their relationships with people from other European powers against the Spanish. Frequently, they found allies in the English and French pirates who raided the Caribbean coast of the Spanish empire. Also, during this period, the Kuna seem to have developed hostile relationships with escaped slaves that formed maroon communities in the lower Bayano River valley. According to historical sources, these communities of escaped slaves fought with the Kuna and captured Indian women to be their wives. Kuna relationships with these different ethnic groups seem to have shaped their belief system in such a way as to strongly enforce their need to keep themselves separate and avoid intermarriage with outsiders.

When the U.S. entered Panamanian society by fostering the independence of Panama in 1903 and building the Panama Canal, the Kuna continued their old practice of seeking relationships with powerful outsiders in order to thwart

Spanish domination. The efforts of the new Panamanian state to incorporate the Kuna population in the San Blas Islands along Panama's northeast coast and force their acculturation to Latino society led to the 1925 Dule (Kuna) Revolution. The Kuna plotted a rebellion and killed a number of Panamanian policemen stationed in their communities along with their mixed race children. Though the scale of this rebellion was small, only twenty-seven people were killed in this uprising, the Kuna were able to utilize their contacts with sympathetic Americans to bring about American intervention with the Panamanian government. An agreement was signed between the Kuna and the government of Panama aboard the U.S.S. Cleveland. As a result, the Kuna were given rights to a large territory of land along the northeast coast of Panama called the Comarca of San Blas. Today the Kuna call it Kuna Yala or Land of the Kuna.

Today the population of Kuna in Panama exceeds 50,000. This study was conducted in the early 1990's primarily in a village called Ipeti, a five-hour bus ride east of Panama City along the Pan American highway, a poorly maintained, narrow dirt road. The village of Ipeti is part of a population referred to as the Bayano Kuna that was also granted an indigenous reserve by the Panamanian government in 1934.

The Kuna of Ipeti are semi-subsistence peasant farmers. They live along the Ipeti River and farm plots in the more fertile land along the river's edge. The main food crop is the plantain but they also raise corn, rice, cassava and other root crops, sour sop(or guanabana), oranges, mango and other fruits. They continue to hunt and fish in the forest although game has become scarcer due to deforestation. Many Kuna supplement their income through selling wood to the lumber companies or working as laborers for those same companies. Deforestation and loss of land from the encroachment of Latino peasant farmers and cattle ranchers are the greatest threats to the continuation of their way of life. Also the lure of the city and the influence of schooling upon the young threaten to undermine Kuna tradition and community.

Kuna communal traditions have, however, proved to be tremendously resilient. Supported by the unusually ample reserves of land granted them by the Panamanian government, they are considered to be one of the more successful and politically savvy Indian peoples in Latin

America. Christian missions have been active in some sectors of the Kuna population. The Baptist Church has had the biggest influence on the larger Kuna population in San Blas. Until the 1970's, the Kuna in Bayano were more isolated than the Kuna in San Blas and consequently more traditional. Mission efforts in the Bayano region by the 1990's had been sporadic and largely unsuccessful.

Kuna traditional religion can be conveniently divided into three areas of practice: meetings of the gathering house, diagnosis and curing of illness, and communal puberty festivals that center around the maturation of the young girls. The gathering house (*onmakke nega*) is at the heart of Kuna community and ritual life. It is a large thatch-roofed structure with enough seating for most of the members of the community to be present in it. In Ipeti, meetings of the *onmakke nega* are held almost nightly, beginning just after sunset and continuing for two to four hours. There are two kinds of meetings, singing meetings and talking meetings. Both kinds of meetings are presided over by the chiefs. The singing meeting is led by two chiefs who sing in responsorial format seated on hammocks strung up in the center of the building. The leader for the evening sings about the myths of the Kuna people as well as about dreams or visions that people have had in the community. This is the forum where predictions of an imminent end of the world or reversal of the social order were publicly proclaimed.

The talking meeting is for discussion of problems in the village, whether it is regarding policy towards the lumber companies, an upcoming puberty festival, or a case of adultery in the village. Issues are discussed at length with extended speeches by men of the community until a consensus is reached and the first chief announces a decision. Because the gathering house is both a political and religious institution, it provides the opportunity to bring religious ideas to bear on social problems confronting the Kuna and also where political issues shape the formation of religious ideas.

Kuna social organization and orientation toward the outside world fits very closely Eric Wolf's model of a "closed corporate community." Gathering house ritual is the vital center of that community. According to Wolf, such communities typically possess

> a system of power which embraces the male members of the community and makes the achievement of power a matter of community decision rather than a matter of individually achieved status. This system of power is often tied into a religious system . . . The political-religious system as a whole tends to define the boundaries of the community and acts as a rallying point and symbol of collective unity.
> (Wolf 1964, 507-508)

Curing ritual involves two key figures: the *inadulet*, literally medicine man, and the *nele*, or village prophet(ess). It is the job of the *nele* to diagnose the illness, i.e. determine what evil spirit is causing it, and it is the job of the medicine man to treat it with herbal medicines and magical singing. Cure is accomplished as the good spirits associated with the medicine, instructed and guided by the medicine man's chanting, battle and overcome the evil spirits (*bonis*) that cause disease. Kuna medicine and its practitioners encounter a serious challenge from modern medicine practiced by Latino society. Kuna are pragmatists and will seek healing where they can find it. But the success of modern medicine is perceived as a threat by traditionalists. They often argue that Kuna medicine is better than the medicine of the *waga*. For example, it is argued that Western medicine cures rapidly, but that Kuna medicine resolves the real problem, not just the symptoms.   Also, Western medicine is often viewed with suspicion as a kind of black magic, drawing power from macabre and sinister practices such as surgery and the drawing of blood.

The third major dimension of Kuna ritual life is the ritual of the *inna nega* or chicha house. When a girl reaches puberty, a lengthy ceremony must be held to prepare her for womanhood. The most important part of the ceremony for the people of the village is the feasting, drinking, and dancing that accompany it. These festivals may last as long as three days and nights and involve considerable investment of time, labor and expense by the girl's family and the community as a whole.

Puberty ceremonies are linked to another important dimension of Kuna communalism and ethnic identity. Women are the core of the Kuna household. Residence rules among the Kuna are uxorilocal, that is, young men at the time of marriage go to live with their wife's family. They serve their father-in-law and wife's family for many years. Household structure is a key difference between the Kuna and Latino ways of life in Bayano. The Latino way of life is more individualistic. Latinos live in nuclear family households usually with common-law marriage. The conjugal bond tends to be unstable and men and women may have a number of partners over the life span. Kuna life in the uxorilocal household is more stable and less individualistic. It is regulated by the community as a whole. Domestic problems will be adjudicated in the gathering house. The uxorilocal household also is linked to communal ownership of land. A young man works his father-in-law's plots on behalf of the household. Although use rights to plots of land are inherited through both sides of the family, one does not work one's own land for oneself alone.

Syncretistic Millenarianism as a Product of Oppositional Ethnicity

All of this serves as background to the main focus of this study, the millenarian rhetoric and beliefs expressed in gathering house ritual and in discussions in the village in the early 1990's. Kuna beliefs at this time seem to have been stimulated by the approach of the year 2000 that also provoked speculation among the Latino population about the end of the world. Kuna millenarian beliefs closely parallel those observed in the cargo cults of Oceania. For example, here is a description of the ideology of the Tuka movement, initiated by the prophet Navosavakandua in Fiji in 1885.

> The ancestors were shortly to return to Fiji. When they did, the millennium would begin: the faithful would enter the Mburoto Kula, the Glorious Paradise, and the ancient lands and independence of the past would be restored. Eternal life and eternal pleasure were to be the lot of the faithful . . . The shops would be jammed with calico, tinned salmon and other goods for the faithful, but unbelievers would die, or be condemned to everlasting hell-fire, or become the slaves and servants of believers. Navosavakandua's message was also directed against the Whites: government officials, missionaries and traders were to be driven into the sea.
>
> (Worsley 1957, 21)

In the above quote there are basically three parallels with Kuna conceptions. First of all, there is the hope of an imminent reversal of the relative poverty and subordination of the people. The Kuna talked about how the land would be restored to them. All of Panama would be theirs. Second, they expressed the hope that they would have access to the goods of modern society. The stores of Panama City would be theirs. They would own cars and airplanes. Third, they talked of punishment for the Latinos or *wagas*, the non-Indians. They would be slaves of the Kuna or thrown into the sea.

The ethnographic record is full of many examples of beliefs like these among indigenous peoples around the world. What is particularly striking about Kuna millenarian beliefs are the strong emphases on ethnic distinctions. Kuna describe themselves as the golden people, the chosen people of Great Father. They decry racial mixture as against the will of Great Father. A kind of "heavenly apartheid" along ethnic lines is a part of their vision of the afterlife. When they discussed the afterlife, they often stated that the good Kuna would be close to Great Father in Father's place. Other ethnic groups would be in separate islands or places farther from Great Father. One problem with marriage outside of the Kuna people, they said, is that the children of such unions would not be in the same place after death as their parents. These ethnic distinctions expressed in Kuna notions of the afterlife are also developed in their millenarian ideology.

The reality of opposition vis-à-vis other ethnic groups provides the key to understanding much about Kuna millenarianism. It is a product of Kuna ethnic opposition to Latino society and its domination. Thus, the development of this syncretistic religious ideology is best explained in terms of ethnic opposition. The logic of ethnic opposition is woven into Kuna millenarianism as well as into Kuna mythology more generally.

In a discussion we had one day, one of my informants, a chief of Ipeti and a highly regarded medicine man, summarized Kuna beliefs about a coming reversal. It was summarized in my field notes. It brings together a striking collection of ideas from Kuna mythology, Christianity and other sources. The logic that ties these diverse components together is one of ethnic opposition.

He said Jesus would come in five years because it is the year 2000. I asked him about the Kuna race. He said it was a pure race or blood (ablis *okinnoet*), a blood which is fragrant, he said. On the other hand, Latinos have black or bad blood (*ablis kutturreget*, Sp. *color morado, oscuro*, purple color, dark or black). He said that Latinos only have fighting in their hearts (*wagmar e kwake unnila urwe nai*) although there are a few friends (*ai nuedi*). When I asked him what the *daet* (way of life) of the Latinos was, he said that they were Jews (Sp., judios). They fight, they want to kill (*make*) people.

He began to talk about the fate of the wicked. They will go to the fourth level and be punished indefinitely. There is a big river there; there will be earthquakes and other problems. The Latinos in Panama will all drown in the sea, he said. The Americans in their country will not perish. Americans are good people; they have good blood.

He said that before the end comes a golden plate (*olobatte*) will take the good Kuna, who share their food and go to the gathering house, to the mountain of Errey Montezuma(King Montezuma). He says that Montezuma is God's son. Things will be changed in a moment to gold. The Latinos don't know that they will perish. God doesn't let them know. The buildings in Panama will turn to gold and will be inherited by the Kuna. The chief himself will have 32 airplanes and 32 houses. He will have 8 wives. There will be no jealousy in heaven.

He said that God did not love the *wagas* (Latinos) and he spoke of how they had treated Jesus. He mentioned several *waga* kings who rejected Christ. Herod was one and he killed all the children. Later they crucified Jesus. A King Midas (perhaps an identification with Judas in that he sold Jesus for silver) put the sword in Jesus' chest. He also spoke of the Latinos as devils (*niamar*). He said that they have a lot of money and cars while he does not have those things.

This is a fair summary of the beliefs that constituted Kuna millenarianism. Here we can see a fine example of syncretism in the sense of mixing of ideas from different religions and cultures. Apart from the specifically religious elements, there are thoughts from European folklore (King Midas) and the history of Indian America (Montezuma). The idea of a coming cataclysm combines notions from traditional Kuna cosmology of repeated destructions and recreations of the world with the Christian belief in the Second Coming of Christ and Judgment Day. However, these ideas are not mixed randomly; they are put together in terms of the logic of ethnic opposition. Syncretism is not a passive process here, where ideas from two religious systems are linked together because of a lack of understanding and the desire to hold on to old beliefs. Rather, ideas from different belief systems are put together according to the logic of ethnic opposition for the purpose of maintaining ethnic boundaries.

> Syncretism is not a passive process here.....[r]ather, ideas from different belief systems are put together according to the logic of ethnic opposition...

The chief combined racial and ethical notions in his understanding of the coming end. The *wagas* are conceived to be racially and physically inferior (they have bad blood), and also morally inferior (they only have fighting in their hearts). He also describes the rich Latinos as devils. This was characteristic of Kuna rhetoric and has been noted by other observers. This is of course not unique to the Kuna. Demonization of the enemy is a common sociological phenomenon and the identification of the non-Indian with the devil or demons has been observed elsewhere in Latin America (Howe 1991, 22; Warren 1978, 47).

Another way the Latinos are demonized is by associating them with the Jews and Herod. This too has been observed elsewhere in Latin America. This seems to be a product of the Passion plays of colonial Catholicism. It was opportune for the Indians to associate their oppressors, the Latinos, with those who killed Christ. A study of Maya mythology and ritual has documented the same phenomenon.

> The leaders of the nineteenth-century Indian rebellions in highland Chiapas and the Yucatan peninsula tried to revitalize Indian culture by reinterpreting Catholic symbols in terms relevant to Indian experience. In both cases, the reworking took the form of "Indianizing" the concept of the Passion: Christ became an Indian, and "Ladino" became synonymous with Jew. (Bricker 1969, 162)

The account of Jesus' passion here has been worked into the Indian religious ideology but with a significantly different meaning. The meaning of Jesus' death is not as the means of redemption from sin but rather is an illustration of the evil of the oppressor, the ethnic other.

The Kuna often fit Jesus into their scheme of ethnic contrasts. The most important culture hero in Kuna mythology is a figure called Ibe Orgun. He is an idealized image of a Kuna chief and teacher and is said to have taught Kuna the most important elements of their way of life. He taught them their medicine, for example. He made them a truly human people. In contrast, Kuna mythology often depicts other Indian groups as animal-men, not truly human. In the Kuna mind, Ibe Orgun is often equated with Jesus. Some said Ibe Orgun and Jesus were brothers. Both Jesus and Ibe Orgun are sometimes referred to as God's Son (*Bab machi*-Father's Son). When Jesus came to the *waga* on the other side of the sea, Ibe Orgun was already teaching the Kuna. Just as Ibe Orgun taught the Kuna their culture, so Jesus taught the *wagas* their culture and as Ibe Orgun taught the Kuna their medicine so Jesus taught the *waga* their medicine. In conceiving of Jesus and Ibe Orgun as parallel to each other the meaning of each one is altered. Ibe Orgun was not *Bab machi* in the original Kuna conception. His place in Kuna mythology is altered by the need to oppose the figure of Jesus. And of course, Jesus is not primarily a teacher of culture for the Latino. But His role is construed this way for the purposes of Kuna ethnic ideology.

The Kuna use the crucifixion of Jesus as the basis for a claim to superiority over the *waga* and a reason to reject their way of life and their religion. The claim is made that the *wagas* killed Jesus when He came to teach them whereas the Kuna treated their teacher well. Here is an account from a compilation of Kuna myths published in Spanish:

> When Ibeorgun came down here, Jesus Christ came down on the other side of the sea, and he also was charged with teaching all the people over there. But the people of that region did not listen to him, they threw rocks at him and insulted him. Here, on the other hand, everyone listened to the counsels of Ibeorgun and treated him with respect.
>
> (Chapin 1970, 43)

The cultural logic of this is one of ethnic opposition. Kuna religious ideology is constructed in opposition to the Latinos and to Latino domination. Even the message of Christ is utilized for this purpose. This kind of response has characterized indigenous encounter with European Christianity throughout the Americas. The Moravian missionary David Zeisberger encountered similar thinking among the Iroquois in 1773. Zeisberger recorded one Iroquois man stating that "Indians are men, even as are the whites, but God has created them differently." When Zeisberger told the man about Jesus' death on the cross, he replied, "Then the Indians are certainly not guilty of His death, as the whites are" (Dowd 1992, 42). Both the Iroquois and the Kuna were involved in the same sociological process, the attempt to claim parity or superiority for Indian beliefs and ways in contrast to those of the Europeans. Consequently, there is a parallel development of religious ideology.

Millenarianism can be understood in terms of what Max Weber calls "theodicy". A theodicy for Weber is an attempt to explain misfortune or good fortune in a world where one's fate is uncertain. Kuna millenarianism would correspond to what Weber terms a "theodicy of misfortune" (Weber 1946, 274). The Kuna struggle with the fact that they are in a subordinate position within society. They do not have the same access to wealth and influence in Panamanian society that others have. At the same time they value their communal existence and traditions. They view themselves as the golden people of Great Father, yet they find themselves in a difficult and subordinate position. Millenarianism explains their current misfortune by claiming that their situation will soon be radically altered. They will find themselves on top in the social system of Panama. They will no longer be deprived; they will enjoy the consumer goods, cars and airplanes that the wealthy Panamanians have.

This millenarian idea is not just an expression of ethnic resentment. It is understood in moral terms. Though the millennium will bring judgement on the Latinos, it will also bring judgement on those Kuna who do not follow the ethical norms of the community. The criteria for salvation are moral criteria, but they are moral criteria shaped by the Kuna and understood in ethnic terms (see Crumrine 1977 for a similar perspective on moral conceptions of a Native American group). From the perspective of Christian understanding, the Kuna, like all people, live their lives in a moral framework. This is part of the "law written upon the heart" of which Paul wrote in Romans 2:15. The conditions of existence require all people to understand the basic elements of God's law. Thus, Kuna millenarian notions do have a genuine ethical core to them. They are not just an excuse to justify the Kuna vis-à-vis the Latinos. But every people has particular understandings of these basic moral principles based on their own culture and society. Thus, Kuna moral conceptions are understood in terms of their own values and way of life. They understand that Kuna will come out on top in the coming judgment because Kuna by nature of their ethnicity and commitment to the communal values of the group are believed to be morally superior to the non-Kuna.

Kuna communalism is under siege. Their claim to their land is based on ethnicity and they hold their lands as a people, not under individual titles. But land hungry Latino peasants living on the edge of the reserve see unused land there. They claim that the Kuna are not utilizing the land so they should be entitled to farm it. During the 1990's there were a number of clashes between Kuna and Latino peasants due to squatting on the reserve.

The Kuna are also under siege from within. The draw of city life and wage labor with the lumber companies draws young men away from a commitment to Kuna communal traditions. As people are increasingly drawn into the cash economy, they are no longer as oriented toward communal ownership of land and forest and communal labor to build houses and prepare for puberty festivals. Young people whose schooling has inclined them to participation in urban life are less inclined to submit to the rules and authority of the community as promoted and enforced in the gathering house.

The table on the following page diagrams what is at stake for the Kuna as they strive to maintain their ethnic boundary. It follows the logic of Kuna ethnic ideology and opposition to the *waga*. Sometimes they speak of this as a conflict between "tradition" and "civilization." Millenarianism defends against the loss of their communal order. They fear the moral disorder of a world where individual interest prevails over community interest. The world of wage labor and private property is one where the moral value they hold in highest regard, the obligation to share, is undermined. Many in the community, especially the young men, strain at the leash of village controls and expectations. Traditionalists use the promise of an overturning of the social order as a way to keep

The Social Consequences of the Difference Between "Waga" and "Kuna"

"Waga"		"Kuna"
1. "civilization"	vs.	1. "tradition"
2. secularization or Christianization	vs.	2. *onmakke nega* (gathering house), "millennium"
3. "moral disorder"	vs.	3. communal control of moral disorder
4. nuclear household with tendency towards conjugal instability	vs.	4. uxorilocal household, relatively stable conjugal unions
5. women relatively unprotected	vs.	5. family structure offers protection for women
6. individual freedom	vs.	6. social control by the village
7. wage earning and commercialization of agriculture	vs.	7. peasant agriculture, "closed corporate community"
8. loss of control of land and proletarianization	vs.	8. control of land based on ethnic identity
9. mestizaje and dispersion	vs.	9. ethnic solidarity and identity

others committed to Kuna ethnic communalism. The Kuna way, *dule daet*, defines Kuna expectations vis-à-vis the world and way of the *waga*. The uxorilocal household as part of the village community stands over against the unstable conjugal bond and individual families of the *waga*. Communal ownership and control of land stands against individual ownership and loss of the land. Maintaining ethnic purity through endogamy is opposed to the alternative of racial mixture and the dispersion of the ethnic community.

Kuna millenarianism and concepts of afterlife promise to reward those who are faithful to Kuna tradition and communalism. Peasant farming is exalted. Commitment to traditional ritual knowledge, medicine chants and gathering house ritual will be rewarded. Violation of the ethnic boundary, especially race mixing, is severely condemned. Politics and religion are woven together, both in gathering house ritual and in millenarianism. Millenarian rhetoric provides a means of social control against that which threatens the integrity of the community.

Missiological Lessons from Kuna Millenarianism

This case study demonstrates the importance of an approach to understanding syncretism that integrates the social and religious. Dualism has been an Achilles heel of much thinking about missions and the church (cf. Schwarz 1999, 35). For example, Donald McGavran stated, in *Understanding Church Growth*, that "the great obstacles to conversion are social, not theological" (McGavran 1990, 215). McGavran meant that we need to think seriously about social factors as we attempt to reach the lost peoples of the world. Kuna millenarian religious thought demonstrates this since it clearly shows how important ethnic boundaries and group identity are to them as they wrestle with spiritual questions. However, McGavran's statement, though correct from the perspective of social science, dichotomizes our conception of how mission works. Either obstacles to conversion are conceived to be social, and therefore not theological, or they are conceived to be theological, and therefore not social. Such thinking leads to distorted perspectives. Surely Scripture teaches that the primary obstacle to conversion is the sinful, darkened heart of human beings. This is an important issue of theological truth. Nevertheless, this truth does not mean that McGavran was wrong in saying that there are very great social obstacles to conversion. The social is not separated from the spiritual since our human existence is lived in the framework of our social relationships. In Kuna millenarian beliefs, issues of human sinfulness, divine justice, and ethnic identity are bound together. To proclaim the Gospel contextually, we must think both sociologically and theologically.

In missiological perspective, the issue of syncretism can benefit from an analysis focusing on ethnicity and ethnic boundaries. Syncretism is not just a mixing of elements from a pagan religious system with elements from Christianity. Because the Gospel message comes to people in an interethnic and indeed global context, elements from Christianity are often adopted and adapted by peoples specifically to address issues of ethnic identity. Understanding this dynamic provides insight into syncretistic religious systems and reveals underlying identity issues that powerfully motivate people. True repentance for the Kuna means to give up a self-righteousness based on ethnicity and to recognize that they have no righteousness apart from Christ. The Kuna in Bayano see their identity as a people being threatened by forces from without and by those from within who would break away from communal life. The millenarian defense of ethnic identity demonstrates how important corporate ethnic identity is to the Kuna. It serves as a reminder that the message of Christ is not just a call to individual conversion but a proclamation of the Kingdom of God. Those who bring the Gospel to the Kuna need to show them that accepting the Gospel would not lead to their destruction as a people but rather to their incorporation as the people of God and that the coming Kingdom they long for is found, not in their ethnic group, but in Christ.

> **The issue of syncretism can benefit from an analysis focusing on ethnicity and ethnic boundaries.**

Sources Cited

Barth, Fredrik, ed. 1969. *Ethnic Groups and Boundaries: The Social Organization of Cultural Differences.* London: Allen and Unwin.

Bricker, Victoria Reifler. 1981. *The Indian Christ, the Indian King: The Historical Substrate of Maya Myth and Ritual.* Austin: University of Texas Press.

Chapin, Mac. 1970. *Pab Igala: Historias de la Tradicion Kuna.* Panama: Centro de Investigaciones Antropologicas de la Universidad de Panama.

Crumrine, N. Ross. 1977. *The Mayo Indians of Sonora: A People Who Refuse to Die.* Tucson: University of Arizona Press.

Dowd, Gregory Evans. 1992. *A Spirited Resistance: The North American Indian Struggle for Unity, 1745-1815.* Baltimore: John Hopkins Press.

Howe, James. 1986. *The Kuna Gathering: Contemporary Village Politics in Panama.* Austin: University of Texas Press.

_____. 1991. "An Ideological Triangle: The Struggle Over San Blas Kuna Culture, 1915-1925," in *Nation-States and Indians in Latin America.* Eds. Greg Urban and Joel Sherzer. Austin: University of Texas Press.

McGavran, Donald A. 1990. *Understanding Church Growth, 3rd Edition.* Revised and edited by Peter Wagner. Grand Rapids: Eerdmans.

Montgomery, Robert L. 1999. *Introduction to the Sociology of Missions.* Westport, CT: Praeger.

Schwarz, Christian A. 1999. *Paradigm Shift in the Church: How Natural Church Development Can Transform Theological Thinking.* St. Charles, IL: Church Smart Resources.

Taber, Charles. 1991. *The World is too Much with Us: "Culture" in Modern Protestant Missions*. Macon, GA: Mercer University Press.

Warren, Kay. 1978. *The Symbolism of Subordination: Indian Identity in a Guatemalan Town*. Austin: University of Texas Press.

Weber, Max. 1946. *From Max Weber: Essays in Sociology*. Trans. and ed. by H.H. Gerth and C. Wright Mills. New York: Oxford University Press.

_____. 1978. *Economy and Society*. G. Roth and C. Wittich, eds. Berkeley: University of California Press.

Wolf, Eric R. 1964. *Anthropology*. Englewood Cliffs: Prentice-Hall.

Worsley, Peter. 1957. *The trumpet shall sound: a study of "cargo" cults in Melanesia*. London: MacGibbon & Kee.

Wuthnow, Robert. 1987. *Meaning and Moral Order*. Berkeley: University of California Press.

15

Building Bridges to Muslims or Syncretism: A Test Case

Gareth Lee Cockerill

Introduction

As evening shadows fell the old man rode his donkey toward home. His young grandson ran along behind, taking two steps for every step of the trotting donkey. As they passed through the first village, a woman shouted from her veranda, "Old man, why are you treating that boy so harshly, making him run behind. Can't you see his legs are short?" The old man got off, put the boy on, and the donkey plodded ahead. They passed a farmer on the road who stopped, scowled at the boy, and said,

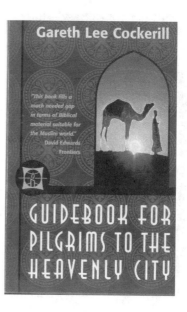

Gareth Lee Cockerill

"This book fills a much needed gap in terms of Biblical material suitable for the Muslim world."
David Edwards
Frontiers

GUIDEBOOK FOR PILGRIMS TO THE HEAVENLY CITY

"Shame on you, son. You should respect the age of your grandfather and let him ride." Both grandfather and grandson sat astride the donkey. As they passed the next village, people began to shout: "Poor donkey, what are you doing overloading your beast so!" The old man and boy arrived home carrying the donkey on a pole. Needless to say, the villagers laughed them to scorn!

I often felt like this old man (I wish I could say the boy!) while writing *Guidebook for Pilgrims to the Heavenly City* (Cockerill 2002, herein after referred to as *Guidebook*). Some people who reviewed the manuscript wanted the book to be more "Muslim-friendly," others cautioned against inadvertent syncretism. For example, each chapter begins with a description of some aspect of the *Hajj*. One missionary to the Muslim world who vetted the manuscript for William Carey Library said, "I like the way he [the author] begins each chapter with reference to the Hajj." On the other hand, Warren Larson, in his very favorable *EMQ* review of *Guidebook*, suggested that these summaries should have been omitted to avoid any hint of syncretism (Larson 2002: 526, 528). Thus it seemed appropriate to study *Guidebook* as a test case of the struggle between building bridges to Muslims and syncretism.

Figure 1

The C1 – C6 Spectrum					
C1	**C2**	**C3**	**C4**	**C5**	**C6**
Christ-Centered Community Description					
A church foreign to the Muslim community both in culture and language	Like C1, but speaking the language used by Muslims, though their religious terminology is distinctly non-Muslim.	Like C2, but using non-Islamic cultural elements (e.g., dress, music, diet, and arts	Like C3, but with some Biblically acceptable Islamic practices	Like C4 with a "Muslim follower of Jesus" self-identity	Secret believers, may or may not be active in the religious life of the Muslim community
Self-Identity					
"Christian"	"Christian"	"Christian"	"Follower of Isa"	"Muslim follower of Isa"	Primarily "Follower of Isa" or "Muslim follower of Isa"
Muslim Perception					
Christian	Christian	Christian	A kind of Christian	A strange kind of Muslim"	Muslim

from (Massey 2000, 7)

First, this study will survey the purpose, appropriateness, and content of *Guidebook*. Second, it will identify the sources of tension between bridge building and syncretism that arose in its writing. Third, it will discuss how this tension was addressed. This project grew out of my ministry in Sierra Leone, West Africa. About ten people with rich and varied experience in Muslim ministry representing the Middle East, South Asia, and Africa reviewed *Guidebook* in draft form. Their comments led to very significant rewriting and (I trust) improvement. I am also indebted to Rick Kress, of William Carey Library, for his constant encouragement. It is the purpose of this investigation to stimulate further discussion of these issues with the hope that such discussion will lead to interpretation of Scripture for Muslims and Muslim Background Believers (hereinafter "MBBs") that is both more effective and more faithful.

Guidebook for Pilgrims to the Heavenly City—An Overview

Guidebook is a holistic interpretation of Hebrews written to disciple MBBs. [1] It targets C4 and C5 MBBs (Massey 2000, 5-14; Travis 1998, 407-408), who do not identify themselves as "Christians" but as "followers of Jesus" and who follow many biblically permissible Islamic practices (see Figure 1). This book is especially useful as a teaching resource for English speaking workers who are discipling such believers. It may also be appropriate for some Muslims on the verge of turning to Jesus. The rationale and method for this project were laid out in an article entitled "To the Hebrews/To the Muslims: Islamic Pilgrimage as a Key to Interpretation" (Cockerill 1994, 347-359).

Why use Hebrews to disciple Muslims? First, the message of Hebrews is appropriate. Hebrews was written to a minority group who faced considerable pressure from the larger religious society to compromise their commitment to Jesus and return to their former religion (deSilva 2000). Even in a C4 or C5 context MBBs eventually face such pressure.[2]

---

[1] *Guidebook* is based on a very careful exegesis of the text of Hebrews. I have written a commentary on Hebrews for lay people and am under contract with Eerdmans to do a new volume on Hebrews in the NICNT series.

[2] Massey (2000, 7-8) says of C5 believers, "In time, however, their deviance from mainstream Islamic theology may lead to their banishment

Second, the answer Hebrews gives is the answer such MBBs must hear—the full sufficiency of Christ as the only way to God. Third, both Hebrews and Islam give a prominent place to the idea of religious pilgrimage, which serves Guidebook as an interpretive bridge. Fourth, Hebrews and Islam have many other points of contact rooted in Hebrews' use of the Old Testament and Islam's exposure to both Judaism and Christianity (Green 1989, 233-250).

Guidebook uses religious pilgrimage as a bridge to span the gap between the original recipients of Hebrews and MBBs.[3] The phenomenological model of pilgrimage developed by H. B. Partin as a tool for studying the Hajj (1967) and applied to Hebrews by William G. Johnsson (1978, 239-251) supplied the conceptual framework for this bridge. According to this model religious pilgrimage is characterized by four essential elements: separation from home, a sacred destination, a fixed religious purpose, and hardship along the way. It was easy to compare Hebrews'

Why use Hebrews to disciple Muslims?

1. **The recipients of Hebrews and Muslims face similar challenges.**
2. **The answer Hebrews gives is what Muslims need – the full sufficiency of Christ.**
3. **The prominent place of religious pilgrimage in Hebrews and Islam.**
4. **Many points of contact from Hebrews' use of the OT and Islam's exposure to Judaism and Christianity.**

teaching on the pilgrimage to the Heavenly City with pilgrimage to Mecca using these four categories. It was also fascinating to see how concrete this comparison could be due to the other points of contact between Hebrews and Islam mentioned above. For instance, as will be noted below, Abraham plays an analogous role in both pilgrimages. The

---

from the Muslim community." Of course, some C5 MBBs may not (yet) feel this pressure. Like the first readers of Hebrews, however, they face the possible imminent escalation of such pressure.

[3] The very title of this book, *Guidebook for Pilgrims to the Heavenly City*, is drawn from the publication and use of "guidebooks" for pilgrims to Mecca.

standing at Arafat on the ninth day of the month of pilgrimage provided a ready analogy for interpreting the standing before Sinai/Zion in Heb 12:18-29.

The pilgrimage motif also gives cohesiveness to *Guidebook*. Part One of *Guidebook* compares the pilgrimage to the Heavenly City described in Hebrews 10:29-12:29 to the *Hajj*. Part Two uses various aspects of the *Hajj* to show how the Christ described in Hebrews 1:1—10:18 is the one who enables us to successfully pursue this heavenly pilgrimage. Jesus is likened to our *Ka'bah* (Heb 1:1—2:4), to Muhammad as the founder of the pilgrimage (Heb 2:5-18; 4:14—5:10), and to our *mutawwif* or guide on the pilgrim way (12:1-17). His sacrifice, which takes up so much of Heb 8:1—10:18, is compared to the sacrifice commemorated by the Feast of Sacrifice at the conclusion of the *Hajj*. In addition, Christ's heavenly intercession (Heb 7:1-28) is compared to the intercession of Muhammad on the Day of Judgment. Hebrews designation of Christ as "Apostle" (Heb 3:1) paves the way for a comparison with Muhammad as the Apostle of God (Heb 3:1—4:13). The stoning of the devil (Heb 10:19-31) and the pilgrim state of *ihram* (Heb 13:1-25) are both used to describe the purity of the believer's life. The first of two appendices in the book gives an overview of *Hajj*, the second gives a chapter-by-chapter summary of *Guidebook* so that one can quickly get a sense of its content and direction.

This cohesiveness provided by the pilgrimage motif is in accord with the unity of the theology of Hebrews. The message of Hebrews is that Christ is the one, the only one, who can help us persevere until we enter the Heavenly City.

Building Bridges or Syncretism—Sources of Tensions

The resultant tension in *Guidebook* between bridge building and syncretism arises from at least four sources. First, the attempt to overcome Islam's objections to the crucifixion and divine Sonship of Jesus always involves such tension. Second, struggle with syncretism comes from addressing C4 and especially C5 believers. Writing such a book is made more difficult because C5 MBBs are a moving target.[4] Third,

---

[4] Some C5 MBBs still identify closely with Muslim religious observance (e.g. keeping the fast, attending the Mosque prayers) and some, while culturally Muslim, have moved away from those practices.

while common mention of Old Testament persons often serves as a bridge, problems arise when Hebrews and Islam offer conflicting reports of those persons. Fourth, the chosen method of communication causes this tension. Comparing the pilgrimage to the Heavenly City with the *Hajj* means that one must compare Christian practice and teaching with Muslim practice and teaching. On the one hand *Guidebook* had to describe Muslim practices without demeaning them or offending the sensitivity of the readers. On the other, I did not want to affirm the validity of those practices or let my descriptions draw readers back to Islam. *Guidebook* used Muslim practices and quotations from the Qur'an pedagogically to get the readers' attention and to explain the unknown by the known. It did not handle these quotations confrontationally. As a general rule *Guidebook* did not argue directly for the superiority of the pilgrimage to the Heavenly City and of the Christ who makes that pilgrimage possible. This book says, "Muslim practices can help us understand the wonderful pilgrimage to the Heavenly City that God has provided for us through Christ." Then it lets the text of Hebrews itself speak for the unsurpassable greatness of Christ and his saving work.

Building Bridges or Syncretism—Possibilities for Resolution

In the rest of this paper we will discuss examples of how this issue of building bridges/syncretism was addressed (1) in the choice of language, (2) in quoting the Qur'an, (3) in dealing with conflicting accounts of Old Testament personages, (4) in describing Muslim practices/teachings and comparing them with Christian, and (5) in communicating the Sonship and atoning death of Jesus.

Choice of Language

It was of first importance to avoid language that might be offensive to people in a C4 or C5 context. Thus it was necessary to exclude such expressions as "Christian" and "Church." Instead *Guidebook* uses terms like "believers" (Cockerill 2000, 13, 14, 70, 83, 94, 153, 159, 160), "followers of Jesus" (Cockerill 2000, 8, 12, 13, 14, 33, 48, 54, 60, 61, 71, 87, 111, 152, 159, 160, 169), "people of God" (Cockerill 2000, 33, 34, 35,

102, 103, 113, 114, 120), or "fellowship of Jesus' followers" (Cockerill 2000, 161). Nor is there use of such terms as "Israel" or "Jew." Where possible, phraseology familiar to Muslims was appropriated in a positive context. For instance, in the introduction the pilgrimage to the Heavenly City is identified as "the straight path": "Let us study our guidebook so that we will be able to follow the straight path to the Heavenly City" (Cockerill 2000, 8). "The straight path" is then used as a description of the journey to the Heavenly City throughout the book (Cockerill 2000, 12, 13, 14, 16, 17, 20, 33, 48, 53, 91, 112, 117, 149, 151, 164). On the other hand, it was not as easy to use the familiar language of "right guidance," since the salvation Jesus provides is so much more than "guidance." Thus although on page 112 *Guidebook* reads: "These commandments are the heart of the *Tawrah* and give clear guidance on how to walk the straight path," on page 98 it says, "Sin is more than the result of weakness and its cure requires more than right guidance." It might have been possible to use the language of "taking refuge" in God more effectively than I did. This language occurs only once: "As pilgrims to the Heavenly City we have a great resource for resisting temptation. Through the sacrifice of Christ we can take refuge from Satan by drawing 'near to God' (Heb 10:22) and receiving His victorious grace" (Cockerill 2000, 149).

Another terminological question arose with regard to the names of persons mentioned in both the Qur'an and the Bible. Should the book use "Isa" or "Jesus," "Musa" or "Moses," "Ibrahim" or "Abraham"? *Guidebook* uses the normal English names, that is, the ones found in our English Bible, which are also used in many English interpretations of the Qur'an. The first time such a person is mentioned a transliteration of the person's Qur'anic name follows in parenthesis: e.g., "Moses (*Musa*)" (Cockerill 2000, 8). If it has been a long time since a character was mentioned, the parenthesis may be repeated. A time or two the Qur'anic form has been used for effect, e.g. page 11: "Dauda explained to me that he wanted to become a follower of *Isa al Masih*." One reason preference is given to the normal English spelling has already been intimated. *Guidebook* is in English and so it seemed natural to use the forms of these names that occur in English Bibles and in many English interpretations of the Qur'an. Since *Guidebook* is commentary on the NIV text, it would have been necessary to change the Biblical text if Qur'anic names had been used.

If *Guidebook* is translated into other languages, as one reviewer hoped it would be, then the form of names and the Biblical text appropriate for those languages should be used. English-speaking Christian workers can use this book as a resource and make adjustment for their target language or group.

Another difficulty was whether or not to use the "honorifics" with these names and, of course, with the name of Muhammad, "may the blessing and peace of Allah be upon him." One reviewer of an earlier pre-publication manuscript strongly urged their usage. This reviewer, whose helpful comments were given anonymously, was the staunchest advocate of making the book more "Muslim-friendly."

It is true that Muslims and perhaps C5 MBBs, who by definition are living in a Muslim environment and following Muslim practices, might consider omission of these titles disrespectful. After consulting with several people I did not use them for fear of affirming the prophethood of Muhammad and thus turning MBBs back to their Muslim heritage. One could not use them for the other prophets without using them for him. Because C5 believers follow Jesus, even they must eventually deny the ultimacy of Muhammad's prophethood. Having raised these

> ## Why *Guidebook* cited the Qur'an?
>
> 1. **To show that the Qur'an and the Bible hold some teachings in common.**
> 2. **To show parallels between Biblical pilgrimage and the *Hajj*.**
> 3. **To answer objections by suggesting alternate interpretations of Qur'anic passages.**

objections, it still might be best to use these honorifics if *Guidebook* is translated into predominately Muslim languages. The same reviewer who urged use of honorifics also helped *Guidebook* avoid other errors when speaking of the prophets. For instance, in an earlier edition (there were many!) the text read: "Moses was not a coward." He felt that even making this statement would be offensive because it suggested that someone might think Moses a coward. Also, at his suggestion,

I did not try to explain the difference between the Biblical idea of prophet and the Muslim one. The Bible can treat Abraham and Moses as prophets, even if it does not primarily think of them in prophetic categories.

Quotations from the Qur'an

In order to build the interpretive bridge that is the basis of *Guidebook* it was necessary to cite the Qur'an. On the one hand, such citation ran the risk of implying to the new MBB that the Qur'an is Scripture on a par with the Bible. On the other was the danger of insulting such a new believer, or an interested Muslim inquirer, by referring to the Qur'an in a derogatory way. Earlier editions of *Guidebook* used such phrases as "Muslims believe" when citing the Qur'an. Due to reviewers' response this terminology was changed to a more straightforward "the Qur'an teaches" or "the Qur'an says" despite the risk involved. We can categorize the use of Qur'anic citations in *Guidebook* as follows:

First, citations are used to show that the Qur'an and the Bible hold beliefs in common. *Guidebook* cites Qur'an 53:4-11 and Luke 1:16-28 to show that both believe in angels (Cockerill 2000, 86). The Qur'an is also cited to show that both the Bible and the Qur'an refer to some of the same prophets (Cockerill 2002, 38).

Second, the Qur'an is cited in a number of places to show parallels between the *Hajj* and the pilgrimage to the Heavenly City. The following is a comment on Heb 11:8-22:

"The Qur'an says that God told Abraham to proclaim pilgrimage to Mecca (22:26-30). Abraham calls us on the pilgrimage to the Heavenly City. He is the first person to demonstrate clearly what it means to be a pilgrim."
(Cockerill 2000, 17)

Or again,

"As noted above, the Qur'an teaches that Abraham was the first to make the pilgrimage to the *Ka'bah* in Mecca and that God commanded him to call all people to pilgrimage. Heb 11:8-22 describes Abraham as the fist clear example of one who is a pilgrim to the Heavenly City. By his example Abraham calls us to follow." (Cockerill 2000, 23)

331

This type of quotation is in no way degrading to the Qur'an.

Third, when talking about the divine Sonship of Jesus and his atoning death *Guidebook* offers interpretations of Qur'anic texts that differ from standard Muslim interpretations. Thus the Qur'an is quoted positively, but the proffered interpretation may give offense. Of course Muslims normally understand Qur'an 4:158, "they did not slay him, neither crucified him," as a denial of the crucifixion. *Guidebook* suggests that this verse be understood to say that the Jewish leaders did not kill Jesus by their own power.[5] It also suggests that God's raising Jesus to Himself in Qur'an 4:159 may support the resurrection. Finally, it uses the designation of Jesus as God's "Word—the word which He [God] imparted to Mary" in 4:171 to explain what followers of Jesus mean when they call Jesus the "Son of God" (Cockerill 2002, 71).

Such interpretations are not likely to repulse C5 MBBs because they have already accepted Jesus. Nevertheless they are offered suggestively and undogmatically. After all, how do we feel when Muslim friends try to tell us that the "comforter" in John 15-16 is a reference to Muhammad?

Finally, there is at least one place where *Guidebook* comes close to actually contradicting a Qur'anic citation. I quote at length from the beginning of chapter eight, "An Intercessor Before the Day of Judgment!" on page 125:

> Will you intercede for me on the Day of Judgment?
> No, none of us will be able to intercede for friend,

---

[5]"The Qur'an pronounces the following judgment on those who hated Jesus so—'they did not slay him, neither crucified him' (4:158). Although the Gospels report that Jesus was crucified, they are also clear that his crucifixion was not the result of the schemes or power of his enemies—'they' were not the ones who brought about his death" (Cockerill 2002, 72). "The *cross* refers to Jesus' death for us by crucifixion. In one sense followers of Jesus agree that 'they did not kill him' (Qur'an 4:158) for Jesus himself said, 'No one takes my life from me, but I lay it down of my own accord' (see John 10:18). He could have called twelve legions of angels for his defense (Matthew 26:53) but he willingly let his enemies take him and freely gave up his life for our salvation (Matthew 27:50)" (Cockerill 2002, 48). It was necessary to use the word "cross" here because this quotation is comment on Heb 12:2 "endured the cross." All words quoted from the text being explained are in italics. Thus in context the use of italics does not emphasize the word "cross."

brother, sister, mother, father, son, or daughter on that Day (Qur'an 39:43). "Every soul earns only to its own account; no soul laden bears the load of another" (Qur'an 6:164). Each one will be responsible for himself alone. And so we often think that we must do many good deeds so that they will outweigh our evil deeds on that day. If I pray enough, fast enough, and give enough alms I will be accepted at the Judgment Day.

It is certainly true that we are each responsible for our own sins.

The last sentence above affirms the individual responsibility asserted by Qur'an 6:164. The explanation following the above quotation also assumes that "we" cannot intercede for one another on the Day of Judgment, as Qur'an 39:43 says. Nevertheless the text of *Guidebook* goes on to explain that we already owe God our good deeds and so they cannot make up for our evil deeds. Jesus, alone, has provided the way of forgiveness and he is our intercessor now, in the present, administering God's merciful forgiveness and grace for victorious living. Thus the text does not formally contradict the quotations from the Qur'an. It does contradict what "we often think" (on the basis of the Qur'an?)—"that we must do many good deeds so that they will outweigh our evil deeds on that day." It also presents a very different understanding of intercession. Intercession is not getting somebody off the hook on the Day of Judgment. It is Jesus' taking our sin now, giving us forgiveness now, and supplying grace now for right living. Thus at this point *Guidebook* avoids direct contradiction of the Qur'an while giving a very different vision of grace and salvation.

Conflicting Accounts of Old Testament Persons

The fact that both the Qur'an and Hebrews refer to people like Noah, Abraham, and Moses provides a significant point of contact. What happens, however, when their accounts of these characters differ? *Guidebook* only addressed differences if those differences are so obvious that reading the Biblical text is likely to raise questions in the reader's mind.

This issue comes to the fore in Heb 11:17, which says that God ordered Abraham to sacrifice his son "Isaac." Muslims normally believe that God commanded Abraham to sacrifice Ishmael. And, of course, the remembrance of this sacrifice is basic to the Feast of Sacrifice at the conclusion of the *Hajj*. Fortunately, the Qur'an does not actually name the son Abraham was told to sacrifice. Some Muslim scholars have believed that it was Isaac. In commenting on Heb 11:17 *Guidebook* simply says, "The Qur'an does not say which son Abraham was commanded to sacrifice. Most Muslims believe that God commanded Abraham to sacrifice his eldest son Ishmael. However, some great Muslim commentators have agreed that Isaac was to be sacrificed" (Cockerill 2002, 28). When not constrained by Heb 11:17 I have just referred to Abraham's sacrificing his "son" without mention of the name (Cockerill 2000, 149, 167).

Muslim Practices Compared with Christian

As noted above, Larson suggested removing the descriptions of various aspects of the *Hajj* at the beginning of each chapter "to avoid any hint of syncretism" (Larson 2003, 528). Each of these descriptions leads into the particular aspect of pilgrimage to the Heavenly City that the given chapter develops. Thus their purpose is to get and hold the readers attention and then to act as a bridge from the known to the unknown. Here are a couple of examples. Chapter one begins by describing pilgrims approaching Mecca and the "faith" which motivates them (Cockerill 2002, 19). This description of their faith serves as a bridge to a description of the faith of pilgrims to the heavenly city as described in Heb 11:1-7 and following verses. There is a transition sentence on the top of page 20: "The pilgrim en route to the Heavenly City has a faith similar to those on the way to Mecca."

Chapter six, "The First Pilgrim," begins by describing Muhammad's flight to Medina, his eventual return and conquest of Mecca, and his establishing the pilgrimage by the "Great Pilgrimage" of 632 A.D./ 10 A.H. This description is used as a basis to describe the "eternal Word's" leaving heaven, coming to earth, and returning again to heaven in order to open the way and establish our pilgrimage to the Heavenly City (Cockerill 2002, 97-98).

I did my best to make these descriptions graphic enough to be interesting, but not so graphic or detailed as to focus the reader's attention or emotions on the pilgrimage to Mecca rather than on the pilgrimage to the Heavenly City that these practices were used to illustrate.[6] There is nothing in these descriptions that would be offensive. Muslim practices and teachings are not set in sharp contrast to the Biblical truth that is compared to them. There are no direct contrasts— here is the Muslim practice, but the Christian is far superior. The transition sentence given above is fairly typical: "The pilgrim en route to the Heavenly City has a faith similar to those on the way to Mecca." Of course as the discourse develops the greatness of the pilgrimage to the Heavenly City becomes evident. However, the pilgrimage to Mecca is not used as a foil to bring out this greatness. Rather it is used as a

> **The Divine Sonship of Jesus and his crucifixion are most crucial in any exposition of Scripture for MBBs or Muslims because of Muslim objections, because of the centrality of these teachings to Christian faith, and because of the resultant difficulty in adequately explaining them within a Muslim context.**

starting point to help the reader understand the pilgrimage to the Heavenly City. There may be a "hint" of syncretism here. It seems to me, however, that the use of these descriptions is worth the risk. As executed, they provide a bridge for understanding without offending Muslim sensitivities, nor are they likely to draw an MBB back to Islam. They also help to tie the entire book together and give it a sense of coherence.

The Crucified Son of God

Many of the concerns we have been discussing pale when we turn to consider the Divine Sonship of Jesus and his

---

[6] An earlier edition of *Guidebook* had the following description of pilgrims' feelings at first sight of the *Ka'bah*. On the advice of a reviewer I removed this quotation for fear that its emotional intensity would draw the reader toward Mecca and away from the Heavenly City: "I became suddenly dazed. My wife clung to my arm, trembling and sobbing. This time my daughter shuddered as if an electric current had shot through her, and my son was speechless" (Abdul-Rauf 1978, 584).

crucifixion. Of course in a book like *Guidebook* the parameters of one's discussion are set by the Biblical text under consideration. Thus concern for effective treatment of these two issues determined the very order of commentary on the text of Hebrews. In order to first build bridges and postpone detailed consideration of these tough Christological issues Part One is a discussion of Heb 10:32—12:29, in which pilgrimage rather than Christology is the dominant motif. It didn't seem very wise to begin with Hebrews one, for the second verse says that God has spoken to us through His "Son."

Heb 5:11—6:20 is used as an introduction to Part Two. In this passage the writer of Hebrews prepares his readers for teaching that they will find difficult—in his case the atoning death of the Son of God understood in terms of High Priesthood. Thus it was easy to use this passage as an introduction to teaching that MBBs and especially Muslims might find difficult—the eternal Sonship and atoning death of Jesus. After this introduction, Part Two deals with Heb 1:1—10:31; 13:1-25 and uses the *tawaf* around the *Ka'bah*, Muhammad's establishment of the pilgrimage to Mecca, Muhammad's apostleship, the idea of intercession, and the Feast of Sacrifice as analogies for explaining the Christology of these chapters. As noted above, stoning the devil and the practice of *Ihram* are used to describe the life of the pilgrim.

The commentary on Heb 5:11—6:20 sets the basic strategy for dealing with Jesus' divine Sonship and atoning crucifixion (Cockerill 2002, 69-80). First, of course, one must try to remove false understanding. When they call Jesus "Son" followers of Jesus do not mean that God had a wife who bore a son. After dealing with misunderstanding, *Guidebook* turns to Qur'an 4:171 as the basis for a positive explanation. Jesus is God's "Word—the word which He imparted to Mary" (Cockerill 2002, 71, 83-95). Thus when followers of Jesus call Him God's "Son" they mean that He is the full expression of what God is like. God's Word was spoken through the prophets. His Word became "embodied" in Jesus. When we hear the words of the prophets it is like listening to someone on the radio. When we meet Jesus we meet the speaker face to face. It is also noted that the Qur'an calls Jesus God's "Beloved" and "Companion." These lines of thought are expanded in the commentary of Heb 1:1—2:4; 3:1-6; and 7:1-28 (Cockerill 2002,

81-96, 111-114, 125-134). The contrast in Heb 1:4—2:4 between the "Son" and the angels makes an implicit, though not explicit, contrast between Jesus the Son and those prophets, like Muhammad, who received revelation through angels.[7] This implication of the angels/Son contrast is, however, left unstated.

As suggested above, the introduction to Part Two addresses the issue of the crucifixion by suggesting an alternate meaning for the relevant Qur'anic passages. Perhaps these passages do not deny Jesus' crucifixion. Perhaps they deny that it was the power of the proud and envious Jewish rulers that brought him to death. To use Qur'anic language, these rulers "plotted," but God was the greater "Plotter." He used Jesus' death, and resurrection, to achieve His purposes and to receive greater glory than He would have received by merely rescuing Jesus from death. But, assuming Jesus was crucified, one must still answer the question, "Why was his death necessary and how did it obtain our salvation?" To answer this question one must counter the Islamic belief that sin is weakness, salvation is through right guidance, and paradise is obtained by one's good works outweighing one's bad. Thus using the images availed by Hebrews, *Guidebook* builds up a picture of the holiness of God, the resultant inability of good works to ever pay for bad since we already owe God our good works, and the consequent corruption of the human heart. In Jesus His eternal Word, God has taken that sin on Himself so that we can be both forgiven and cleansed and thus have eternal fellowship with Him. These ideas are developed particularly in commentary on Heb 2:5-18; 4:14—5:10 (Cockerill 2002, 97-110) and 8:1—10:18 (Cockerill 2002, 135-148). Comparison is made with the Feast of Sacrifice at the conclusion of the pilgrimage

> "They [Jesus' enemies] plotted and Allah plotted, but Allah is the best of plotters."
>
> **Qur'an 3:54**

---

[7] "The Qur'an teaches that the Archangel Gabriel appeared often to the prophets and brought the revelations of the Qur'an to Muhammad (53:4-11). In Luke 1:26-38 Gabriel appears to Mary. The writer of Hebrews shows that the Son is superior to the angels in order to demonstrate that God's revelation in the Son is greater than any revelation given through angels" (Cockerill 2002, 86).

(Cockerill 2002, 135-148). *Guidebook* quietly but attractively emphasizes the resulting fellowship with God (Cockerill 2002, 12, 14, 26, 42, 50, 52, 55, 60, 61, 64, 73, 74, 78, 82, 85, 94, 98, 102, 110, 118, 119, 120, 122, 130, 131, 147, 148, 150, 154, 161, 162). Only once is the consummation of this fellowship implicitly contrasted with the Muslim view of paradise.[8]

In dealing with these issues it is easy to fall into syncretism from the best of motives. Our desire to reach Muslims and understandable frustration in trying to overcome these barriers makes us susceptible to over simplification and dilution. One reviewer wanted me to explain the title "Son of God" as merely a royal title for Jesus' kingly rule. He based this suggestion on an article by Rick Brown (Brown 2000, 41-52).

> **"You are the Son of God, you are the King of Israel."**
> **-Nathaniel** (John 1:49)
>
> **"You are the Messiah, the Son of the Living God."**
> **-Peter** (Matthew 16:16)

Although there is much that is helpful in Brown's work, his well-intentioned approach is marred by what we might call the "no-more-than" fallacy: because the term "Son of God" was used in Second Temple Judaism as a designation for the divinely anointed King-Messiah, it can mean "no more" when applied to Jesus.[9]

In fact, the New Testament does the exact opposite. The New Testament writers show how the meanings of Jesus' titles have been deepened and extended through application to Him. The new referent makes all the difference.[10] After all, this Jesus is the one who interpreted the Old Testament with

---

[8] "How can we enter the Paradise that He has promised us, a Paradise that is not merely a place of ease and enjoyment but of intimate fellowship with God?" (Cockerill 2002, 74).

[9] Brown is correct in saying that "Son of God" was used as a title for the Messiah and that this usage was derived from such passages as Psalm 2:7 and 2 Samuel 7:14 (Brown 2000, 44-46). However, based on the sources we have, "Son of God" probably wasn't used this way as frequently as Brown's work might imply. Thus its frequency and prominence in Scripture is surprising.

[10] It was definitely not loss of the original meaning of "Son of God" at the time of the Council of Nicea that brought about this deepening of meaning, as Brown supposes (Brown 2000, 49). Nicea built on the richer meaning already given to this term in the New Testament.

sovereign authority (Matt. 7:28-29), claimed the divine right to forgive sins (Mark 2:1-12), and performed miracles with a mere (Divine) word, miracles of unprecedented variety and intensity and with unheard of frequency. "What sort of man is this, that even winds and sea obey him?" (Matt. 7:28, ESV).

Thus in some of the examples cited by Brown, such as Nathaniel's and Peter's confessions, the speakers probably did understand "Son of God" as "Messianic King" (Brown 2000, 47). However, when we get to John 3:16, especially in light of 1:14, 18, "Son of God" has a much deeper and richer meaning.

Indeed, a look at Nathaniel's confession, "You are the Son of God, you are the king of Israel" (John 1:49), shows us this process of transformation in progress. Although Nathaniel may have used "Son of God" as a synonym for "King of Israel," we the readers have information Nathaniel did not have. By giving us this privileged information in the prologue John has equipped us to understand this term on a different level. We already know that the eternal Word incarnate is "the only

---

The "Son" in John 1-3 Greek and English

John 1:15 *monogenēs*
"only begotten"

John 1:18 *monogenēs theos*
"only begotten God"

John 1:34 ho huios tou theou
"the Son of God"

John 3:16 *monogenēs huios*
"only begotten Son"

---

begotten" (*monogenous*) from the Father" (1:14) and "the only begotten God (*monogenēs theos*), who is at the Father's side" (1:18), whom John the Baptist has declared to be "the Son of God" (*ho huios tou theou*, 1:34). When Nathaniel declared that Jesus was "the Son of God" (*ho huios tou theou*, 1:49) he "spoke better than he knew" (Carson 1991, 162).[11]

---

[11] Compare Schnackenburg, "The titles used by Nathanael are meant as Messianic, but provide the reader with the possibility of a deeper understanding" (Schnackenburg 1968, 319). Raymond Brown goes into greater detail: "It may well be, however, that John intends to give 'Son of God' a more profound meaning. In the theological progression indicated by the titles of ch. i which capsulizes the disciples' gradual growth in insight throughout the whole ministry of Jesus, John may well have wished to include in "son of God" a confession of the divinity of Jesus" (Brown

Indeed, Jesus says that Nathaniel will see much more! He will come to know Jesus as the "only begotten Son" (*ton huion ton monogenē*) of John 3:16.

Certainly in Hebrews "the Son" is used of Christ's deity. It is as "Son" that He is "appointed heir of all things," it is through him as "Son" that God "made the universe." It is as "Son" that he "is the radiance of God's glory and the exact representation of his being, sustaining all things by his powerful word" (Heb 1:2; on Heb 1:1-3 see Hughes 1977, 35-49). It is as eternal "Son" that he "founded the earth" and the heavens (Heb 1:10) in the beginning and as "Son" he will "roll them up" at the end (Heb 1:12). It is his very character as eternal "Son" that makes God's revelation through him superior to all others[12] and that shows his superiority to created angels and to men, such as Moses (Heb 3:1-6) and the Aaronic priests (Heb 5:1-10). The divinity of the "Son" is absolutely fundamental to Hebrews' teaching that in Him we have both God's final revelation and the effecting of God's ultimate salvation (Heb 1:1-2; 5:6-19; 10:5-19). Thus to reduce "Son" in Hebrews to "enthroned Messianic King" would be a complete betrayal of Hebrew's intention.

At the same time, as indicated above, I have followed Brown's lead by using the Qur'an's designation of Jesus as the "Word" of God to explain his Sonship. In my judgment this approach makes more sense than any other.[13]

Conclusion

Although I have served as a missionary where there was a significant Muslim presence, witnessed to Muslims, and worked with believers from a Muslim background, my greatest strength is in the field of Biblical studies. It would not have been possible to write *Guidebook* without the help of all those in

---

1977, 88).

[12] In commenting on Heb 1:3 Lane says, "The anarthrous *en huiō* [in son] is qualitative. The eternal, essential quality of Jesus' sonship qualified him to be the one through whom God uttered his final word" (Lane 1991, 11).

[13] I did not compare Jesus as God's Word to the Qur'an, which, of course, many Muslims believe to be eternal with Allah. This comparison has possibilities, but it could easily have led to the kind of confrontation I was trying to avoid: "You believe the Qur'an is God's eternal Word, we believe Jesus is God's eternal Word."

Muslim ministry who read the manuscript and took the time to give serious, thorough, and sometimes quite critical comment.

I hope *Guidebook* will encourage others to discover parallels between the original recipients of Biblical books and Muslims and to find bridges for communication. I offer this paper to stimulate further discussion about the issues raised: How can we communicate the divine Sonship and atoning death of Jesus to MBBs and to Muslims? How can we cite the Qur'an without offense but without affirming it as Scripture? What language communicates the truth without offense or compromise? What bridges of communication are available to us based on commonalities?

Furthermore, I welcome any suggestions that might increase *Guidebook's* effectiveness and use in making disciples. One reviewer, who is deeply involved in outreach to Muslims, expressed the wish that the book might be translated into other languages so that its message would be more accessible to MBBs. Another suggested that the material might be recast as a daily devotional structured for reading during Ramadan or the month of Hajj—perhaps *Guidebook for Pilgrims to the Heavenly City: Daily Readings for Dhu-l-Hijjah.* Others might want to rework this material in English or in other languages for local audiences. Perhaps the material in this book should be made available anonymously or with a suitable pseudonym and where appropriate with the Arabic spelling of Bible names. Input, suggestions, or inquires from readers of this study are most welcome.

Sources Cited

Abdul-Rauf, Muhammad. 1978. "Pilgrimage to Mecca." *National Geographic*. 154 (November): 581-607.

Brown, Raymond. 1977. *The Gospel According to John (i-xiii)*. (The Anchor Bible). New York: Doubleday.

Brown, Rick. 2000. "The 'Son of God': Understanding the Messianic Titles of Jesus." *International Journal of Frontier Missions*. 17 (Spring): 41-52.

Carson, D.A. 1991. *The Gospel According to John*. Leicester/Grand Rapids: IVP/Eerdmans.

Cockerill, Gareth Lee. 2002. *Guidebook for Pilgrims to the Heavenly City*. Pasadena, CA: William Carey Library.

Cockerill, Gareth Lee. 1994. "To the Hebrews/To the Muslims: Islamic Pilgrimage as a Key to Interpretation." *Missiology* 22 (July): 347-359.

deSilva, David A. 2000. *Perseverance in Gratitude: A Socio-Rhetorical Commentary on the Epistle "to the Hebrews."* Grand Rapids: Eerdmans.

Green, Denis. 1989. "Guidelines from Hebrews for Contextualization." In *Muslims and Christians on the Emmaus Road*, ed. J. Dudley Woodberry, 233-250. Monrovia, CA: MARC.

Hughes, P. E. 1977. *A Commentary on the Epistle to the Hebrews*. Grand Rapids: Eerdmans.

Johnsson, William G. 1978. "The Pilgrimage Motif in the Book of Hebrews." *Journal of Biblical Literature* 92 (June): 239-251.

Lane, W. L. 1991. *Hebrews 1-8* (Word Biblical Commentary). Dallas, TX: Word.

Larson, Warren. 2003. Review of *Guidebook for Pilgrims to the Heavenly City*. *Evangelical Missions Quarterly* 39 (October): 526-528.

Massey, Joshua. 2000. "God's Amazing Diversity in Drawing Muslims to Christ." *International Journal of Frontier Mission* 17 (Spring): 5-14.

Partin, H.B.1969. "The Muslim Pilgrimage: Journey to the Center." Ph.D. dissertation, University of Chicago.

Schnackenburg, R. 1968. *The Gospel According to St. John, Volume One: Introduction and Commentary on Chapters 1-4*. (Herder's Theological Commentary on the New Testament) New York: Herder and Herder.

Travis, John. 1998. "The C1 to C6 Spectrum: A Practical Tool for Defining Six Types of 'Christ-Centered Communities' ('C') Found in the Muslim Context." *Evangelical Missions Quarterly* 34 (October): 407-408.